PERSPECTIVES IN LEADERSHIP

SOCIAL JUSTICE, EQUALITY AND EMPOWERMENT

Additional books in this series can be found on Nova's website
under the Series tab.

Additional e-books in this series can be found on Nova's website
under the e-book tab.

PERSPECTIVES IN LEADERSHIP

JERRY D. VANVACTOR
EDITOR

nova publishers

New York

For permission to use material from this book please contact us:
Telephone 631-231-7269; Fax 631-231-8175
Web Site: http://www.novapublishers.com

NOTICE TO THE READER

Additional color graphics may be available in the e-book version of this book.

Library of Congress Cataloging-in-Publication Data

Perspectives in leadership / editor, Jerry D. Vanvactor.
    p. cm.
  Includes index.
  ISBN 978-1-62417-170-3 (hardcover)
  1. Leadership--Case studies. I. Vanvactor, Jerry D.
  HD57.7.P466 2013
  658.4'092--dc23
                        2012040507

Published by Nova Science Publishers, Inc. † *New York*

CONTENTS

PREFACE

To lead an organization or group of people, one must have skills related to setting and ensuring that a corporate direction is followed. Albeit somewhat difficult to define, leadership can apply as much to oneself as it can to leading other individuals, groups, organizations and societies. Many people among contemporary society are seeking to better understand concepts and practices related to leadership. One need look no further than a search of Google, Amazon.com, or other such mechanisms to find that there is a plethora of information available concerning such an apparently well-defined topic. There is more than one definition of leadership and depending on a person's background, education, and experience, multiple definitions of this simplistic word may apply. Arguably, then, to be an effective leader, a broad view of leadership must exist.

The nature of leadership is contextual and can vary significantly in situation, perspective, and the nature and needs of involved individuals. Leadership is personal and a distinctly human activity. Understanding leadership requires more than reading articles and books, attending classes on the subject, or hypothesizing leader effectiveness. Leadership must be practiced, in situ, to be best understood.

This is not a typical book about leadership. This book is a variety of perspectives concerning leadership wherein several theories and ideas have been collectively shared so that the reader can have a broader view of the many tenets of leadership. Among these pages, a collection of independent ideas concerning leadership, from an international faculty, come together to demonstrate the broader applications of leadership. Each chapter brings a host of considerations to the forefront of any student's mind when delving into such a topic as influencing people to accomplish tasks through purpose, motivation, and a desire to perform.

Thematically, leadership is the only thread that holds each chapter together. The reader is encouraged to read the information in any order desired as, in the end, he will be armed with new knowledge concerning the topic of leadership itself. There is no need to feel restricted to reading each chapter in order from beginning to end. There is no plot or climax for which the reader should be searching.

Dr. Glenys Drew launches us on our multi-perspective journey by suggesting that leadership infers a relationship of some kind, and posits from data, literature and a brief case study of some key aspects of the leadership role that most require, indeed are dependent upon, a relationship-centred, action-oriented approach for achieving high quality outcomes. Employing the Quality Leadership Profile (QLP) 360 degree feedback survey for leaders in education and knowledge organizations, Drew reveals an overview of a trend noticed on individual result reports that high scores in the survey items under the factor, 'Staff Motivation and Involvement', where a leader places emphasis on fostering strong interpersonal relationships, high scores on all factors can be predicted. This information is then applied to a case study involving a knowledge organization for readers to gain understanding and comprehension.

Chapter 2 provides a different perspective in the 'ordinary' discussion of leadership. Mrs. Maria Johnson recognizes skills for effective leadership through a personification of leadership among the characters in the story The Wizard of Oz. As Johnson discloses for readers, Dorothy, the Scarecrow, the Wicked Witch of the West and the Wizard of Oz all provide examples of leadership characteristics, such as organization, flexibility and responsibility. Some of these characters, however, are more effective in motivating their followers in the pursuit of their goals than others.

In Chapter 3, Dr. Karina M. Nielsen leverages cognitive theory to investigate the relationship between leaders' self-appraisal of transformational leadership behaviors, how these link to levels of work engagement, and how followers' group climate may enhance this link. Nielsen determined, through her research, that the exertion of transformational leadership behaviors significantly predicted leaders' work engagement and a general collaborative climate among a work group enhanced this relationship. As stated by Nielsen, understanding how behaviors specific to the leadership role is related to leaders' work engagement provides valuable knowledge of how we may increase leaders' engagement. As leaders play a vital role in maintaining staff well-being and obtaining organizational objectives, their own levels of work engagement are important to ensure organizational health.

Chapter 4 is a timely discussion as many countries are in the throes of reforming health care and re-evaluating the availability of limited resources in the continuance of care for aging populations. Health care organizations tend to operate routinely within a resource-dependent environment. Dr. Tracy L. Buchman expounds upon the concept that many organizations trade their autonomy by collaborating to share critical resources and maintain a clinical center for excellence, to encompass the best technology available for their patients, and to maintain their status as a technological leader in the community. External resources are often required in the sustainment of health care operations; managers among health care organizations need to understand this variable and factor it into the health care equation.

Chapter 5 provides a dynamic evaluation of previous research showing a surprisingly low correlation between leader intelligence and leader performance. In this chapter authors Roland S. Jacobs, Ronald E. Smith, Fred E. Fiedler and Thomas G. Link discuss one contributive factor concerning low overall correlation is that under conditions of high interpersonal stress, intelligent leaders seem unable to fully utilize their superior cognitive resources, often resulting in a null or negative correlation between intelligence and leader performance in highly-stressed leaders. The authors conclude through a scientific study that although high situational stress is endemic to many leadership settings and cannot be easily reduced, interventions can be applied that are designed to help individuals within those settings be made more resilient in responding to the stressors. The results of this study suggest that structured coping skills training that enhances emotional self-regulatory skills can be an efficacious means for maximizing the ability of leaders to utilize their intellectual abilities and thereby perform at a higher level in stressful conditions.

In Chapter 6, Dr. James M. Lewis provides a somewhat different perspective of leadership. While leadership always involves two factors - one leading and one being led - there is a relationship aspect that must be considered and therein discusses the influence of spirituality upon leadership and the workplace. Lewis adeptly discloses that while leadership is about motivating, inspiring, energizing, and empowering followers, a leader should possess a vision and be able to articulate it, emphasize an order among priorities, persuade others to comply with guidance and instruction, and must constantly include a self-oriented review of what is being done. Leadership involves an endearment of things of value. How, though, does this concept apply to defined leadership and how does a leader's demonstrated behaviors and ideals influence those being led?

Chapter 7 involves a necessary discussion each leader needs to consider in everyday practice. Dr. Jerry D. VanVactor provides a discourse in ethics and applies ethical decision-making to leadership in situ. As stated, leadership is a generalized skill set inculcated among supervisors and managers at various levels of organizational operations and processes and is not specific to any job title, rank, or role. Ethically driven behaviors affect everyone throughout an organization and are likely to be a valuable consideration in any decision-making scenario. Leaders have an inherent responsibility to develop and plan tactics, operational templates, and strategies based upon a strong ethical foundation. Arguably, a critical path to success involves a contiguous consideration of the implications that misdirected ethics may have on organizational outcomes.

In Chapter 8, authors Drs.Chiara Rollero, Filippo Rutto, and Norma De Piccoli discuss political leadership from a gender perspective. The authors posit that although women have gained increased access to leadership positions, they often remain subordinated to men in competition for top executive roles. Even in most industrialized societies women are still suffering disadvantage in access to major leadership posts. The authors express their findings and conclusions via several theories that have been formulated to explain the sparse representation of women in leadership roles.

Chapter 9 continues a gender-oriented discussion as authors Drs.Chiara Rollero and Norma De Piccoli consider perceptions associated with female leaders through the gendered image of power. The authors demonstrate that prejudice is sometimes shown toward female leaders because of inconsistencies between the communal quality associated with women and the agentic qualities stereotypically required to be a successful leader. The results of the associated study demonstrate that both the male and the female leaders were described through agentic traits exclusively.

In Chapter 10, Mr. Tony J. Gill reflects upon the Curt Flood effect on workplace leadership. As described in Gill's chapter, in 1969, Curt Flood, an outfielder with the St. Louis Cardinals, refused an inter-team trade to the Philadelphia Phillies thereby violating the terms of baseball's Reserve Clause. As a result, Flood sat the entire 1970 season out and filed a lawsuit against his organization. Although he lost his suit in the U.S. Supreme Court, the action set in motion new ideations of free agency among professional sports. Just as sports teams had to adjust to the newfound power of players, corporations too had to evaluate and adjust the manner in which they maximized the productivity of employees and success among organizations.

Chapter 11, authored by Drs. William L. Tullar and Dianne H.B. Welsh, provide a perspective in entrepreneurial leadership. The authors posit that economists, public policy experts, and the popular press have noted the contribution that entrepreneurs make to society in general and the economy in particular. Many leading authors view the entrepreneur as an economic hero, launching and growing new ventures against a growing plethora of regulations, monopolistic big businesses, and increasing foreign competition, while worldwide currency valuation has continued to affect import and export costs. Entrepreneurship has long been believed a driver of economic development. Academicians are cognizant of this type of view and have led many business schools, both in the U. S. and abroad, to develop curricula oriented toward the enhancement of emerging skill sets among students through internships, experiential learning, practicums, and real stores on campus. However, there is cause for concern about such programs and the authors elucidate one area in which academic programs are not focused.

In chapter 12, Dr. Shih-ying Yang highlights leadership through renowned leaders in history: Solomon, Confucius, and Mother Teresa. Yang expounds upon the different levels of positive influence among each of the three's leadership that they achieved, respectively. Yang states that the ultimate goal of wisdom is to promote a meaningful and satisfying life for everyone involved. When wisdom is manifested through leadership, it can generate positive effects not only for the leader, but also for others at the individual, organizational, and societal level. This chapter suggests that multiple levels of positive influence should be emphasized when discussing wisdom in leadership.

Finally, in Chapter 13, Mr. Brocato and Dr. Theodori provide a discourse related to emerging management principles potentially requiring a new theoretical paradigm that expands previous attempts to describe the efficacy of a more democratic, cooperative work environment. The authors advance a new theoretical orientation of leadership. The chapter concludes with a discussion related to the need to use more robust operational constructs to meet leadership needs in the postmodern era

Collectively, the authors have presented each reader with a toolkit of ideas related to leadership. It is the authors' desire that this information will contribute to the literature and practice of leadership among organizations.

In: Perspectives in Leadership
Editor: Jerry D. VanVactor

ISBN: 978-1-62417-170-3
© 2013 Nova Science Publishers, Inc.

Chapter 1

AN EXCITING JOURNEY OF LEADERSHIP LEARNING: A CASE STUDY OF ONE SCHOOL'S LEADERSHIP AND ACTION

*Glenys M. Drew**

QUT (Queensland University of Technology), Brisbane,
Queensland, Australia

ABSTRACT

This chapter suggests that leadership infers a relationship, and poses from some data, literature and a brief case study, some key aspects of the leadership role that most require, indeed are dependent upon, a relationship-centred, action-oriented approach for achieving high quality outcomes. In terms of insights from data, the Quality Leadership Profile (QLP) 360 degree feedback survey for leaders in education and knowledge organisations, is fruitful. This survey has enabled hundreds of leaders in education/knowledge settings to gain feedback on a relevant set of capability items for continuous improvement purposes. The QLP item/question set was developed over six years of research at QUT. The items for the QLP 'General' survey (designed for senior administrative/professional leaders) cluster into the areas: 'Staff Motivation and Involvement', 'Strategic and Operational Management', 'Service Focus' and 'Community Outreach', while the QLP 'Academic' survey includes an additional factor, 'Academic Leadership', which contains items relevant to academic development. More recently, the Australian Centre for Educational Leadership (ACEL), the Association of Heads of Independent Schools in Australia (AHISA) and the Queensland University of Technology (QUT)[+] partnered to produce a spin-off instrument specifically for the use of school principals and senior leadership teams in schools.

This instrument, known as the Quality Leadership Profile for Schools (QLPS), like the QLP, is fully accessible on-line and also is attracting very positive reviews as an

---

* Glenys M. Drew works at QUT (Queensland University of Technology), Brisbane, Queensland, Australia, and within a range of education/knowledge organisations as a practitioner and researcher in leadership and organisational development.
Correspondence contact: Dr Glenys Drew at g.drew@qut.edu.au.
+ It was the school's choice to be named in the case study

intensely relevant tool for practice enhancement purposes. This chapter reveals an overview of the trend noticed on individual result reports that high scores in the survey items under the factor, 'Staff Motivation and Involvement' - in other words, where the leader is seen to place emphasis on fostering strong interpersonal relationships - predict high scores on all factors. This chapter considers briefly what this trend suggests, with observations from this data, some theory and a case study. The case study relates to the leadership journey of one school, John Paul College, located in the Logan Shire near Brisbane city in Queensland, Australia.

When this school's headmaster and senior leadership team undertook the QLPS, they received noticeably higher scores in 'Staff Motivation and Involvement' against the longstanding survey aggregate norms and, true to the predictive trend abovementioned, their scores concomitantly were high overall, spanning strategic planning, gaining ownership of strategy, articulation of future vision, operational management, service, representing the organisation effectively, and strategic, relational and personal capability. We explore here some 'touchstones' of leadership and action that are evident in a brief examination of the leadership learning journey embarked upon by John Paul College; how one organisation is shaping culture and pulling together in unity by identifying and communicating particular values, developing and prosecuting a consistent message concerning key goals, and by forging active relationships across the school and stakeholder community. This chapter draws upon some leadership literature in exploring the essence of the quest of the chapter; namely, what it means, and what it takes to engage and mobilise others as a leader. An underpinning paradox of the observations is that, for the leader, the seemingly 'lost' time spent connecting with people may be the richest investment that the leader may make for better outcomes.

Keywords: Communication, 360 degree feedback, leadership development, schools

ATTENTION TO INTERPERSONAL RELATIONSHIPS

It has long been said that paying attention to interpersonal relationships promoting the engagement of others with a level of inspiration and support, is a good idea. Indeed, it is likely true to any definition of the word 'leadership' that the role involves forging a relationship via communication. While few may dispute the correlation in practice, how often, however, do we see leaders inspiring, empowering and mobilising others with clarity of purpose towards achieving strategic aims? Fortunately, such leaders exist, and I put to you: If you have experienced such a leader then, most likely, you will remember that person.

It may be that when you reflect on that person and the impact that he or she had upon you and others, you might recall this as a rewarding and fulfilling professional experience; perhaps even something of a 'landmark' or 'watershed' where valuable lessons were learned and confidence was gained. This may be because that leader repudiated wielding power for power's sake and used influence to empower others (Drew, 2010). Such a leader may have contributed to building 'self-efficacy' that is so necessary to personal learning and development – that is, the belief that one can learn, change and grow (Maurer, Mitchell & Barbeite, 2002).

Not many years ago I conducted a research project with a group of leaders in universities. Some participants were in academic leadership roles and some were leaders in administrative areas like human resources and finance. I asked these participants, leaders themselves, to consider the most effective leader they had encountered in their experience to date and I asked them to describe something of the qualities demonstrated by that person in the leadership role. I wanted to know not what the literatures says but how they experienced what they viewed as high-order leadership. Their answers conclusively related to what they saw as relationship-centred qualities of empowerment, trust, motivation and support demonstrated by a leader whom they saw as having been very effective (Drew, Ehrich & Hansford, 2008). The research study did not extend to asking the participants how often such leaders were represented in their organisational histories, but I recall that each participant tended to describe the experience as having been somewhat 'special'; something that 'stood out' for them as having made a difference in multiple ways.

Noting that definitions of 'leadership' see leadership as focused on others, I find it interesting to ask serving leaders and managers how they perceive their practice of leadership in their roles and how their staff view their leadership practice, and ascertain the dissonance or alignment between those perceptions. I describe gathering feedback from others as not creating anything new but garnering the perceptions that already exist as a 'gift of information' for the leader. Via this 'gift of information', I have seen leaders affirmed in positive leadership practice and equipped to adjust practice where useful to do so. Working in this way with leaders in light of the information received, co-developing strategies and plans for enhancements, leaders have made appreciable gains for themselves, their teams and their organisations.

Over twelve years I have received emails from leaders undertaking this process reporting that engagement levels have increased, and from the staff members of leaders saying that they have noted and appreciated that their leader is giving feedback, consulting more, communicating the rationale for decisions and strategic agenda, listening more, or whatever the case may be, following the process. All credit to the leaders/participants: it is one thing to undertake a feedback survey and to engage in the feedback conversation, and quite another to act on two or three development aspects and see the gains as little as three months later. The 360 degree feedback survey I have been using as a springboard for these discussions is the fully online and globally accessible Quality Leadership Profile (QLP) that is outlined briefly in the next sub-section.

In my practice, I find that people attain their leadership roles chiefly through excelling in a particular skill or discipline, whether it be engineering, government, policy, medicine, economics, trades work, school education, humanities, university or non-university tertiary education, business, construction, policing, industrial relations or a multitude of other possible domains. Often, leaders take on their roles on the basis of strong performance in their sphere of specialist knowledge with little or no preparation for the role of leadership with its demands for a range of inter-relational and communication capabilities. This makes for a somewhat 'hit or miss' approach to handling the complexities of interpersonal and strategic communications, conflict resolution and so on. Indeed, some leaders anecdotally report feeling unsupported in the areas of navigating change and handling difficult situations involving people. I believe that fostering self-awareness at an early stage via feedback helps the leader to be in touch with his/her staff and provides a valuable focus for refining practice to perceived needs for greater effectiveness.

A leader's investment in establishing early a communication environment of recognition, mutual respect and goodwill is said to be foundational to growing a culture of cohesion, innovation, opportunity and growth. The Director of Coach Pty Ltd (www.ownthegame.com.au) in Brisbane, Australia, Leanne Drew-McKain, who works in this strategic space for individuals and organisations, identifies these qualities in the leadership team of the subject of our case study, John Paul College (2012). Drew-McKain maintains that, conversely, without that healthy communication environment, when people most need their powers of communication, under pressure, they feel disempowered in their communication. She proposes that the manner in which an individual commences an interchange predicts the end result. The more tension-laden the issue, Drew-McKain argues, the less likely it is that the individual commences the interchange in a respectful, positive dialogue built on recognition and professional courtesy, virtually spinning off the end result as a self-fulfilling prophecy. The end result is an impasse, or accelerated conflict, which leaves individuals and organisations further away from resolution or constructive outcome. Having encountered this somewhat paradoxical phenomenon time and time again in feedback conversations, I repeatedly observe that the more complex and 'laden' the issue, the less managers tend to take action to help resolve or help others resolve the matter, and long after people have forgotten the nature of the offending issue, the sense of disaffection and resentment palpably remains. Tension hangs in the air, people divide into factions and the amorphous situation becomes ever more difficult to address. A circuit-breaker is required to gain or re-establish connection. A well-facilitated feedback process that says, implicitly, 'I am listening', followed by useful development action in response – sometimes requiring little more than the leader's increased 'mindfulness' to communicate more often, consult more effectively, provide strategic clarity, and rationale for decisions made - have been just the platform needed to make or regain connection.

So why is effective leadership not necessarily 'run of the mill'; why does experience *of* leadership often run counter to the plethora of seemingly obvious statements *about* what leadership should be? A leader recently said to me: 'I can take the paperwork home if I need to but I can't take the people home. For me as a leader the people must be my priority. I must be there for them.' This executive understood that it was the relationship that she fostered with her staff that catalysed most the entire outcome for herself and her group. There is evidence that supports absolutely this treatise - that it *pays* in every area of strategic and operational outcome to invest properly in positive interpersonal engagement, communicating shared goals with the team with clarity and vision. The background to this assertion is outlined next.

INSIGHTS OF QLP '360' FEEDBACK PROCESS AND OTHER RESEARCH FINDINGS

The Quality Leadership Profile (QLP) was researched and developed over six years at QUT (Queensland University of Technology), Brisbane, Australia. The QLP was developed primarily for use by leaders in education/knowledge organisations. Scott, Coates and Anderson (2008), reporting on their large-scale research study of Australian academic leaders, support the increased use of 360 degree feedback surveys for development purposes, with the caveat that the survey must be valid and relevant to context for capability building, and they cite the QLP factor structure as an example of such a survey fostering leadership insight and development in the education/knowledge sector.

Aggregate data from almost twelve years of repeated usage of the QLP 360 degree feedback survey for leadership development by hundreds of senior leaders in education/'knowledge' organisations in Australia, New Zealand and Hong Kong, shows a small upward trending of QLP scores over time (Drew & Kerr, 2003; Drew, 2006). The table below shows the international average aggregate scores on all factors of the QLP at the start of 2012. The first three factors on the QLP survey, 'Staff Development', 'Consultative Management' and 'Team Environment', which all relate to interpersonal aspects of leadership, yield aggregate scores that are slightly lower than those for all other factors in QLP aggregate data (see below). These first three factors are where most development needs lie, as identified by respondents.

Quality Leadership Profile (QLP) 'Academic' Survey Data at 2012 International Averages on QLP Factors on a 1-5 scale, 5 being the highest

Staff Development	3.63
Consultative Management	3.82
Team Environment	3.80
Systems and Processes	3.89
Making Decisions	3.98
Managing Change and Innovation	3.92
Service Focus	3.95
Community Focus	4.25
Academic Leadership	3.95

Number of feedback responses represented in the data: 16,031.

Debriefing a large percentage of these survey reports in feedback interviews, I have observed two interesting trends. The first is that in the majority of cases, individuals improve on their base line scores when undertaking the survey a further time or times. It should be noted that the QLP aggregate data comprises, at any one time, first time users gaining base line data for feedback insight and enhancement of practice, and those having used the process multiple times (Drew & Kerr, 2003; Drew, 2006, Drew 2009A). Seeing a small upward trend in the international aggregate data over time is noteworthy. The second observation is that when scores in the first three factors, 'Staff Development', 'Consultative Management' and 'Team Environment' are high, the results of the entire survey report invariably are high. This suggests that sound interpersonal engagement is foundational to all else working well in the leadership/management role.

To expand briefly on the two observations mentioned, the data yielded from respondents to the QLP-related surveys show consistently that the relationship-centred elements of leadership are the areas where scores are lower, and, hence, where leaders find that with increased 'mindfulness' and action in these areas, the perceptions on their leadership are enhanced. Most people going into management/leadership roles either have, or may rely on direct reports for, specialized skills for managing functional aspects such as finance and implementing technological and administrative systems; they may access skill-building in time management or strategic planning. However, the vital areas of communications, gaining strategic ownership, building an effective team, making decisions and communicating outcomes, handling disagreement, providing feedback and developing and mentoring others, are aspects that lie squarely with the leader and, to some extent, with the leader's capacity for reflection and empathy (Drew et al., 2008). However, as suggested above, these are areas in which incumbents of leadership and management roles may have had little or no prior experience or preparation. This, at least, is implied in the aggregate QLP data over time (See Drew & Kerr, 2003 and Drew, 2006). Of the second observation, it is noted in individual survey result reports that when the candidate/leader scores highly in survey items clustering under 'Staff Motivation and Involvement', which have most to do with these inter-relational, communication aspects, this predicts high scores throughout. This gives the lie to any notion that 'people' skills may be semi-dismissed as 'soft' skills, tacked on for those thus inclined. The data trend shows that a preparedness to communicate positively with others, provide feedback and support, listen, consult, help resolve conflict, and offer development guidance against clear strategic objectives, albeit out of different leadership styles, is to invest in better outcomes. Two QLP items which appear most frequently in 'lowest scoring items', and on which gains have been made following feedback, are 'provides regular feedback to staff' and 'manages conflict within teams successfully'. Positive communication and empowering behaviours may be the province of all. These characteristics are pivotal if we agree that the leadership role entails, indeed that its success may turn upon, the engagement and mobilisation of others.

While there is a place for distributed leadership models, roving leadership and the like, I find that, in organisations, staff members look to the person to whom they are responsible in their role to provide a measure of guidance, support and feedback. I once asked a group of leaders in a study what they wanted most in a leader; what characteristics they saw as most critical when they recalled a person who, for them, demonstrated most effective leadership. The answers that individuals gave were that they wanted someone who could be trusted to follow through on what they said they would do; someone who communicated clearly, demonstrated empathy and provided positive support (Drew et al., 2008). This study found similarly to the findings of Scott et al. (2008) on academic leaders in Australia that a blend of supportive and empowering characteristics and the more instrumental functions were critical.

The comprehensive study of Scott and colleagues (2008) sought to identify prescient leadership challenges and development needs as reported in interviews with leaders within the Australian university sector. Both the studies of Drew et al. (2008) and Scott et al. (2008) found that trustworthiness and integrity, two key requirements, had an 'action' edge relating to the leader's 'follow through' on, for example, decision-making and addressing conflict issues. The studies found that 'self-organisation' – ability to prioritise and organise one's time and attention – importantly should go hand in hand with the affective capabilities to lead effectively. Moreover, a Leximancer-based study of qualitative comments made by respondents as they completed the QLP survey on leaders revealed that supportive leadership behaviours were most in mind for respondents in writing open comments as this was the general topic of the majority of qualitative comments that respondents provided (Rafferty & Neale, 2004).

Collins' (2001) extensive research found that outstanding leaders who imprinted their organisations sustainably for good demonstrated a unique combination of strong professional will and humility; they demonstrated persistence and rigor to see goals accomplished, combined with a listening, learning attitude. In the QLP 360 feedback survey there are four items relating to perceptions on the leader's role in strategic thinking and action. Those items, in different parts of the survey, invite respondents' perceptions on aspects of the leader's activities relating to strategic planning and action as follows: the strategic plan being place; the strategic plan, together with budget, being monitored; gaining staff 'ownership' of the strategic plan; and articulation of future vision. Most leaders score more highly on the first two than the latter two. Why might this be? It is one thing to formulate a strategic plan (or restructure a department or organisation) and another to have the strategic treatise or structural change embraced and 'owned' by those involved. It is an excellent challenge to see leaders use the QLP survey process iteratively to activate more inclusive approaches and communicate their messages more consistently, clearly and effectively, to foster greater engagement in strategy and a sense of the vision for the future. Willing adoption of a strategic plan is unlikely without pertinent scaffolds of consultation, communication and engagement in place. I find repeatedly in feedback conversations with leaders over their feedback survey reports that every management function that they exercise in a leadership/management role depends on interpersonal ability to communicate concerning that function, be it a fiscal and resource matter, direction setting, organisational restructure or other change process.

I endeavour to maximise the impact from the strategic feedback process by encouraging leaders to communicate the general learning from their 360 feedback results with staff. This practice 'closes the loop' and sends a positive message that the leader is listening. Staff-leader relationships are known to strengthen through this element of 'humanness' and honesty showing forth. For example, with the leader imbued with greater 'mindfulness' on effective strategic communication, staff members tend better to accept a decision or strategic direction, whether they agree with the decision or not, if their leader communicates the relevant rationale to them. I have come to believe that the essence of leadership relates to spirit – a spirit of goodwill, of other-centredness; a listening and learning attitude; a preparedness to develop and communicate strategy and mission, and then of empowering others in the shared achievement of goals. Such a spirit is evident in the case study that is discussed below. The case study refers briefly to the Quality Leadership Profile for Schools (QLPS), a spin-off instrument to the QLP, which is now in place. The QLPS survey is designed specifically for principals/heads and their senior leadership team members wishing to gain feedback in best practice continuous learning mode for themselves and their schools. The background to the development of this instrument is outlined briefly before turning to the case study.

QUALITY LEADERSHIP PROFILE FOR SCHOOLS '360' LEADERSHIP FEEDBACK SURVEY

The Quality Leadership Profile for Schools (QLPS) survey, designed specifically for the use of school principals and their senior teams, is gaining currency in Australia with significant usage by independent schools. The QLPS is a fully customised survey mapped to the Capability Framework of the Australian Council for Educational Leaders (ACEL). As ACEL is described as the peak educational leadership organisation in Australia, this capability framework was deemed to provide a very relevant suite of capability items as a focus for development in the school leadership sector. As many of the QLP and QLPS survey items/questions are the same, the data on pre-existing factors in relation to prior usage of the

QLP in schools was brought forward into the new QLPS instrument. Hence, the QLPS offers important comparative benchmarking data for current and future users for leaders in schools.

HALLMARKS OF A LEADERSHIP LEARNING JOURNEY CASE STUDY DISCUSSION

The story of John Paul College so far recognises the challenges as well as the fruits of persistence; and seemingly bountiful gains they are. John Paul College, commenced in 1982, has approximately 2500 students spanning childcare to year 12. It is an independent co-educational school with ecumenical affiliation, located on thirty hectares of land at Daisy Hill, Logan, Queensland, Australia. I acknowledge my involvement intermittently over the period of a year with the school as a leadership development practitioner and researcher, where my main involvement has been facilitating the QLPS at the invitation of the headmaster and senior leadership team. As I talked with the headmaster and senior leadership team members, the chairperson of the board of the college, front office staff and a handful of students in my comings and goings over a period of the year, the passion for the school, its motto and its values, was palpable. As suggested so far in this chapter, achieving strategic vision is ever a work in progress and, ever, turns upon the engagement of those who are meant to mobilise that vision. Not every decision will be right, there will be flaws, but genuine commitment, passion and excitement to see shared goals accomplished go a very long way to achieving outstanding outcomes. John Paul College offers an effective case study of spirit, passion and commitment which is explored briefly here, with the permission of the authorities of the college, with the caveat, from the leaders, that the story of their leadership learning journey is a 'work in progress'.

The case study proposes a number of potential 'touchstones' of leadership and action reflecting the spirit of a positive leadership learning journey aimed at best strategic outcomes. My contribution to the topic of perspectives in leadership here is an interest in exploring what leaders do to 'take others to *their own* places of independent and unique capability, operating on a platform that is not endlessly upheld in a spirit of frustration or exhaustion' (Drew & Bensley 2001, p.64). For me, this is the picture of the most effective leader. Such leaders 'make it look easy'. They are extraordinarily busy people but they are energised because they love what they are doing, and they are buoyed because goodwill returns to them. The case study presents an example of a leader who credits his leadership team and the college board chair and members to whom he reports. When speaking with the chairperson of the board, he in turn credits the headmaster and the leadership team for the achievements gained. Co-operation, trust and acknowledgement were evident as a sound foundation. In my conversations with the college's headmaster, the following series of actions were revealed. I propose these as 'touchstones' of leadership which reflect actions taken to foster an inclusive culture aimed at communicating and achieving clear organisational mission and goals.

Reinforced a Sense of the Unique, Characteristic Qualities of the Organisation

What became very evident as I spoke to this headmaster was that there was something, as he described, 'in the "DNA"' of the college relating to 'values'. The headmaster said that the college operated in the spirit of Christian ecumenical culture which is accepting of all religions and faiths. They have counted some twenty-seven different faiths represented in the school and the school celebrates all of them. While school observances are based on the Uniting Church in Australia, Anglican and Catholic faiths are foundational in the school's history. The point of difference, the headmaster believes, is respect for all people, and promoting a clear and proud sense of community for students and their families, staff and stakeholders of the college. This includes welcoming visitors to the school. I had noticed when visiting the school on a number of occasions that students stopped along a school pathway and greeted me with 'Good afternoon, Ma'am'. The headmaster said that traditional values are the basis of encouraging students in respectful and pleasant interchanges, such as the greetings to school visitors as I had experienced. The headmaster said that: 'the school acts out its ethos in these ways: respect for all; a practical faith; strong values relating to family; cutting edge education and technology; and linking these through to our vision and curriculum'. He added: 'We have a very strong culture around our motto, "Unity, Christ, Learning". We seek to make learning enduring and embedded wherever possible; we show how theory bears out in practice, but there is ever more to do.' This led me to ask what the headmaster would describe as the unique characteristics and strength of John Paul College.

He said: 'It is the culture, and the ability of people to go the extra mile. People work long hours enthusiastically for success. The pride, the spirit and the goodwill that we have here are points of difference. It is noticeable in the Alumni. For example, the 'JPC Spirit' video was recently released. Alumni students prepared the video. They donated their time, technical skill and musical talent because they wanted "to put something back" to a school that still held their allegiance and interest.' The headmaster avowed that culture is always a 'work in progress' and 'things are never perfect', but that it is exciting to be part of a school community that is focused on pulling together to create something special. Such an attitude is winsome and contagious, and the fruits of the 'work in progress' inevitably are evident. The headmaster demonstrated passion for the goal, a service orientation, clarity of purpose, and evidence of being an empowering leader. Clearly, empowerment had occurred, and was occurring, as considerable change and transition had been navigated over the years.

It was clear in this example of John Paul College that, as I have proposed in an earlier paper (Drew, 2009B), CEOs can influence organisational culture; that formation of culture emanates mostly 'from the top' in terms of behaviour modelling with the reinforcement and reward of 'ways of being' (ontology) being as vital as 'knowledge' (epistemology). It may be others' experience and observation, too, that culture is created not by mottos or value statements but by the actions of people within the organisation as they interact with each other. I argue that the sinecure role of the CEO tends to have, for good or ill, considerable influence by virtue of what constituents imbibe about 'what gets rewarded' and 'how things really work' in their organisation. An attitude evident in the headmaster and the chairperson of the board at John Paul College in my observations and interactions with them is reminiscent of Collins' (2001) findings that a paradoxical combination of 'humility and strong professional will' are the powerful indices of 'Level 5 leadership', characterised by rigor (p. 39). Some of this rigor is exemplified in some evident hard work undertaken by the headmaster and executive to develop connectedness within the team, the college as a whole and with external stakeholders, bound together in clear vision developed consultatively and executed collaboratively.

Avowed the Importance of Coherence and Connectedness at All Levels

It might be said that where the stakes are high and spirit is high, a certain amount of disagreement around 'territorial' interests may arise and may militate against a full sense of connectedness within an organisation. I asked the headmaster of John Paul College how he manages tension between collegiality and competition. He said that, in his communications, he places strong emphases on team accomplishment and on a sense of shared success. Similarly, Carlopio, Andrewartha and Armstrong (2001, p. 491, 495) argue the benefits of building 'dynamic, continuous improvement and innovation' based on building 'multifaceted relationships among team members' to create 'an advanced, high-performing quality culture', emphasising that the leader's ability to unite people with a sense of purpose is crucial. The headmaster claimed, as Renz and Greg (2000) also posit, that a flatter, more inclusive culture makes for a greater sense of connectedness in organisations, and that greater participation occurs when members feel comfortable to express their points of view. In speaking with the headmaster, it was clear that he understood that if an organisation is to present a compelling concerted face to its various publics it must demonstrate coherence within its walls and that, to be credible, the organisation must clearly communicate and 'live' its mission.

For example, if part of the mission is respect for others, the person at the reception desk, or the person who answers the telephone *is*, for the caller, the organisation at that point. Should the encounter run counter to the stated 'mission', then the mission seems hollow. The leadership at John Paul College seeks to make abstract ideals come alive for students, embedding notions of coherency and connectedness within the school. For example, creating a sustainable environment for the school became a key element of mission.

Sustainability principles prevailed in the college's infrastructure and, subsequently, curriculum. It was a commitment to integration and coherence that drove the concept of students 'living' with sustainability practice while learning about sustainability principles at the school. Hence students' experience matches the learning of the curriculum, from water conservation to cost-effective solutions saving money, time and carbon-emissions. Similarly, learning about wellness at the school is reinforced by having 'healthy' food available for students and staff, together with resources and encouragement for practising wellness and maintaining physical fitness. It is ironic that while organisations preoccupy themselves with structure and restructure, clients and stakeholders typically are unconcerned with how people assemble themselves within an organisation, but they do want to engage with an efficient, coherent, integrated organisational presence. Integrating learning with practice for students, wherever possible, greatly assists this sense of coherence for students and teachers at John Paul College as they 'develop the capacity to transfer knowledge...by collaborating and sharing expertise and information...' (De Simone, Werner & Harris, 2002, p. 597).

The John Paul College leadership learning journey demonstrates moving towards a 'listening' leadership style. The leader is far from remote. He puts in place strategies to ensure close connection with external stakeholders, staff and with 'clients' – in this case, students and parents. The theory is not new. Yuill (1985) recommends the careful assessment of external and internal impact factors relating to power, policies and structure, in any community of practice. The theory developed by Yuill is illustrated by empirical evidence from a wide range of Australian organisations with respect to the effectiveness of their policies, strategies and structures and aspects of the organisation's behaviour. Yuill argues that 'maps' (standing for 'management assessment of power and strategies') allow management teams to plot their future course of action by assessing factors in their environment representing major influences, and evaluating the insipient power variables to cope with their impact. Yuill's model includes assessing the organisation's 'capacity to act or react with respect to the needs or demands of [its] environment', then 'evaluat[ing] the policies, strategies..and management styles to determine their effectiveness' (p. 4). The headmaster spoke of many instances where the school was ably supported by the chairperson and members of the board of the college and by parents and families of students, to provide advice on external changing influences, and to question and promote improved practice. Clearly, maintaining close connection with these external stakeholders gives vital 'perspective' in the school's decision-making towards pursuing the best 'life' experiences, educational and lifelong learning outcomes for students.

Consistent with Yuill's model, which 'identifies [any] weaknesses' and 'strategy options based on future scenarios consistent with corporate planning' (p. 4), maintaining important linkages and preserving a sense of 'connectedness' helped, and continues to help the college prepare for major external influences of impact. The Lantern model of organisational development (Drew & Ehrich, 2010) offers a contemporary framework for an organisational development approach based on clarity, communication and coherency. The model proposes an organisational environment that is well illuminated by important relevant data such as information on external influences that may affect the organisation's strategy and operation, clarity on goals and values and on the capabilities by which these will be supported, and having in place ways of assessing and developing capability in line with strategic goals and mission via 360 degree feedback surveys and the like. The Lantern model thus seeks to 'cover the bases' of the multiple imperatives for leaders, expanding on Yuill's model to embrace a continuous development ethos. The John Paul College experience is an example of this model in action.

As the headmaster of John Paul College put it: 'The biggest thing for us was encompassing everyone together, to say, in effect that "if you engage and listen, you will be part of something exciting", and seeing students change in the way they act towards each other each day; they are proud of who they are.' The headmaster felt that it was timely to acknowledge that change had occurred and was occurring in terms of embracing a clear strategic vision. He felt that a 'binding metaphor' was timely. The symbol of the eagle had been used in the past at the school. The eagle was restored as a metaphor with a clear sense of meaning, representing the college motto. The students had embraced this readily. The symbol of the eagle represents the ethos of strength in support as in 'wind beneath my wings' and reflects renewal and inspiration of Scripture (Isaiah 40:31) 'But they that wait upon the Lord shall renew their strength; they shall mount up with wings as eagles; they shall run, and not be weary; they shall walk, and not faint.' This symbol works well because it reflects emphases already in place as a meaningful reminder of how the 'walk' should match the 'talk' of mission and values, while understanding that such alignment is ever 'in progress'. As

Delahaye (2000) states, consciously aspiring towards ever increasing alignment between 'how we say we act' (the 'legitimate system') and 'how we act' (the 'shadow system') in organisations is the organisation's best armoury when needing to navigate change (p, 394). Prosecuting such an alignment in organisations can vest only in individuals' behaviours. It is a mark of credibility. At John Paul College, the eagle is embroidered on uniforms and a marble eagle donated to the college several years ago is being erected in the school grounds. 'Now', the headmaster said, 'it means something special. It is the students' mascot as a reminder of change and growth'. He and the team see this as becoming a symbol of connectedness and unity in which the whole college community takes part.

The headmaster said: 'It is about their pride; they connect in the pride they take in their school and how that, in the way they act, they reflect upon their school, their families and themselves. Enrolments have turned around; we have flipped. We gained two hundred and ninety-five new students in 2012 against a depressed market.' The headmaster was delighted to share the following dialogue which took place at a supermarket some suburbs away when there with his daughter who attends John Paul College. He said that the lady at the check-out asked his daughter 'How old are you?' The daughter answered: 'I am thirteen, going into year eight at John Paul College, ma'am'. Response: 'I have heard massive things about that school lately. I've heard the headmaster is pretty good. Do you know him?' 'Yes, we know him, ma'am', the daughter said as she kept her counsel, happy to hear the positive feedback on the school impartially given.

I noted that the headmaster tries to be as 'visible' for staff as he can. He makes a point of connecting with them as often as possible in both formal and informal ways. He said: 'It is important to take time. It is a physical and mental marathon. If you don't look after yourself physically the body will stop. I try to encourage staff members to be smarter with time and to care for themselves. I take time out to read helpful things, to have a cup of tea with the staff, and to come back to them on issues raised.' The headmaster said that he tries to be considered and not go with knee jerk reactions under pressure, believing that it is quicker in the long run to invest in staying well, keeping to the priorities and being consistent and considered in decision-making. He said that two mentors in particular had helped him stay the course. He emphasised the value of the 'reality check' of being mentored by trusted others as an important element of his leadership learning journey. He said that organisations do not need a figurehead. His view was that the school didn't need a figurehead; it needs a leader who is in touch, provides feedback, who is visible, and with whom staff can raise any matter, discuss a conflict issue, put a different view, and know that it will be a positive interaction. This, he felt, was where mentoring helped leaders, sometimes in fairly isolated roles, to be accountable in their actions and reflective practice, and to remain 'learners'. He spoke of the 'bucket' metaphor: You fill someone's bucket with something good – in other words, recognise them openly for what they have done while they do the same for others as genuine opportunities arise, thus building the mindfulness of goodwill, respect and connectedness, which inevitably, he said, 'rubs off' on the students.

Developed an Action Strategy and Mobilised a Collective Vision

It might be agreed that rallying people, inspiring trust and building strategic unity, the test of strong leadership, entails winning hearts and minds, outweighing a 'command-and-control' type of leadership (Buss, 2001). Klinge (2000) refers to the need for more affective, relationship-building leadership qualities in reaching objectives especially in the environments of education and development. Researchers, Bordage, Foley and Goldyn (2000) conducted an international survey of deans, department heads and chief executive officers in United States universities to identify what potential employers saw as appropriate capabilities for directors of educational programs. The study identified strategic leadership and being able to articulate and inspire vision as the most beneficial elements. Few would argue that this finding is surprising; however in practice, what frequently becomes lost in the 'white paper' of the strategic plans is the notion of 'action'. As I have suggested already, the measure to which the words of the mission statement translate to action is the measure to which any articulated strategy and vision resonates with members as a compelling unifying force. The question for the leader is to address whether strategic vision is being clearly communicated and whether it is 'owned' by those involved. According to 'Participatory Democracy' theory, a participative approach to generation of vision successfully may unify action as members pursue strategic goals which they 'own' as meaningful (Byrne & Davis, 1998). I asked the headmaster of John Paul College what steps he took to mobilise a vision. This was of interest having noted in the QLPS feedback survey that the headmaster and his executive team members had gained as high scores for gaining 'ownership of strategic vision' as for understanding that the strategic plan was in place and was monitored. This was counter to the trend normally seen in the data of result reports.

On the issue of gaining strategic 'ownership', the headmaster explained that earlier the school was attempting to put together a key performance indicator (KPI) document but was not really getting it accepted. He said: 'We had gone backwards to a large degree. I decided to recall the document that they had come up with. I mobilised the entire leadership team and said: 'Where do we *want* to go? What do you think our priority areas are? I asked the board members similarly. We then went to a two-day retreat, all senior staff and board members, thirty people in all, and we nutted out what we wanted to do. We came up with eight key priority areas. The senior leadership team took those key priorities back to staff and from there set up sub-groups, each led by members of the team, to write key performance statements for every one of those KPI goals, with objectives, measures, timelines by which they had to be achieved, and the group responsible for each. These were written up and bought back, finalised in a system with which we are *all* happy.' The headmaster emphasised: *'Now* - and I think this is a point of difference - all of these KPIs are on-line; they are on an on-line chart; every project run at the school is linked to one or other of the KPIs. Progress on projects is documented on this e-chart as threads to the [relevant] performance objective. This is there for all staff and board members to see.' He was justifiably proud of this living, evolving document linking action with mission and strategy at every turn. The document was consulted and updated continually. There was a note of celebration evident as the document mapped the 'wins' along the way, presenting a coherent picture of progress to the staff and board.

The headmaster reflected that they had worked on improving the management of the college: 'The board is much more into transparency, with a clear model for leadership and accountability, with us all moving forward as a learning community.' He outlined that, for every board meeting, all senior leadership team members provide a one-page document on the project or projects for which they are responsible. They show how the projects link to the KPIs and progress of projects in summary each five weeks. The headmaster said: 'My report sits on top of that with any readings I want them to do; it becomes an educational document which board members read on-line a week before the board meeting.' He added: 'For the next stage, we are taking the entire group away this year; we will reflect on the model. This will be about visionary management rather than planning. We will revisit the specific priorities we are trying to work towards in accountability to the board who are keepers of the strategic plan. We will look at different impact factors that might come into play and which might suggest making minor adjustment but we will not be distracted from the plan. If there is an opportunity aligned to the plan, we will consider it.'

As the headmaster recounted these elements as a leadership journey I noted once again that it is clarity on strategy and vision which most catalyses organisational coherency and integration within, and which furnishes a coherent face to the external world, as touched upon earlier as a key touchstone of leadership effectiveness. Fragmentation has no place here – simply no place at all – and yet our organisations build veritable fifedoms of fragmentation, falling so readily to 'silos' and guarded 'territories', and where organisational structures and funding models, leaning to competition rather than collaboration, act as impediments to collective achievement. For leaders, such challenges are to be anticipated and mitigated. It is here that a further 'touchstone' emerged.

Managed the Nexus between 'Individual' and 'Collective' Achievement

Research (for example, see Drew & Kerr, 2003; Stiles 2004) suggests that innovation rarely occurs in silos but where people repudiate the boundaries that artificially separate them. For example, Stiles (2004) suggests that when exploring new possibilities, those involved acknowledge early the inevitable biases residing in the team and seek to 'understand the allegedly different worlds they [the members] have built on their respective sides of the divide' (p. 160). This may entail discovering what parties are willing to offer, trade, share or commit to the venture. Clarifying roles and responsibilities early in the team's life may well offset potential misunderstandings on delineation of responsibility. Simply having these conversations tends to build trust and goodwill. In my experience, sound leaders welcome difference to gain richer perspectives on an issue. No leader worth the title should covet the stasis and mediocrity of 'groupthink'. Nevertheless, it may take the strong influence of a leader to see different personalities within a team willingly coalesce and subjugate their personal interests for the interests of what is best for end users.

As mentioned, a goal at John Paul College was to build sustainability experientially and theoretically for students. In building outstanding approaches to natural resource acquisition and utilisation, the leaders of the college recognised that this would entail looking beyond functional boundaries at the college to explore paths to integrate learning and lived experience in the important contemporary realm of environmental sustainability. The first step was taking the time to engage in the relevant conversations as a team, with the ultimate aims of 'client'/ student benefit in view.

Clearly the headmaster made every effort to meld a team that is focused on 'the whole picture', and he said that, as this focus increases, fragmentation lessens. He said: 'The unity pledge has broken down the silos. I try to cultivate collaboration and to recognise individual and collective achievement. If someone wants a lot of money to achieve a particular initiative we weigh it up as a group. The answer might be "no" or it might be "yes", but it is shared consideration with the decision always linked to priorities. Staying with those priorities makes it really easy, as at any one time there are a hundred good ideas.' The headmaster further explained: 'With [the ethos of] sustainability such a big focus for the college, we sought ventures to create the most environmentally responsible and resource economic infrastructure here, and to demonstrate sustainability values in practice and in the curriculum.' He said that now students observe and experience sustainability principles in an integrated approach to learning and practice, and that this has a binding, uniting effect for the school community at the college. He added: 'Our property manager does a great job, but because of needing to put money into other areas I said to him recently that we will need to drop his budget at this time, but this was done in a way that honoured the leader's passion, and again the sense of pulling together even when there may be a sense of disappointment at a decision not going a particular way, always held the group together.'

The headmaster believes that consistency is most important, together with having a strong relationship already in place. Indeed, it is not possible to 'invent' a strong relationship 'on demand'. Robust professional relationships aimed at collective achievement present a powerful force for reaching goals, and in such a climate all can share in the 'small wins' and significant successes.

Identified Ways of Navigating Change and Transition, Cultivating Flexibility

In a changing education leadership environment, change relating to external influences may be presumed upon as an ever-present reality (Hanna, 2003; Kotter, 2002). Authors such as Barnett (2004), Boyatzis, Stubbs and Taylor (2002), Collins (2001), Delahaye (2000), Healy, Ehrich, Hansford and Stewart (2001) and Sauer (2002) argue in different ways and contexts a similar message - that change-adept organisations have leaders who can engage others in responding flexibly to new initiatives. The headmaster at John Paul College clearly believed that the capacity to navigate transition is absolutely vital, and that a number of elements were crucial to success. The leadership had taken deliberate steps to promote adaptation and flexibility. At the outset of significant change, the leader spoke to the executive team about what this entailed for executive team members and their staff. The headmaster saw his and the executive team's commitment to personal/professional development as a vital part of being able to get through the rough spots at a time of transition. He said that the college had undergone a major change in culture, which can never 'happen overnight' but by consistent effort, and consolidation and 'reality check' was timely.

The college headmaster and team, with the support of the college board, sought opportunity to expand the evidence-based portfolio of attributes and capabilities of the executive by investing in a systematic means of leadership and management performance assessment. The headmaster saw this as the only way to be sure that individuals were best equipped in the capabilities that would help ensure maximum outcomes for the school. The headmaster and executive members, with the board's full support, committed to using the Quality Leadership Profile for Schools. The purpose was to gain feedback in order to 'plot', as it were, where they were currently in the perceptions of their staff, peers including board representation, and supervisor. The goal was to identify perceived areas of strength and areas for improvement. The results, while providing some guidance for further enhancement such as ensuring full penetration of mission and goals to all levels of staff, were overwhelmingly positive for individuals and the group.

The results typified the point made early in the chapter that investing in relationships in tandem with strong processes for achieving clarity on strategy and vision pays dividends. Outcomes of high quality in all dimensions were noted. The headmaster is the first to say: 'We are not there yet, we have a way to go; this is always a work in progress, but it is such an exciting journey!' I term it 'enlightened passion', and it is, as ever, contagious. Following the QLPS, the executive team was brought together for an overview of the QLPS exercise where it was possible to consider, further to individual results, the whole picture presented by the feedback. The team was keen to continue sound practices of communication, knowing that their respective staffing groups registered a sense of 'ownership' of strategic mission and vision, and they felt this was not to be taken for granted but consistently reinforced. For example, linking strategic clarity to a greater sense of role clarity for each person reporting to executive members was suggested as a way to help ensure that every staff member sees the contribution that their efforts are making to overall mission and goals. The headmaster emphasised that he depends on each executive team member to communicate these messages as it is impossible to communicate this personally to all staff as he would like. I was reminded of Aristotle's 'appeals' to *logos*, *ethos* and *pathos* in seeking engagement – firstly logical appeal; secondly ethical appeal vesting in the credibility of the speaker; and thirdly appeal to the emotions recognising the human element in all undertakings. I felt that the leadership at John Paul College demonstrated these three precepts in a genuine approach to communication and work that fostered mutual respect as it galvanised action, bringing the college through changeful times and continuing to enlist the school community with zeal and passion.

The QLPS process also reinforced that strong working relationships had been established and there was evidence that these were embedded in strong values, with strategic clarity as the guiding light for all decisions. The headmaster reflected upon 'a good saying from a mentor' that he said he tried to live by – 'Always do what is right no matter how hard it is. If you concentrate on doing what is right you'll never go wrong.' He said he had learned that if strategy is clear and relationships are as sound as they can be, people feel more inclined to be flexible and accommodating when called upon to change the way things are done. This echoes the views of Delahaye (2000) and Barnett (2004) that sound relationships, the 'lived' values of an effective 'shadow' system, attending to positive behaviours and 'way of being' are the organisation's best investments for capacity to be flexible and respond to change. This suggests, again, that paying attention to effective relationships is not peripheral but crucial to strategic organisational capability.

CONCLUSION

This chapter has suggested a number of themes as 'touchstones' of leadership and action. These touchstones have emphasised pursuing distinctiveness of purpose, building coherency and integration, mobilising a vision, consistently communicating strategy and values, focusing on collective achievement, and cultivating ability to respond to needed change. These themes, far from purporting to be inclusive of all factors, offer a scaffold by which leaders and teams might audit a collaborative team's positioning for rich performance, and for development of leadership. The case study celebrates leadership as essentially a generous-spirited relationship, centred on others rather than self, with a clear purpose in view, and a robustness and passion for communicating and acting upon strategy. The chairperson of the board of the college put it this way: 'Because we all understand "why" what we are doing contributes to the overall plan, this focuses, aligns and motivates us all. John Paul College has had a wonderful history, but I do believe that the best days are still ahead of us.'

It seems to me that the leader who is open- minded, canvassing others' views and embracing a learning orientation, has nothing to fear, while closed-mindedness has everything to fear, as the interest is with self and with safeguarding a 'position'. The narrative here proposes leadership as a collaborative experience of direction-setting where collective will conspires to benefit all participants. The case study exemplifies a leadership model that tends towards 'reproducing itself' for learning and growth. As the literature enjoins, effective leaders do well to avoid the inertia of fence-sitting as much as the stasis of habitual rejection of other possibilities. Accordingly, the last word goes to the headmaster of John Paul College: 'We must allow ourselves and others to make mistakes rather than slip into safe mediocrity; so long as it is a learning journey!' The sense of forward movement is compelling, reminding of the sage words attributed to one Eric Hoffer (undated): 'Learners inherit the earth, while "the learned" [those who believe that they have arrived at all there is to know] are equipped for a world that no longer exists.'

REFERENCES

Barnett, R. (2004). Learning for an unknown future. *Higher Education Research & Development, 23*(3), 247-260.

Bordage, G., Foley, R., & Goldyn, S. (2000). Skills and attributes of directors of educational programmes. *Medical Education, 34*, 201-202.

Boyatzis, R.E., Stubbs, E.C., & Taylor, S.N. (2002). Learning cognitive and emotional competencies through graduate management education. *Academy of Management Learning and Education, 1*(2), 150-162.

Buss, D. (2001). When managing isn't enough: Nine ways to develop the leaders you need. *Workforce, 80*(12), 44-48.

Byrne, J. & Davis, G. (1998). Participation and the NSW policy process: A discussion paper for the Cabinet Office, New South Wales, New South Wales Government, Sydney, (pp. 3-6).

Carlopio, J., Andrewartha, G., & Armstrong, H. (2001). *Developing Management Skills: A Comprehensive Guide for Leaders* (2nd ed.). Frenchs Forest NSW: Pearson Education Aust. Collins, J. (2001). *Good to Great: Why some companies make the leap.and others don't*. New York: HarperCollins.

Delahaye, B.L. (2000). *Human resource development: principles and practice*. New York: John Wiley & Sons Australia.

De Simone, R.L., Werner J.M., & Harris, D.M. (2002). *Human Resource Development* (3rd ed). New York: Harcourt College Press.

Drew, G. (2010). Enabling or 'Real' Power and Influence in Leadership. *Journal of Leadership Studies 4*(1), 47-58.

Drew, G. (2009A). A '360' View for Individual Leadership Development. *Journal of Management Development, 28*(7), 581-592.

Drew, G., (2009B). Leadership and Organisational Culture: Can the CEO and Executive Leadership Teams in Bureaucratic Organisations Influence Organisational Culture? *Academic Leadership OnLine Journal, 7*(1).

Drew, G. (2006). Balancing Academic Advancement with Business Effectiveness: The dual role for university leaders. *The International Journal of Knowledge, Culture and Change Management, 6*(4), 117-125.

Drew, G.M. & Ehrich, L.E. (2010) A Model of Organisational Leadership Development Informing Succession Development: Elements and Practices. *Academic Leadership Online Journal, 8*(4).

Drew, G., Ehrich, L.C. & Hansford, B.C. (2008). An Exploration of University Leaders' Perceptions of Leadership and Learning. *Leading & Managing 14*(2), 1-18.

Drew, G. & Kerr, C. (2003). Learning partners in discovery and innovation. *Proceedings of the Women in Research Conference*, November (pp. 1-16). Central Queensland University, Rockhampton, Queensland.

Drew, G., & Bensley, L. (2001). Managerial effectiveness for a new millennium in the global higher education sector. *Higher Education in Europe, XXVI*(1), 61-68.

Drew-McKain, L. (March, 2012), Personal communications

Hanna, D.E. (2003). Building a leadership vision: Eleven strategic challenges for higher education. *Educause*, July-August, 25-34.

Healy, L., Ehrich, L.C., Hansford, B. & Stewart, D. (2001).
Conversations: A means of learning, growth and change. *Journal of Educational Administration, 39*(4), 332-345.

Klinge, B. (2000). Leadership in academic institutions: raising the value of Teaching. *Medical Education, 34*, 201-202.

Kotter, J.P. (2002). *The Heart of Change*. Boston, Mass.: HBS Press.

Maurer, T.J., Mitchell, D.R.D., & Barbeite, F.G. (2002), Predictors of attitudes toward a 360-degree feedback system and involvement in post-feedback management development activity. *Journal of Occupational and Organizational Psychology, 75*, 87-107.

Rafferty, A.E. & Neale, M. (2004). What do followers say about supportive and developmental leadership? Paper presented at the *18th Annual conference of the Australian and New Zealand Academy of Management* (December). Full paper on CD ISBN 0-476-01131-0, University of Otago, NZ: ANZAM.

Renz, M.A., & Greg, J.B. (2000). *Effective Small Group Communication in Theory and Practice*. Needham Heights: Allyn and Bacon.

Sauer, P. (2002, June). CEOs speak: Executive leadership. Chemical Market Reporter, pp. 1-14.

Scott, G., Coates, H. & Anderson, M. (2008). *Learning leadership in times of change: Academic leadership capabilities for Australian higher education*. Sydney: Australian Learning and Teaching Board.

Stiles, D.R. (2004). Narcissus revisited: The values of management academics and their role in business school strategies in the UK and Canada. *British Journal of Management*, 15, 157-175.

Yuill, B. (1985). *Power and Strategies: Assessment of Australian Organisations*. Melbourne: Vital Instant Print.

In: Perspectives in Leadership
Editor: Jerry D. VanVactor

ISBN: 978-1-62417-170-3

Chapter 2

RECOGNIZING SKILLS FOR EFFECTIVE LEADERSHIP: A CASE STUDY OF LEADERS WITHIN THE WIZARD OF OZ

*Maria M. Johnson**

MA from Eastern Kentucky University, Richmond, KY, US

ABSTRACT

Using *The Wizard of Oz* as a case study, this article examines leadership skills employed by some of the movie's primary characters, and their effectiveness at directing the actions of their followers. The relationship between power, authority and leadership is established, providing a framework for identifying the skills used by the characters. Throughout several scenes within the movie, Dorothy, the Scarecrow, the Wicked Witch of the West and the Wizard of Oz all provide examples of varying leadership characteristics, such as organization, flexibility and responsibility, but some of these characters are more effective in motivating their followers in the pursuit of their goals than others. By identifying and analyzing the skills demonstrated, the effectiveness of the characters can be determined. Whether the leaders serve in a formal or informal setting, however, has little bearing on their success, and equally important, the nature of the characters does not determine the effectiveness of the leaders; "good" leaders are not necessarily any more effective than "bad" ones.

Although *leadership* can be defined in its most simple form as the role fulfilled by a person who guides or directs a group (http://www.dictionary.com), it can also be used to describe the ability employed by someone who motivates others to follow his/her direction for a common goal. Sometimes the goal is clearly defined, such as in the workplace, but in less formal settings the common objective might remain ambiguous to the casual observer, and leadership skills may go unnoticed. For both scenarios, however, pop culture offers a prime venue to explore the characteristics of leaders in each of these situations, and to

---

* Correspondence concerning this article should be addressed to maria_johnson184@EKU.edu

determine the effectiveness of each type of leader in influencing the actions of his followers. Through an examination of some of the key characters in *The Wizard of Oz*, this article hopes to establish some basic tenets related to leadership in order to demonstrate that a leader becomes effective by developing and employing a "leadership" skill set.

To begin, the concept of leadership must be distinguished from that of power and authority; although these three often go hand in hand, they are distinct and cannot be used interchangeably. Next, certain skills and traits, when applied adeptly, offer a greater degree of effectiveness to anyone fulfilling a leadership role. Third, leadership can be either formal or informal, and the skills exercised in each can remain the same to achieve the aims of the group, regardless of which category better defines the group. Last, "good" and "bad" leaders do not equate to effective and ineffective leaders; bad leaders are often very effective in recognizing their ambitions, and good leaders can just as easily lose sight of their goals. While each of these four principles is important in understanding effective leadership, the primary focus of this essay will identify and analyze the leadership skills displayed by some of the characters within *The Wizard of Oz*; the other three will provide parameters for understanding how these skills enhance the effectiveness of the same players.

Leadership can invoke images of power and authority, and an effective leader generally possesses both. However, power and authority are attributes of leadership, and these qualities may be granted, either explicitly by another holder of power (such as another leader), or implicitly by a group of followers. Because these qualities are bestowed, they do not necessarily imply an ability to lead. Instead, leadership emerges when a set of skills are employed effectively in such a way as to maintain power and authority. In *The Wizard of Oz*, Dorothy travels over the rainbow and lands on the Wicked Witch of the East, killing her. Glinda, the Good Witch of the North, bestows the ruby slippers on Dorothy, granting her power that the Wicked Witch of the West desires. Although Dorothy now possesses an artifact of power, she is not necessarily awarded the qualities of an effective leader, and it is only as the story progresses that she displays her leadership skills. Glinda also shares knowledge with Dorothy, as the young girl searches for a way to return home. Follow the yellow brick road to the Emerald City, Glinda instructs her, and seek the Wizard of Oz for a way to return to Kansas, as he is a grantor of wishes. Dorothy's companions yield to her authority as she makes decisions for the group, based upon her knowledge, which then inspires her use of leadership skills. Because she knows of the Wizard's powers and believes in his ability to help each of them, Dorothy is able to convince her followers that it is to their benefit to accompany her so that their wishes can be met as well as her own. By persuading each of them to align their goals with hers, Dorothy exercises her authority, given to her tacitly by each of her followers, based upon her knowledge of the Wizard.

While power and authority are important attributes of leadership, however, they are not independent of the skills and traits possessed by a leader. Dorothy assembles a crew of companions on her travels from Munchkinland to the Emerald City by motivating them to marry their goals to hers. Her listening and communication skills, as well as her empathy, first come into play when she discovers the Scarecrow's desire to possess a brain. Through a singing dialogue, Dorothy listens, distinguishes his need, and communicates her knowledge of the wizard's power to grant wishes. Equally important, she recognizes and understands the similarity of the Scarecrow's goal to hers, and encourages him to accompany her to achieve his own goal. More subtly, Dorothy allows the Scarecrow to participate in the decision-making process throughout the story, despite his belief that he does not have the intelligence to do so. Because Dorothy understands his longing, she permits the Scarecrow to step into a role that fulfills his needs. As her path carries her toward her other two companions, Dorothy likewise identifies the commonality of her personal wish to return home with those of the Tin Man (to acquire a heart) and the Lion (to achieve courage), and she offers each of them the opportunity to join her on her journey, so that collectively they might all attain what they most desire upon meeting the Wizard. Without these skills, Dorothy might not have been able to identify and understand the needs of others, nor to share her knowledge about the Wizard with her followers, and in the end she may very well have made her journey alone.

With the progression of the story it becomes clear, however, that these are not the only skills at Dorothy's disposal, as she tells each of her companions about her belief that the Wizard will offer his help. Dorothy possesses the courage to remain true to her course. From the meeting with her first companion, the Scarecrow, Dorothy displays the courage of her convictions, and she emanates sincerity throughout the dialogues she shares with her followers. Consecutively, Dorothy explains to the Scarecrow, Tin Man and Lion the Wizard's ability to grant them what they need, even though her knowledge is limited to what she has been told by Glinda, and not what she has experienced herself. When Dorothy and her followers reach the Emerald City and are at first denied audience with the Wizard, Dorothy does not waiver in her belief that he can help them. Unfortunately, during their first audience with the Wizard, the four travelers realize that despite their long journey, their trials are not yet over. The Wizard instructs them to go away and return only when they have secured the broom of the Wicked Witch of the West if they want to obtain his help in achieving their aims. The emotional strain of such a blow after traveling so far pushes Dorothy to feel defeated, but she realizes that her goal of returning to Kansas is still worthwhile. Eventually, with the support of the Scarecrow, Tin Man and Lion, she rallies her strength and decides to forge ahead. Had she allowed doubt to color her judgment of the Wizard's abilities to grant her particular desire, Dorothy may not remained persuasive in her efforts to convince her followers to travel with her, and it is possible that she would have eventually failed in the pursuit of her goal.

Her courage is not limited to this one aspect, however, as Dorothy also possesses the courage to face a number of obstacles on her journey. Along the yellow brick road near the Tin Man, the Wicked Witch of the West appears, threatening Dorothy and her followers if they continue on their journey to the Emerald City. Realizing the danger to the others after the witch throws a fire ball at the Scarecrow, Dorothy offers to travel the remainder of the trail alone, and leave her companions behind in relative safety. Although the Scarecrow and Tin Man exhibit courage by refusing to part from Dorothy's side, Dorothy, too, displays her determination by making the difficult decision to choose the safety of her companions over her own. Later, as the travelers move forward, they journey through a dark forest and face the dangers posed by unfriendly trees and unknown predators. Again, they travel on despite the peril, following Dorothy's lead. When Dorothy and her followers are attacked by a seemingly vicious lion, Dorothy takes cover behind a tree, until the Lion threatens bodily harm to her dog, Toto. The moment that real danger emerges, Dorothy steps in and defends her companions, swatting the Lion on the nose. Regardless of the possibility of harm to herself, she shames the Lion for lashing out at them, and forces him to admit that his own shortcomings make him act out of fear. Finally, when the Great Oz reveals his seemingly impossible requirement -- that the group must return with the broom of the witch -- Dorothy faces the possibility of failure at a time when she thought her journey to be at an end.

Although emotionally and physically drained, Dorothy pushes aside her despair and chooses to stand firm in the face of these obstacles. She does not expect her followers to go before her and make her path easier, but instead leads them toward the witch's castle while relying on their support.

In the last instance, Dorothy also displays another important skill of effective leadership: flexibility. Glinda, a leader in her own right, provides Dorothy with an initial plan to achieve her goal of returning to Kansas -- follow the yellow brick road to the Emerald City where the Great Oz resides -- but Glinda's guidance could carry Dorothy only so far. When the Wizard refuses to accommodate Dorothy and her fellow travelers, they must establish another means to achieve their goals, even though it might involve a direct confrontation with the Wicked Witch of the West. Rather than admit defeat, they leave the Emerald City with renewed determination, even though Dorothy and her group now had to change course. At first the additional challenge seemed daunting to Dorothy, but her adaptability allowed her to continue to lead. Unfortunately for the group, Dorothy is soon captured by the witch's flying monkeys, and the remaining three are left without a leader despite her ability to bend to the circumstances.

Because of Dorothy's abduction, the possibility arises that the band of travelers could fall into disunity. Instead, the Scarecrow steps up to assume leadership, displaying his own flexibility as he exchanges his role of follower to leader, in spite of his own self-perception of being brainless. He devises a plan for Dorothy's rescue from the witch's castle, but when presented with a better opportunity, he quickly devises another, showcasing both his adaptability and his ability to organize the actions of the group. While the Scarecrow, Tin Man and Lion observe the Wicked Witch of the West's guards marching along her castle's perimeter, the Scarecrow explains the tactic that he's devised. However, in the middle of their discussion, Dorothy's followers are attacked from behind by three stray guards, and the Scarecrow recognizes the potential of a better strategy. After triumphing over the soldiers' ambush, the Scarecrow, Tin Man, and Lion don scavenged uniforms and blend in with the witch's forces until they ascertain Dorothy's position within the castle walls. Because of the Scarecrow's versatility and organization, Dorothy escapes death at the hands of the witch, and the other three travelers eventually have their wishes fulfilled.

Thus far, Dorothy and her followers have remained the principal focus for the identification and analysis of leadership skills, but there are other, equally important leaders in *The Wizard of Oz* who display their own abilities to command a group. The most apparent of these is the Wicked Witch of the West, as she organizes forces to act on her behalf against Dorothy and her ensemble. Whereas Dorothy assembles a small group of three to accompany her to the Emerald City, the witch coordinates the command of both land troops and air forces to help her achieve her primary ambition, recovering Dorothy's ruby slippers and their inherent power. After Dorothy's departure from the Emerald City, the Wicked Witch of the West directs her flying monkeys to capture the girl and deliver her to the castle. When the Scarecrow leads the Tin Man and the Lion on a rescue mission, the witch mobilizes her ground troops to entrap them, along with Dorothy, in a tower along the castle wall. Repeatedly, the Wicked Witch of the West demonstrates her organizational expertise in mounting a preemptory assault against Dorothy and her companions.

While the Wicked Witch of the West possesses an affinity for organization, she also demonstrates an unquestionable aptitude for maintaining discipline among her followers. When Dorothy is first captured, the witch threatens harm to Toto in an effort to coerce

Dorothy to give up her ruby slippers. Toto, however, manages to escape his imprisonment, and the Wicked Witch commands her troops to stop him as he attempts to leap from the drawbridge of her castle, and they rush to attack the little dog in an attempt to do so. Later, as the Scarecrow plots Dorothy's rescue outside the castle wall, Dorothy's followers observe the witch's troops marching in formation. The military precision of the soldiers' steps, their uniformity of handling weapons, and their chanting a cadence as one voice all work together as elements of intimidation against Dorothy's would-be rescuers. The Scarecrow, Tin Man and Lion realize that only through establishing absolute obedience through strong discipline could the Wicked Witch of the West maintain power over so many.

Upon closer examination of this same example, a leadership skill shared by both the Wicked Witch of the West and Dorothy reveals itself and provides a stark contrast of two distinct leadership styles. Both endeavor to provide and maintain security for their followers, but they do so through the application of contradictory methods. Dorothy, recognizing the dire consequences to her loyal follower, tosses a bucket of water to extinguish the Scarecrow as the Wicked Witch of the West ignites him with his worst fear, fire. Unfortunately for the witch, she becomes an unintentional victim of death by melting, prompting the guards to salute Dorothy. Such action of the witch's soldiers demonstrates their service to her through fear. Whereas Dorothy provides security by protecting her followers from external dangers when they arise, the Wicked Witch of the West offers security against harm that she herself might inflict upon her followers.

Throughout the scenes explored thus far to identify the leadership skills displayed within *The Wizard of Oz*, another significant skill or trait has remained constant, underpinning those previously analyzed: responsibility. Dorothy, the Scarecrow, and the Wicked Witch of the West all engage in responsible acts that guide and protect their followers as each of these leaders pursue their goals. Dorothy's empathy allows her to understand the needs of her followers, but she does not exploit them for her own personal gain. The Scarecrow recognizes the danger in his plan to rescue Dorothy, but he does not send the Tin Man and the Lion into the witch's castle while he hides in safety. The Wicked Witch of the West maintains order among her troops, despite the amount of energy required for her to do so. However, one other leader in this story remains to be examined, and his conduct better illustrates a lack of responsible action in the guidance of his followers. As previously noted, the Wizard of Oz did not act in the manner expected by Dorothy and her followers when they first approached him. Rather than grant them their wishes as the Good Witch of the North indicated that he would, the Wizard sent Dorothy's group on the quest to acquire the Wicked Witch of the West's broom. This assignment could be interpreted as an act of responsibility if the Wizard's true intent had been for Dorothy and her crew to rid the land of Oz of evil. His purpose, however, was not so benevolent. Instead, the Wizard sent them off on what he regarded as an impossible task, hoping that they would not return. He did so to conceal his own inability to perform as the group expected; his purpose was not to further the goal of the group.

As the examples provided here indicate, not every leader possesses the same skills and traits, yet all leaders can be classified as belonging to one of two broad categories, either formal or informal, regardless of the skills they employ. Political and military rulers, teachers, and priests are all examples of formal leaders, with specific duties to their followers defining their role as leaders. Political and military rulers are entrusted with the power and authority to maintain security (physical, capital) for their followers, and often have specific dictates within a defined realm. Informal leaders, on the other hand, have no specific instructions on what they are to accomplish or maintain. The class bully, the friend who always organizes activities for the group, and the person who steps up in a crisis depict informal leaders. Even though there is no explicit expectation that these people share a responsibility to accomplish anything, they often create a goal, and convince others to join them in its pursuit.

Glinda, the Wicked Witch of the West, and the Wizard of Oz all lead within a formal framework. Glinda acts as a political leader of the munchkins, speaking for the group upon Dorothy's arrival from Kansas, as she welcomes the young girl and questions her motives for killing the Wicked Witch of the East. When the Wicked Witch of the West appears, threatening Dorothy, Glinda intervenes, and reminds the Wicked Witch of the West of her lack of power outside her own dominion. The Wicked Witch of the West, on the other hand, serves as a military commander, effectively wielding her power through her armed forces, but only within her own domain. When Dorothy departs from the Emerald City, the witch plots and executes Dorothy's kidnapping and ensuing imprisonment through a few simple commands to her forces. The Wizard of Oz reigns within the Emerald City, acting as a political-religious leader. His ascendancy there arose from his miraculous journey to Oz in a hot air balloon, whereupon the citizens of the green metropolis legitimized the wizard's leadership as an act of divine intervention.

As informal leaders, however, Dorothy and the Scarecrow each take on the role of leader with no specific parameters to define their duties. Dorothy leaves Munchkin City on a journey unescorted with only one aim, to find a way home via the Wizard's intervention, and her group of followers join together naturally. The Scarecrow propitiously guarded a cornfield at the crossroads of the yellow brick road, the Tin Man rusted in place near the unfriendly apple trees, and the Lion rushed the others in an attempt to frighten them as they entered the dark woods. Through no planning on her part, Dorothy assembles a small following, and serves as their de facto leader. Similarly, the Scarecrow steps into the role of leader only after Dorothy is kidnapped by the flying monkeys; no elections were held, no coronation occurred, and no portent revealed him to be the chosen one. He simply saw the need to guide the others on a rescue mission of a young girl, and acted upon it. Neither Dorothy nor the Scarecrow pursued a role in leadership, yet each of them demonstrated skills that the others recognized as belonging to leaders.

Regardless of the formality surrounding a leader's role, it is equally important to note that both "good" and "bad" leaders can employ some of the same qualities, and a bad leader can be just as effective as a good leader. A classroom bully, for instance, is often viewed as a bad influence, but she can maintain a group of followers if she practices qualities of effective leadership. By the same token, a benevolent ruler might find his domain in disarray if he is unable to clarify his goals and provide guidance to his followers. The scenes examined here demonstrate that the terms "good" and "bad" remain independent of "effective" and "ineffective" when applied to leadership. In *The Wizard of Oz*, the Wicked Witch of the West is a bad ruler, but she is not ineffective. She forces others to bend to her will, and menaces those that stand in her way. However, she has a clear goal -- recovering the ruby slippers from Dorothy -- and she exploits her personal leadership skills to the fullest so that she might achieve it. She demonstrates her skills by organizing the actions of many and maintaining discipline among all who serve her. The Wizard of Oz, however, is cast in the role of a good leader, a grantor of wishes. Despite all the power and authority bestowed on him by the Emerald City citizens, though, he has denied admittance into his chamber for as long as anyone can remember. Only after seeing the witch's sky-writing does the Wizard make an exception for Dorothy and her fellow travelers. Unfortunately, he does not have the leadership skills necessary to live up to their expectations, and chooses to hide behind a remote and forbidding façade so that no one will notice his inadequacies. Later, the Wizard is exposed as a fraud when Toto whips open the control room's curtain, but only then does the Wizard demonstrate his generosity as he presents the Scarecrow, Tin Man, and Lion with totems that fulfill their wishes. His goodness, however, does not equate to effectiveness.

All of the characters examined herein derived power and authority either from an established leader or from followers, but only some fulfilled the requirements of effective leadership. Dorothy, as an informal leader, acquires her authority by exercising her abilities to listen, communicate, and empathize with her followers. She hears their needs, understands them, and shares her knowledge of how they might all achieve their goals by following the same path. The Wicked Witch of the West, on the other hand, maintains her power through strict discipline and careful organization of her land and air forces, so that her minions might help her attain her personal objective. In spite of his straw-filled head, the Scarecrow capitalizes on his flexibility in transforming from a follower into a leader when the situation demands it. Unfortunately for Dorothy and her followers, however, the Wizard of Oz utilizes his power irresponsibly, and commands them to fulfill a seemingly impossible task so that he might hide his inability to meet their needs in the manner that they envision. In each case, power and authority served as attributes of leadership, but not as a substitute for it.

Skills such as empathy and responsibility provide a leader with tools to accomplish his goals effectively; so do an ability to communicate and listen. Others, such as organization, flexibility and discipline allow a leader to control their circumstances or to change with them. While the leadership skills identified above do not exhaust the possible faculties available to succeed, these traits can be developed or enhanced by those fulfilling a leadership role, thereby increasing their effectiveness in attaining the goals of the organization. The success of their performance, however, remains independent of the formal nature of the group's structure. Dorothy led only three followers who happened to join her along the way, while the Wicked Witch of the West controlled the actions of all those residing within her domain; yet each displayed effective leadership, by successfully motivating a group to help them reach their aims. The Wizard of Oz, however, was unable to do so despite his official position within the Emerald City. While an effective leader may possess one or many skills to accomplish her goals, the same set of skills serves a successful leader in either formal or informal circumstances.

Similarly, both "good" and "bad" leaders can achieve their goals, therefore the focus of analysis should remain on effective and ineffective leadership, rather than the subjective qualities defining good and bad. Glinda, Dorothy, the Scarecrow and the Wizard of Oz are all "good," in the sense that they desire to help others achieve their own aims, but they are not all effective. The Wicked Witch of the West follows a darker path, because she pursues her goal regardless of the harm she may cause to those who stand in her way; yet she is effective in guiding her followers to persevere on her behalf. Leadership can be categorized in a number of ways, but the skills a leader uses, and the method in which she implements them, that determine effective leadership.

REFERENCES

Fleming, V. (Director). (1939). The wizard of oz [Film]. Los Angeles: MGM.

leadership. (n.d.). Dictionary.com Unabridged. Retrieved February 28, 2012, from Dictionary.com website: http://dictionary.reference.com/ browse/leadership.

In: Perspectives in Leadership
Editor: Jerry D. VanVactor

ISBN: 978-1-62417-170-3
© 2013 Nova Science Publishers, Inc.

Chapter 3

WORK ENGAGEMENT IN TRANSFORMATIONAL LEADERS: A MULTI-LEVEL, MULTI-SOURCE STUDY

Karina Nielsen

National Research Centre for the Working Environment
Copenhagen, Denmark

ABSTRACT

Purpose – Building on cognitive theories, the aim of the study was to investigate the relationship between leaders' appraisals of their own transformational leadership behaviors and levels of work engagement, and how followers' group climate may enhance this link.

Design – The study was a multi-method, multi-source study. Experience Sampling Method was used to collect leaders' own ratings of their transformational leadership behaviors and work engagements states in the situation (N = 58) and followers completed a questionnaire on their group collaborative climate (N = 653).

Findings – Exerting transformational leadership behaviors significantly predicted leaders' work engagement states and a general collaborative climate in the group of followers enhanced this relationship.

Implications – Understanding how behaviors specific to the leadership role is related to leaders' work engagement provides valuable knowledge of how we may increase leaders' engagement. As leaders play a vital role in maintaining staff well-being and obtaining organizational objectives, their own levels of work engagement is important to ensure organizational health.

Originality/value – Previous research has primarily focused on how transformational leadership is related to followers' work engagement, however, in this study I examined the link between transformational leadership and leaders' own engagement levels, testing cognitive theories. Furthermore, I extend current research by examining characteristics specific to the leader role, e.g. transformational leadership behaviors and leading a group of followers, whereas previous research has focused only on general work characteristics, such as job autonomy, social support and opportunities to learn.

Keywords: Experience Sampling Method; Work Engagement; Transformational Leadership; Team Collaborative Climate; Multi-level Analyses

Previous research on leaders' work engagement (e. g. Schaufeli, Taris, & van Rhenen, 2008) has focused on general job characteristics irrespective of the role leaders have in the organization. In this multi-level, multi-source study I extend previous research by focusing on work characteristics specific to the leader role, i.e. whether the degree to which leaders exert transformational leadership behaviors and whether the characteristics of the teams they manage predict leaders' own engagement levels. In doing so, I provide valuable information on how the leaders' role is related to their engagement.

Organizations today face new challenges in their efforts to be competitive in the global market. Recent efforts to ensure organizational performance have begun to emphasize positive organizational behavior and positive states at work (Koyuncu, Burke, Fiksembaum, 2006). In today's competitive environment, leaders are needed to ensure competitive advantage; healthy and strong leaders are at the heart of healthy organizations (Quick, Macik-Frey, & Cooper, 2007). Engaged leaders at the first line level are particularly important for two reasons: First, because such leaders play a decisive role achieving organizational objectives and maintaining staff well-being (Hiller, Day, & Vance, 2006; Nielsen & Randall, 2009; Nielsen, Randall, & Yarker, & Brenner, 2008; van Dierendonck, Haynes, Borril, & Stride, 2004) and second, because engaged leaders at this level may engage their followers through contagion processes (Bakker, Westman, & van Emmerik, 2009). The cross-over of the mood and emotions of leaders to their followers has been established (Glasø & Einarsen, 2006; Sy, Cote, & Saavedra, 2005). Furthermore, unengaged leaders may make faulty decisions or leave the organization and the costs may be far-reaching (Little, Simmons, & Nelson, 2007). However, it is important to note that leadership does not occur in a vacuum, previous studies have found that leaders' opportunities to exert leadership is related to the characteristics of their followers (Nielsen & Munir, 2009, Nielsen et al., 2008). It is therefore important to understand the antecedents of work engagement in leaders. In this study I examine how characteristics specific to the leader role may influence leaders' own levels of work engagement. Both in terms of their own leadership behaviors but also in terms of the context in which they act as leaders.

Although work engagement has been defined in several ways (Macey & Schneider, 2008), I follow the definition of Schaufeli and Salanova (2011). Scahufeli and Salanova (2011) define work engagement as a positive, affective-motivational work-related state of fulfilment (Schaufeli & Salanova, 2011). According to their definition, work engagement consists of three elements: *Vigor* refers to high levels of energy and activity while working. *Dedication* is characterized by being highly involved in your work and feeling challenged and *absorption* refers to fully concentrating on your work (Schaufeli & Bakker, 2004; Schaufeli, Salanova, González-Roma, & Bakker, 2002). A central tenet of this definition is that work engagement is conceived as an experience and a state rather than a trait and therefore occurs as a result of the appraisal of the situation in which an individual finds him- or herself (Bakker, Schaufeli, Leiter, & Taris, 2008; Sonnentag, Dormann, & Demerouti, 2010).

Work engagement in leaders has to date primarily been examined as a stable characteristic using questionnaire designs; however, an emerging body of research has found relationships between daily fluctuations and daily work engagement among non-leaders, emphasizing the importance of examining work engagement at the time and in the situation it occurs rather than studying work engagement as a stable characteristic (Bakker & Xanthopoulou, 2009; Xanthopoulou, Bakker, Demerouti, & Schaufeli, 2009a). Studying work engagement according to the definition of Schaufeli and Salanova (2001) requires a design that allows the researcher to measure work engagement as a transient state that fluctuates within the same individual over shorter periods of time. For example, a leader may feel vigorous, dedicated, and absorbed in a situation where s/he together with followers discusses the solutions to a complex problem and the leader observes followers engaging and taking responsibility for finding a good solution, but the same leader may later feel less dedicated and vigorous when s/he has a conversation with an individual member of the team not living up to performance requirements. The study of work engagement as a transient state carries value in that 1) it enables us to understand psychological variables at the time and level they are manifested, 2) states can explain within-person differences, i.e. why a person at times feels engaged and not at other times, and finally, 3) it reduces recall bias (Bakker et al., 2008; Xanthopoulou, Bakker, Demerouti, Schaufeli, 2009b).

The study extends previous research in three areas: First, it addresses the call by Kark and Shamir (2002) examining within-leader variations of transformational leadership and the outcomes of these. Furthermore, I examine how transformational leaders interpret and react to their own leadership style. Previous research has focused on the effects of transformational leadership on followers; however, due to the central role of leaders in organizations, there is added value in understanding how exerting transformational leadership influences agents themselves. Second, I address the call of Hogg, Martin, Epitropaki, Mankad, Svensson, and Weeden (2005) to consider the importance of social cognition and examine how followers working in a collaborative climate interact with the leaders' behaviors to influence leaders' own work engagement. Finally, I address the call of Bakker et al. (2008) who in their position paper on engagement called for research to investigate the within-individual levels of work engagement to understand the fluctuations of engagement and the day-to-day triggers of state engagement.

THE ANTECEDENTS OF LEADERS' WORK ENGAGEMENT

The antecedents of engagement in leaders have only been sporadically examined. Koyuncu et al. (2006) found that control, rewards and recognition, and value fit all predicted engagement and Schaufeli et al. (2008) found that although engaged leaders worked longer hours in highly demanding jobs, they experienced good mental health and job resources such as social support, social functioning, and job control predicted engagement. Also personal resources have been found to predict engagement in leaders: Bakker, Gierveld, and Van Rijswijk (2006) reported that female school principals high in self-efficacy (an individual's belief about his or her abilities to mobilize cognitive resources and actions to execute a specific task within a given context (Bandura, 1997)) and resilience were more engaged. In a longitudinal study, Schaufeli, Bakker, and van Rhenen (2009) examined the positive gain spiral of engagement in leaders; i.e. they found that engagement lead to increases in job resources (autonomy, social support, performance feedback and opportunities to learn) which in turn predicted engagement.

Although these studies examined the antecedents of engagement in leaders they have not examined characteristics specific to the leader role, i.e. how leaders lead their followers and how the behaviors and norms of followers influence how leaders appraise and react to such behaviors in terms of their levels of engagement. A few studies have focused on how specific leader work characteristics may influence first line leaders' health and well-being. In a study of leaders in five countries around the world, Konrad, Kashlak, Yoshioka, Waryszak, and Toren (2001) found that the least enjoyable activities reported by leaders involved controlling followers and the most enjoyable were related to actually *leading* followers. Knudsen, Ducharme, and Roman (2009) found that demands for high performance and having to make many day-to-day decisions in a centralized environment were related to higher levels of emotional exhaustion, whereas being in an environment that supported innovation and engaged in long-term strategic planning predicted lower levels of emotional exhaustion. During downsizing, Grunberg, Moore, and Greenbirg (2006) found that leaders who had laid off followers reported physical health problems, emotional exhaustion and sleep problems. Having dynamic tasks, i.e. changes in tasks due to an ever-changing environment was found to predict irritation in leaders (Mohr & Wolfram, 2010). In the following I identify two leader-specific characteristics that may be related to leader engagement: Transformational leadership and the collaborative climate of followers.

DO TRANSFORMATIONAL LEADERS ENGAGE THEMSELVES?

The four main characteristics of transformational leadership behaviors are: 1) idealized influence/charisma – the leader acts as a role model and takes the lead in displaying desirable behavior, 2) inspirational motivation – the leader outlines a clear vision and the way forward, 3) intellectual stimulation – the leader encourages followers to make use of their skills and coaches them in making their own decisions and 4) individualized consideration – the leader acknowledges individual differences and adjusts behavior according to the individual's needs and capabilities (Bass, 1985; Bass & Riggio, 2006). Transformational leaders are active in developing a vision and encouraging followers to improve their situation (Bass & Riggio, 2006). Transformational leaders take responsibility for developing followers to take on future challenges. Recent studies have found that transformational leadership is related to followers' work engagement (Moss, 2009, Tims, Bakker, & Xanthopoulou, 2011). It is likely that this leadership role also has an impact on the leaders exerting transformational leadership in terms of their own engagement states. In the following I propose a number of mechanisms through which transformational leadership behaviors may influence leaders' own work engagement states. I base these mechanisms on self-perception theory (Bem, 1972), role holder theory (Neale & Griffin, 2006), and sensemaking theory (Weick, Sutcliffe, & Obstfeld, 1995).

Self-perception theory suggests that individuals come to understand their attitudes, emotions and internal states through the interpretation of their own behaviors (Bem, 1972). This theory suggests that the behaviors of leaders influence their own states of well-being, including their work engagement. According to Conservation of Resources (COR) theory (Hobfoll, 1989) people invest resources in order to avoid resource loss, recover from resource loss and to gain additional resources. It is possible that transformational leaders who focus on developing the resources of their followers and encouraging develop new ways of doing work may become increasingly aware of how they may strengthen both their own individual resources but also the resources of their followers. I therefore propose that exerting transformational leadership behaviors may influence leaders' work engagement through how they appraise these behaviors and the opportunities these behaviors bring about for enhancing and building further resources.

Recent studies of work roles have focused on the self-perceptions of the role holder and how such perceptions shape role holders' behaviors and states of well-being (Neale & Griffin, 2006). Based on the expectations leaders may have of their role as transformational leaders and the meaning attributed to such leadership behaviors, leaders may interpret their own behaviors as desirable as these behaviors are believed to bring out the resources of followers resulting in high-performing and engaged employees (Bass & Riggio, 2006). As such they may evaluate their transformational leadership behaviors in a positive light and experience higher levels of engagement when in situations where they are able to enact such behaviors. At the core of transformational leadership is the encouragement and facilitation of growth in others – this is likely to have a growth effect on the agents of transformational leadership as well. Through encouraging novel ways of approaching challenges, leaders may themselves also feel challenged and have the opportunity to grow and engage.

Sensemaking is the process by which individuals give meaning to the situations in which they find themselves (Weick et al., 1995). Sensemaking is about the interplay between behavior and interpretation: individuals interpret the situations in which they find themselves to create meaning (Weick et al., 1995). Through creating a clear vision the transformational leader may encourage positive reframing: Formulating a clear vision for the future also provides meaning for the leader through a sensemaking process. Meaning is closely related to engagement (Xanthopoulou et al., 2009a). Engagement in followers may be the result of formulating a clear vision and facilitating the development of specific goals and supporting the achievement of such goals (Tims et al., 2011). This clarification is also likely to influence the leader him/herself – s/he becomes aware of the expectations to his/her role in the organization and how s/he may contribute thus increasing engagement. Feedback on one's work has been found to lead to work engagement (Schaufeli et al., 2009). It is thus likely that through exerting transformational leadership behaviors the leader comes to understand the role and values of his/her own work and therefore experience more engagement states.

According to self-persuasion theory (Aronson, 1999) individuals alter their beliefs and reactions based on their cognitive evaluations of themselves. A central tenet of transformational leadership is the function as coach and mentor aiming at developing followers at work. Transformational leaders may keep their job challenging through coaching and mentoring. Through intellectual stimulation and positive feedback, leaders may build positive gain spirals (Salanova, Schaufeli, Xanthopoulou, & Bakker, 2010). When leaders experience their followers growing and developing in their jobs they may persuade themselves that they are successful coaches and mentors and as a result report being more engaged at work. Through encouraging novel ways of approaching challenges, leaders may themselves also feel challenged and that they have the opportunity to grow and engage.

Therefore I propose the following:

Hypothesis 1: Exerting transformational leadership behaviors is positively related to leaders' own states of work engagement.

TRANSFORMATIONAL LEADERSHIP: THE IMPACT OF FOLLOWERS' COLLABORATIVE CLIMATE

Just as leaders may influence their followers, followers may also influence their leaders, their leadership behaviors and the degree to which leaders feel engaged at work. While the personality and developmental needs of followers have been found to support transformational leadership behaviors (Dvir & Shamir, 2003; Hetland, Sandal, & Johnsen, 2008), there has been less interest in how group climate may enhance the effects of transformational leadership behaviors, i.e. act as a moderator. Previous research has failed to consider how leadership may emerge as the result of intra-group social cognitive processes (Hogg, 2001) and therefore neglected to consider the impact of the social context in which leaders operate.

There are several theories that suggest that follower's collaborative climate may impact on leaders' engagement states. These include self-determination, role holder, and value congruence fit theories.

According to self-determination theory (Ryan & Deci, 2000) social context catalyzes within-personal differences in well-being: The extent to which environmental factors hinder or facilitate social functioning (here the exertion of transformational leadership behaviors) influences leaders' levels of work engagement (Ryan & Deci, 2000).

Pillai and Meindl (1998) argued that charismatic leadership (an element of transformational leadership) behaviors are more likely to bring about a positive outcome when followers are closely connected socially and the meaning of the group's goals is shared. An overarching element in the exchange between leaders and followers is the acceptance of leadership behaviors. Leaders and followers jointly form an in-group where they share interdependent roles and the outcomes of transformational leadership behaviors are likely to be moderated by how followers engage in group processes. As such group processes influence how leaders appraise their own behaviors thereby influencing how they react to such behaviors (Balkundi & Kilduff, 2005; van Knippenberg & Hogg, 2003).

Role holder theory suggests that the surroundings play an important role in determining the outcomes of leaders' transformational leadership behaviors depending on the extent to which the leaders' transformational leadership behaviors are in congruence with the demands, norms and values of the group they lead (Neale & Griffin, 2006). Neale and Griffin (2006) use the term system requirements to describe the expectations of the surrounding organization regarding the behaviors of the role holder. Leaders are motivated to live up to these expectations in order to reap the rewards of their job. According to work role theory, role holders experience anxiety in a context where the system requirements are incongruent with the role holder's expectations of role behaviors (Neale & Griffin, 2006). Conversely, when role holders experience that the surroundings accept their role and their behaviors they are more likely to experience higher levels of work engagement. Haslam and Platow (2001) found that degree to which the leader was able to motivate followers and engage followers in activities concerning the group's vision depended on the degree to which the leader was able to display values and ideals shared by the group. It is therefore likely that groups engaging in collaborative processes; trusting each other and engaging in problem solving may enhance the effects of transformational leadership behaviors increasing the appraisals of leaders of their behaviors as acceptable and appropriate and they will be more engaged in their job.

Value congruence refers to the fit between the values and behaviors of the leader and the values and behaviors of followers. If a group of followers value and engage in a trusting relationship with each other and continually work together towards improving their ways of solving problems and making decisions (i.e. have a collaborative climate) they are more likely to welcome transformational leaders' attempts to encourage problem solving and foster trust (Jung, Yammarino, & Lee, 2009). When leaders enact transformational leadership behaviors where there is a value fit between the behaviors of the leaders, i.e. the leader encourages innovative problem solving and fosters trust among his or her followers as transformational leaders do, and a group context where followers report interacting with each other in a trusting manner and engage in problem solving behaviors in a collaborative climate, leaders may appraise their own behaviors as congruent with the values of the group and as a result experience more work engagement states at work.

The transformational leader encourages followers to see beyond their own self-interests serving the greater good and achieving the goals of the entire work group (Bass & Riggio, 2006). Research has found that goals are more easily achieved in groups when members work collaboratively and share information about work-related problems, i.e. have a collaborate climate (West, 1996; West, Brodbeck, Richter, 2004). For leaders to successfully exert transformational leadership behaviors followers must trust each other to be able to conduct the group's tasks and support each other. Jung et al. (2009) found that in both Chinese and US samples collectivistic values and trust enhanced the positive effects of transformational leadership on leadership performance. I propose a similar mechanism for work engagement. Transformational leadership behaviors have a stronger impact when they are enacted in a group environment supportive of such behaviors: where followers report having a collaborative climate characterized by trust and active problem solving leaders will perceive their transformational leadership behaviors more positively and therefore report more work engagement states. As such a collaborative climate may enhance the link between transformational leadership behaviors and leaders' engagement levels.

Hypothesis 2: The association between transformational leadership and leaders' own engagement states will be moderated by followers' collaborative climate. That is the link between transformational leadership and leaders' own engagement states will be enhanced when followers report a collaborative climate.

METHODS

To get a broad view of work engagement in leaders, I included data from two very different organizations: elder care in a public organization and a private accountancy firm. This provides an opportunity to test whether the relationships tested are relevant across diverse organizational settings. I examine which factors predict engagement as it occurs in the situation. I do this in a multi-level, multi-method study combining leaders' own appraisals of their leadership behaviors and levels of engagement using Experience Sampling Method with followers' questionnaire self-reports of the collaborative climate in their work groups. Participants were 58 leaders from two companies; one public elder care organization (28 leaders) and one private accountancy firm (30 leaders). Leaders were first line managers and responsible for between 4 and 30 followers. In elder care 41% of leaders had a nursing background, 26% were healthcare assistants by education, 18% had a health-related education and the remaining 15% had no healthcare related education. The private company was an accountancy firm and all participants were qualified accountants. The average age for leaders in both samples was 41 (SD = 9.88), 58% were women and had on average been working in the organization for 14 years. Participation in the study was voluntary and leaders completed ESM forms. One leader from the elder care did not wish to participate and due to technical problems the responses from one leader in the accountancy were not recorded. In the elder care, 576 employees received the questionnaire and 435 questionnaires were returned (response rate 76%). In the accountancy, 283 employees received a questionnaire and there were 225 returns (response rate 79.5%). Seven questionnaires did not include full information on the team climate scale and the total number of responses therefore amounted to 653. In the elder care 93% were women, followers had an average age of 43 (SD = 11.30). In the accountancy, 44% were female. The average age was 29 (SD = 7.09). I included a control variable for organization at level 1 (0 = Elder care, 1 = Accountancy).

ESM Survey Interface

ESM data were recorded on personal digital assistants (PDAs). Completing the ESM questionnaires required little technical knowledge as PDAs would automatically jump to the questionnaire and close down after completion of the questionnaire; however, researchers provided oral presentations and a written manual, to assist leaders in the use of PDAs. A hotline was also established so that leaders could reach the researchers throughout the working day should problems or questions arise. A signal-contingent ESM design was used, where leaders were asked to provide multiple ratings of transformational leadership behaviors and engagement. Signal-contingent designs are recommended when the objective is to minimize recall bias and the focus is on within-day analyses (Wheeler & Reiss, 1991). Leaders were beeped at random times on weekdays, on average 8 times a day between 9 am to 5 pm over a two-week period. Due to technical problems with the PDAs, not all were beeped the maximum of 80 times. Also, a number of leaders had days off or were on training during the two-week period and therefore did not complete the questionnaires during the days when they were off work. Leaders responded an average of 54.59 times (range 10 to 77). Inspection of response patterns revealed that leaders had been compliant, missing responses were primarily due to days off work.

In the elder care, leaders were beeped in total 1,950 times, and 1,670 ESM questionnaires were completed, yielding an overall response rate of 82%. In the accountancy, leaders were beeped in total 1,841 times, and 1,496 questionnaires were completed, yielding an overall response rate of 81%. These response rates are in line with previous research (Csikszentmihalyi, 1992). PDAs were programmed to have a time lapse of 15 minutes, such that if the respondent did not complete the questionnaire or only completed parts of the questionnaire, it would automatically turn off and jump to the next time slot. This procedure is generally recommended in order to avoid recall bias (Hektner, Schmidt, & Csikszentmihalyi, 2007). No two signals were presented within 30 minutes of each other.

ESM Measures

ESM is a time-consuming method as leaders are required to complete the short questionnaire up to eight times a day. I therefore used short measures of transformational leadership and work engagement to keep the demands on leaders to a minimum.

Work engagement consisted of three items representing each of the three dimensions *dedication*, *absorption* and *vigor*. The three questions were "How active did you feel when you were beeped, "Did you feel able to concentrate?", "How involved did you feel when you were beeped?". A five-point Likert scale was used with the response categories ranging from "*Not at all*" to "*To a very large extent*". Cronbach's α revealed an internal reliability of .70.

Transformational leadership was measured using the items from the Global Transformational Leadership Scale developed by Carless, Wearing, and Mann (2000) and adapted to the immediate situation and by inserting "you" instead of "your leader" (Nielsen & Cleal, 2010). E.g. I asked "To which degree did communicate a clear and positive vision of the future" rather than "your leader communicates a clear and positive vision of the future" from the original questionnaire. The scale consists of seven items. A five-point Likert scale was used. Cronbach's α was .87. Leaders reported being with their team (and therefore completed the questions on transformational leadership) 26% of the times they responded to the ESM.

Multi-level confirmatory analysis (CFA) confirmed the two-scale structure (RMSEA = .04, $\chi^2(63) = 87.87$). In other words, CFA confirmed the interdependency between the levels of analysis (i.e. between-person and within-person-level) and the two-factor structure of work engagement and transformational leadership at the event level.

Survey Measure

A cross-sectional questionnaire survey was conducted among followers. Data were collected among employees on their working conditions. In order to assure confidentiality, questionnaires, together with pre-stamped envelopes, were distributed among the participants, who returned their completed questionnaires directly to the research group. The questionnaire survey was conducted prior to leaders completing the ESM. According to David Kenny (Aug 8, 2011) http://.devidkenny.net/cm/moderation the moderator should be measured prior to the independent measure to rule out the possibility that the moderator is a mediator.

Collaborative climate (5 items) measured the degree to which all team members keep each other informed about work issues and there is a climate of trust (TPI (Team Performance Inventory, West, Markiewicz, & Dawson (2004)). An example of an item is: "We know we can rely on one another in this team". Response categories were: *1 = Strongly disagree, 2= Disagree, 3 = Somewhat agree, 4 = Agree, 5 = Strongly agree*. Cronbach's alpha was .91. To determine the extent to which perceptions were shared within teams, and thereby justifying aggregating team members' scores to the team level, I calculated Intraclass Correlations Coefficients (ICCs) for the scale. It is recommended that ICC(1) exceed .12 which is the median observed in previous studies and ICC(2) exceed .70 in order to justify treating constructs as group level constructs (Bliese, 2000). There was evidence of sufficient convergence of perceptions within teams (ICC(1) = 0.21, F(54, 455) = 3.67, p > .001, ICC(2)

= 0.73) to warrant treating collaborative climate as a group-level construct and therefore the individual scores were aggregated at the team level. The scale was transformed so it ranged from 0-100 with 100 representing a high score on the construct.

Analysis Strategy

In this study I included data at the inter-individual level (team members' aggregated scores of a collaborative climate) and within-individual level (leaders' self-reports of their transformational leadership behaviors and their transient work engagement states). In other words, within-individual data was nested within each leader. Due to the nested nature of the data, Hierarchical Multilevel analyses were used to test the Hypotheses (Bryk & Raudenbush, 1992). The Hierarchical Linear Modelling (HLM) method is an iterative strategy that allows for the investigation of the relationships between situational factors and factors of a more permanent nature at two (or more) levels of analysis (Höckertin & Härenstam, 2006). HLM can most intuitively be understood as a series of regressions: at the first level of analysis (level 1) it is investigated which factors in the situation predict transformational leadership behaviors for each group of observations investigating within-group experiences (this model tests Hypothesis 1). At the second level (level 2), the parameters estimated at level 1 (intercepts and slopes) are regressed on level 2 variables – in this case the followers' accounts of their collaborative climate (testing Hypothesis 2). HLM 6 was used to conduct analyses.

Before conducting HLM, intraclass coefficients were calculated to explore the variance explained at the two levels (within-individual and between-individual variance). This first step is to construct an empty model without explanatory variables to see if and how the variance is distributed over different levels of analysis – in this case individual and situational levels. The model defines the amount of variance that exists around the mean of the dependent variables at the situational level and the individual level (Morrison, Payne, & Wall, 2003). This first step is also a good way of checking whether multilevel analysis is appropriate and whether including several levels (in this case followers' reports of their collaborative climate) adds any explanations or interpretation of the data. The results given in the empty model will show how the variance between the levels is partitioned. This is calculated as an ICC1. Having identified the variance components, predictor variables are added to the model and changes in the residual variances at each level observed. To minimize the threat of self-generated validity statistically, the within-individual variables were centered relative to individuals' scores (group-centering), meaning that the relationships are the net of any within-individual experiences. To reduce possible problems with multicollinearity, level 2 predictor (followers' collaborative climate) was grand-mean centered (Bryk & Raudenbusch, 1992). Improvements in the model fit are assessed with reference to a deviance statistic (-2 loglikelihood ratio) that is distributed as χ^2 with associated degrees of freedom.

RESULTS

Means, standard deviations, and intercorrelations (computed across leaders and their followers) of all variables are reported in table 1.

I explored the differences in engagement between the two sectors and paired sample t-tests revealed that found that elder care leaders experienced more engagement than their accountancy counterparts (t (1, 1975) = 17.06, p < .001) and higher levels of transformational leadership behaviors (t (1, 662) = 7.75, p < .001). These results suggest that the organization play a role in leaders' opportunities to exert transformational leadership behaviors and their subsequent work engagement levels.

Table 1. Means, SDs, and Correlations Among the Study Variables (N = 58)

	M	*SD*	1	2	3	4
1. TF	3.48	.81	-			
2. Engagement	4.52	.37	.38**	-		
3. Collaborative climate	59.99	13.03	.16	.18	-	
4. Organization	1.52	.50	-.42**	-.35**	-.59**	-

** p < .01. Note: situational factors (1-2) were raw scores. TF = Transformational leadership. Values used in the correlation analyses here are aggregated across leaders. Thus, the correlations and significance tests associated with these variables should be interpreted with caution.

Testing Hypotheses

In the first step, the empty model (ICC1) model) was tested. The ICC1 model revealed that 26% of the variance could be explained at the individual (questionnaire) level, while the remaining 74% was explained at the situation (ESM) level (p < .001). This would suggest that both inter-individual factors (e.g. collaborative climate) and within-individual factors (e.g. transformational leadership may explain leaders' transient work engagement states and thus confirms that multi-level analysis considering both levels was an appropriate strategy.

In the second step, the associations between leaders' self-reports of transformational leadership (level 1) and engagement were tested (testing Hypothesis 1). I included organization as a control variable in this step. Analyses indicated that organization significantly predicted engagement (t = -5.27 p < .001) as did transformational leadership (t = 9.87, p < .001). The model showed a significant improved fit compared to the empty model (see table 2). This result confirms the first Hypothesis: In situations where leaders report exerting transformational leadership behaviors, they also report being more engaged.

In the third step, I tested whether the relationship between transformational leadership and work engagement was moderated by followers' collaborative climate (level 2) (testing Hypothesis 2). I found that this was the case (t = 2.13, p = .05). χ^2 likelihood test comparisons of the two models revealed that the model including the level 2 moderator of collaborative climate presented a significantly better fit than model 2 (See table 2). This means that Hypothesis 2 was supported: Leaders reported being more engaged in their work when they exerted transformational leadership if their followers' reported working in a collaborative climate.

Table 2. Multilevel Estimates for Models Predicting Engagement (N = 58 Participants, N = 653 Occasions)

Model	Null			Step 1			Step 2		
Variable	Estimate	SE	t	Estimate	SE	T	Estimate	SE	t
Intercept	4.52	.05	96.08***	5.18	.12	44.09***	5.21	.12	44.06***
Organization				-.40	.07	-5.38***	-.44	.08	-5.80***
TF				.24	.02	9.88***	.23	.03	8.91
CC							.00	.01	-1.7
TF X CC							.01	.00	2.13*
-2 X log	4455.31			3411.93			1044.23		
Δ – 2 X log				1049.48***			5.26*		
Df				3			1		
						R^2			R^2
Level 1 (within person) variance	.33			.26		21%	.26		21%
Level 2 (between person) variance	.12			.05		58%	.05		58%

*p < .05; **p < .01; ***p <.001. TF = Transformational leadership, CC = Collaborative climate.

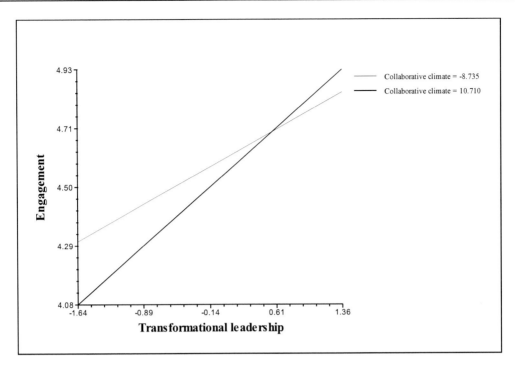

Figure 1. Collaborative climate as a moderator between transformational leadership and well-being.

DISCUSSION

This study extends current research on leaders' work engagement by focusing on the characteristics specific to the leader role: Engaged leaders tend to be those who have the chance to function as transformational leaders in a collaborative team context.

Hypothesis 1 was supported. Enacting transformational leadership behaviors in the situation strongly predicted leaders' own work engagement states. Thus our results support the notion of self-perception theory. It would appear that leaders interpret their own behaviors such that they when they enact transformational leadership behaviors they also report being engaged in their work. A possible explanation may be that exerting transformational leadership behaviors make leaders aware of their own and followers' resources, e.g. innovative problem solving. It is also possible that the transformational leadership behaviors allow leaders to make sense of the situations in which they find themselves. Formulating a clear vision may also make leaders themselves reflect on what is needed of them in order to fulfill the vision and the goals of the team. These results extend the findings of Moss (2009) and Tims et al. (2011) who found a link between transformational leadership and follower work engagement – my results suggest that transformational leadership behaviors are also related to work engagement in leaders themselves. The results support the findings of Knudsen et al. (2009), Mohr and Wolfram (2010), and Grunberg et al. (2006) who found that leader-specific work characteristics and tasks predicted leaders' well-being. In this study I focused on leader-specific behaviors thus expanding our knowledge on the effects on the leader role on leaders' own work engagement.

Hypothesis 2 was also supported. The relationship between transformational leadership behaviors and leaders' own engagement levels was strengthened when leaders interacted with work groups where a collaborative climate existed. The results support the implication of role holder and value congruence theories: When leaders enact transformational leadership behaviors where there is a value fit between the behaviors of the leaders and the values of the group, and the system requirements are congruent with the role holder's expectations, i.e. the leader encourages innovative problem solving and fosters trust among his or her followers, and a group context where followers report interacting with each other in a trusting manner and engage in problem solving behaviors, leaders also report higher engagement states.

I found that the control variable, organization, predicted transformational leadership and work engagement. This finding suggests that the wider organizational context in which leaders fulfil their leader role plays an important part in 1) their experiences of work engagement and that these differences in work engagement may be in part be explained by 2) their opportunities for enacting transformational leadership behaviors. Elder care leaders experienced more engagement states than their accountancy counterparts. Accountants had regular accountancy responsibilities in addition to their leader responsibility and this was associated with some confusion concerning roles and responsibilities - as reported in qualitative interviews. This confusion may have influenced their engagement states. Leaders in the elder care reported higher average levels of exerting transformational leadership behaviors. This is likely because they were full-time leaders as opposed to the mixed role experienced by accountancy leaders. Accountancy leaders may be more reluctant to exert transformational leadership behaviors because their role differed according to projects. One week they may be the project leader and the next week they may be a regular member of a group with their former subordinates having the role of project leader. Leaders in the elder care reported being with either members of the team or the whole team, 28% of the time they were beeped, whereas this was the case for 26% of the accountancy leaders. It would appear that it is not the amount of time spent with followers that determines the level of transformational leadership but the role enacted within a wider context.

Implications for Future Research

In this study I operationalized work engagement as consisting of three items, each representing one dimension of work engagement. Previous research using diary methods have used either six items (Xanthopoulou, Bakker, Demerouti, & Schaufeli, 2009b) or 12 items (Xanthopoulou, Heuven, Demerouti, & Schaufeli, 2008), however, in these studies participants have been asked to complete the questionnaire less frequently than in this study. I decided on a very short measure as leaders who are managing followers when signalled may find it hard to step aside to complete the questionnaire, more so than employees without managerial responsibilities. While it is obvious that short scales are preferred for diary studies, the extent to which shorter scales capture the nature of work engagement compared to longer scales have to established.

Transformational leadership can be seen as a job resource as it promotes followers' well-being (Nielsen et al., 2008; Tims et al., 2011). Results suggest that enacting transformational leadership behaviors also foster engagement in leaders themselves. Previous research has found that transformational leadership predicts followers' engagement (Tims et al., 2011), results suggest that leaders' engagement may mediate this link, possibly through a contagion process. This should be examined in future research.

It is possible that positive gain spirals may be at play. According to Hobfoll's (1989) COR theory, resources may help individuals gain new resources and enhance well-being. As leaders engage in transformational leadership behaviors and these are related to higher levels of engagement, they may in turn be encouraged to exert more transformational leadership behaviors. Previous research on job resources has confirmed such resource caravans. Salanova, Bakker, and Llorens (2006) found that the degree to which managers specify organizational targets were related to flow at work (defined as absorption, enjoyment and intrinsic motivation) which in turn predicted more organizational resources in a positive gain spiral (Salanova et al., 2006). More research is needed to examine the positive gain spirals of job resources and engagement.

Results also indicate the importance of context and social cognition, leaders whose followers work collaboratively reported higher levels of engagement when exerting transformational leadership behaviors. Transformational leadership is but one characteristic specific to the leader role. Other characteristics may also be important in fostering leader engagement. For example, the wider contextual factors for first line leaders may influence their ability to conduct their jobs. In an ever-changing environment leaders are constantly required to shift focus and be ready for change. It is likely that such ongoing changes and the way leaders are supported (in terms of information provided by senior management levels or the level of autonomy they have to implement changes at their level) is likely to influence their engagement levels and also the ability of transformational leadership behaviors to influence work engagement levels of both leaders themselves and their followers. Future research should focus on how the specific role of leaders in a broader perspective may enhance leaders' work engagement.

Although the study included two samples from different sectors I am unable to make firm conclusions about the context. Future research should study organizations within and between sectors to conclude whether work engagement dynamics can be explained by different occupations or by the organizational structures (e.g. size, hierarchical structure, job design).

Practical Implications

Results indicate that transformational leaders are also more engaged leaders. Engaged leaders may also promote engagement in followers through the expression of positive emotions; this is likely to happen through a positive gain spiral: engaged leaders promote employees high in engagement which again increases the leaders' engagement – thus a double contagion effect may be at play (Westman, 2001). Engaged leaders may "contaminate" their followers, but due to their envisioning position and function as role models, the contagion effect may be particularly powerful. Also creating a social climate in which engagement is encouraged in leaders may promote engaged followers. In today's globalized environment, where changes are constant a leader who is engaged and open to change is vital. Research on resilience and work engagement suggests that resilient leaders find it easier to adapt to new situations and are higher in work engagement (Bakker & Demerouti, 2008; Bakker, van Emmerik, & Euwema, 2006) and therefore they may be more willing to accept and implement changes. Leaders may use their experience of state work engagement to mobilize their resources and set high goals for their own behaviors and performance.

The positive outcomes of exerting transformational leadership behaviors may depend not only on the agents of such behaviors but also on how they appraise their context. Leaders are more likely to appraise their behaviors in a positive manner if they act in a group that encourages these behaviors. It is also possible that leaders who try to practice transformational leadership behaviors may find it more beneficial to apply these behaviors in a setting where followers report having a collaborate climate and top executives will find their first line managers create larger and more positive effects when the organizational culture support a group collaborative climate among followers (Jung et al., 2009).

The results suggest that transformational leadership may be incorporated in the Human Resource Management (HRM) cycle (Fonbrun, Tichy, & Devanna, 1984). First, when recruiting managers their transformational leadership competencies should be tested while the recruitment of team members should not only focus on core job tasks but also their interest and ability to work in and promote a collaborative team climate. Second, leaders and followers should receive compensation based on their willingness to engage in behaviors that bring competitive edge to the organization. In annual attitude surveys, leaders' transformational leadership behaviors may be assessed and leader ratings of their followers' rating collaborative climate skills may form the basis for performance pay. Third, by identifying which factors predict engagement in leaders, we may be better able to promote engagement by implementing appropriate interventions. One such intervention may be to train leaders in transformational leadership; this may bring about engagement in leaders and in followers. Research has confirmed that transformational leadership behaviors may be learned. Studies by Barling, Weber, and Kelloway (1996) and Parry and Sinha (2005) found that followers reported their leaders exerted more transformational leadership behaviors after training, and as a result followers reported being more engaged and exerted greater effort. Improving work practices that include the promotion of a collaborative climate in work groups may reinforce the effects of transformational leadership behaviors. The results strongly point to a central element in the training research literature, the concept of training transfer (Burke & Hutchins, 2007) – if leaders return to an environment where followers are little appreciative of their transformational behaviors training may not have the desired effects. As such results point to the importance of multi-level interventions: Both leaders and their followers should be targeted when aiming to increase leaders' work engagement. Finally, with regards to performance management, leaders and their teams should be given targets which contribute towards overall organizational goals. This would help both leaders and their followers to target their efforts in the right direction.

Strengths and Limitations

The major strength of this study is its multi-level, multi-method and multi-source approach. The study offers valuable insight into how we may promote leaders' work engagement at work. Using ESM allows us to investigate leaders' transformational leadership behaviors at the micro-level and how these relate to states of work engagement as well as how the interaction with followers influence leaders' engagement levels. I was thus able to extend the knowledge on the predictors of engagement at work, including micro-level and context (Bakker, 2005; Demerouti, 2006).

The study is not without limitations, three possible limitations of this research include common method bias, the use of short measures of transformational leadership and work engagement, and intrusiveness. First, notwithstanding emerging opinion that problems with common-method bias may have been overstated in organizational research (Spector, 2006), common-method variance may pose a threat to the results in that the measures of transformational leadership and work engagement were self-report. It is possible that the ESM approach caused a form of self-generated validity, where one part of a survey is reactive to another; participants' responses to questions at the beginning of the ESM period influenced their responses to questions later in the period. Furthermore, it is possible to minimize the threat of self-generated validity statistically, and thus the within-individual variables were centered relative to individuals' scores (group-centering), meaning that the relationships are the net of any within-individual experiences. Recent research has indicated that respondents engage in little cognitive processing before responding to questions in ESM (Hektner et al., 2007; Shiffman, 2000). I both tried to minimize common method bias in the design and analysis of the study. First, I included an objective control variable (organization) and another source (followers' ratings of their collaborative climate). It could be argued that it may have been favorable to study objective measures of transformational leadership and work engagement; however, the self-report approach was chosen to test the cognitive theories of how leaders interpret their own behaviors and how these behaviors are related to engagement. Second, common method variance is generally decreased in multiple regression (as opposed to bivariate methods, Siemsen, Roth, & Oliviera, 2010), and correlations between work engagement and transformational leadership were low (Spector, 2006), and the multi-level CFA confirmed a two-factor structure (Podsakoff, MacKenzie, Lee, & Podsakoff, 2003) suggesting common method bias was not a problem. It is possible that leaders rated themselves highly on transformational leadership behaviors due to social desirability. However, I did find variations between and within leaders regarding their ratings of their own transformational leadership behaviors which indicate that leaders critically reviewed their behaviors.

A second limitation is that I used short measures of transformational leadership and work engagement. The measures chosen were well-suited to this kind of study as completing a lengthy questionnaire throughout the working day may impact response rates negatively. The short measures did result in high response rates in both organizations.

A third limitation concerns that of intrusiveness. Leaders were interrupted frequently and their attention was diverted from the activities they engaged in. Furthermore, leaders have much interpersonal contact: with upper management levels, with customers and clients and followers. As a leader it is not easy to "step aside" and complete an ESM questionnaire when you are with others. Nevertheless the ESM survey had a reasonably high response rate (81-82%), indicating that I have captured a representative picture of leaders' daily work experiences. In general, ESM studies have response rates of 70-80% (Hektner et al., 2007). Debriefing sessions with leaders indicated that they had been compliant in responding to the ESM questionnaire.

CONCLUSION

Within the limitations of the study, the present study has four important implications: First, it suggests that the transformational leadership behaviors of first line leaders may not only influence their followers' work engagement levels (as found in previous studies) but also increase engagement in leaders themselves. From the perspective of proactive behavior theory, transformational leaders not only create engagement in followers but also create an engaging working life for themselves. As leaders function as role models and followers may mimic engaged leaders promoting the exertion of transformational leadership in the workplace may not only have direct effects of followers' engagement but also work through contagion. Second, it enhances our understanding of the circumstances under which transformational leadership behaviors may impact on leaders' work engagement. Supporting role holder and value congruence theories, I found that leaders that operate in a context where followers report having a collaborative work climate, leaders may experience higher levels of engagement. Third, the ESM design allowed me to study fluctuations in leaders' self-reported leadership behaviors and how they influence their work engagement states. This design allowed me to study work events as they unravel during the working day. The results of this study enhance our understanding of how leaders' leadership behaviors are associated with their own work engagement states. Finally, the study has important practical implications for organizations and their HRM practices. If organizations wish to optimize organizational performance through promoting leaders' transformational leadership, they need to make sure that also followers share the understanding of the importance of these behaviors in terms of the workplace being characterized by a trusting climate where problems are only discussed and new ways of doing work are encouraged.

REFERENCES

Aronson, E. (1999). The power of self-persuasion. *American Psychologist, 54,* 875-885.

Bakker, A. B. (2005). Flow among music teachers and their students: The crossover of peak experiences. *Journal of Vocational Behavior, 66,* 26-44.

Bakker, A. B., Schaufeli, W. B., Leiter, M. P., & Taris, T. W. (2008). Work engagement: An emerging concept in occupational health psychology. *Work & Stress, 22,* 187-200.

Bakker, A. B. & Demerouti, E. (2008). Towards a model of work engagement. *Career Development International, 13,* 209-223.

Bakker, A. B., Gierveld, J. H., & Van Rijswijk, K. (2006). *Succesfactoren bij vrouwelijeki schooleiders in het primair oderwijs: een onderzok naar burnout, bevlogenheid en prestaties (Success factor among female school principals in primary teaching: A study on burnout, work engagement, and performance).* Right Management Consultants, Diemen.

Bakker, A. B., Schaufeli, W. B., Leiter, M. P., & Taris, T. W. (2008). Work engagement: An emerging concept in occupational health psychology. *Work & Stress, 22,* 187−200.

Bakker, A. B., van Emmerik, H., & Euwema, M. C. (2006). Crossover of burnout and engagement in work teams. *Work and Occupations, 33,* 464-489.

Bakker, A. B., Westman, M., & van Emmerik, I. J. H. (2009). Advancements in crossover theory. *Journal of Managerial Psychology, 24,* 206-219.

Balkundi, P. & Kilduff, M. (2005). The ties that lead: a social network approach to leadership. *The Leadership Quarterly, 16,* 941-961.

Bandura, A. (1997). *Self-Efficacy: The Exercise of Control.* NY: Freeman Press.

Barling, J., Weber, T., & Kelloway, K. (1996). Effects of transformational leadership training on attitudinal and financial outcomes: A field experiment. *Journal of Applied Psychology, 81,* 827-832.

Bass, B.M. (1985). *Transformational leadership and performance beyond expectation.* NY: Free Press.

Bass, B.M. (1990). *Bass and Stogdill's handbook of leadership.* New York: Free Press.

Bass, B.M. & Riggio, E.G. (2006). *Transformational leadership.* Mahwah, NJ: Lawrence Erlbaum.

Bem, D. (1972). Self-perception theory. In L. Berkowitz (Ed.), *Advances in experimental social psychology* (Vol. 2, pp. 1-62). San Diego, CA: Academic Press.

Bliese, P.D. (2000). Within-group agreement, non-independence, and reliability: Implications for data aggregation and analysis. In K.J. Klein and S.W.J. Kozlowski (Eds.), *Multilevel theory, research, and methods in organizations* (pp. 349-381). San Francisco, Jossey-Bass.

Bryk, A.S., & Raudenbush, S.W. (1992). *Hierarchical Linear Models.* Newbury Park, CA: Sage.

Burke, L. A. & Hutchins, H. M. (2007). Training transfer: An integrative literature review. *Human Resource Development Review, 6,* 263-296.

Carless, S., Wearing, A., & Mann, L. (2000). A short measure of transformational leadership. *Journal of Business and Psychology, 14,* 389-405.

Demerouti, E. (2006). Job characteristics, flow, and performance: The moderating role of conscientiousness. *Journal of Occupational Health Psychology, 11,* 266-280.

Dvir, T. & Shamir, B. (2003). Follower developmental characteristics as predicting transformational leadership: a longitudinal field study. *The Leadership Quarterly, 14,* 327-344.

Fonbrun C., Tichy N., & Devanna M. 1984. *Strategic Human Resource Management.* NY: Wiley.

Glasø, L. & Einarsen, S. (2006). Experienced affects in leader-subordinate relationships. *Scandinavian Journal of Management, 22,* 49-73.

Grunberg, L., Moore, S., & Greenbirg, E. S. (2006). Managers' reactions to implementing layoffs: Relationship to health problems and withdrawal behaviors. *Human Resource Management, 45,* 159-178.

Haslam, S. A. & Platow, M. J. (2001). The link between leadership and followership: How affirming social identity translates vision into action. *Personality and Social Psychology Bulletin, 27,* 1469-1479.

Hektner, J., Schmidt, J. A., & Csikszentmihalyi, M. (2007). *Experience Sampling Method; Measuring the Quality of Everyday Life.* Thousand Oaks, CA: Sage.

Hetland, H., Sandal, G., & Johnson, T. B. (2008). Followers' personality and leadership. *Journal of Leadership and Organizational Studies, 14,* 323-331.

Hiller, N. J., Day, D. V., & Vance, R. J. (2006). Collective enactment of leadership roles and team effectiveness: A field study. *The Leadership Quarterly, 17,* 387-397.

Hobfoll, S. E. (1989). Conservation of resources: A new attempt at conceptualizing stress. *American Psychologist, 44,* 513-524.

Höckertin, C., & Härenstam, A. (2006). The impact of ownership on psychosocial working conditions: A multilevel analysis of 60 workplaces. *Economics and Industrial Democracy, 27,* 245-284.

Hogg, M.A. (2001). A social identity theory of leadership. *Personality and Social Psychology Review, 5,* 184-200.

Hogg, M.A., Martin, R., Epitropaki, O., Mankad, A., Svensson, A., & Weeden, K. (2005). Effective leadership in salient group: revisiting leader-member exchange theory from the perspective of the social identity theory of leadership. *Personality and Social Psychology Bulletin, 31,* 991-1004.

Jung, D., Yammarino. F.J., & Lee, J.K. (2009). Moderating role of subordinates' attitudes on transformational leadership and effectiveness: A multi-cultural and multi-level perspective. *The Leadership Quarterly, 20,* 586-603.

Kark, R. & Shamir, B. (2002). The dual effect of transformational leadership: Priming relational and collective selves and further effects on followers. In B.J. Avolio & F. J. Yammarino (Eds.), *Transformational and charismatic leadership: The road ahead* (pp. 67-91). Bingley, UK: JAI Press.

Knudsen, H. K., Ducharme, L. J., & Roman, P. M. (2009). Turnover intention and emotional exhaustion "at the top": adapting the job demands-resources to leaders of addiction treatment organizations. *Journal of Occupational Health Psychology, 14,* 84-95.

Konrad, A., Kashlak, R., Yoshioka, I., Waryszak, R., & Toren, N. (2001). What do managers like to do? A five-country study. *Group & Organization Management, 26,* 401-433.

Koyuncu, M., Burke, R. J., & Fiksenbaum, L. (2006). Work engagement among women managers and professionals in a Turkish bank. *Equal Opportunities International, 25,* 299-310.

Little, L. M., Simmons, B. L., & Nelson, D. L. (2007). Health among leaders: Positive and negative affect, engagement and burnout, forgiveness and revenge. *Journal of Management Studies, 44,* 243-260.

Macey, W.H., & Schneider, B. (2008). The meaning of employee engagement. *Industrial and Organizational Psychology, 1,* 3-30.

Mohr, G. & Wolfram, H.-J. (2010). Stress among managers: The importance of dynamic tasks, predictability, and social support in unpredictable times. *Journal of Occupational Health Psychology, 15,* 167-179.

Morrison, D., Payne, R., & Wall, T. D. (2003). Is job a viable unit of analysis? A multilevel analysis of demand-control-support models. *Journal of Occupational Health Psychology, 8,* 209-219.

Moss, S. (2009). Cultivating the regulatory focus of followers to amplify their sensitivity to transformational leadership. *Journal of Leadership & Organizational Studies, 15,* 241-259.

Neale, M. & Griffin, M. A. (2006). A model of self-held work roles and role transitions. *Human Performance, 19,* 23-41.

Nielsen, K. & Cleal, B. (2010). Predicting flow at work: Investigating the activities and job characteristics that predict flow states at work. *Journal of Occupational Health Psychology, 15,* 180-190.

Nielsen, K. & Munir, F. (2009). How do transformational leaders influence followers' affective well-being? Exploring the mediating mechanism of self-efficacy. *Work & Stress, 23,* 313-329.

Nielsen, K. & Randall, R. (2009). Managers' active support when implementing teams: The impact on employee well-being. *Applied Psychology: Health and Well-being, 1,* 374-390

Nielsen, K., Randall, R., Yarker, J., & Brenner, S.-O. (2008). The effects of transformational leadership on followers' perceived work characteristics and psychological well-being: a longitudinal study. *Work & Stress, 22,* 16-32.

Parry, K. W. & Sinha, P. N. (2005). Researching the trainability of transformational organisational leadership. *Human Resource Development International, 8,* 165-183.

Pillai, R. & Meindl, J. R. (1998). Context and charisma: A "meso" level examination of the relationship of organic structure, collectivism, and crisis to charismatic leadership. *Journal of Management, 24,* 643-671.

Podsakoff, P. M., MacKenzie, S. B., Lee, J.-Y., & Podsakoff, N. P. (2003). Common method biases in behavioral research: A critical review of the literature and recommended remedies. *Journal of Applied Psychology, 88,* 879-903.

Quick, J. C., Macik-Frey, M., & Cooper, C. L. (2007). Managerial dimensions of organizational health: The healthy leader at work. *Journal of Management Studies, 44,* 189-205.

Ryan, R.M. & Deci, E.L. (2000). Self-determination theory and the facilitation of intrinsic motivation, social development, and well-being. *American Psychologist, 55,* 68-78.

Salanova, M., Bakker, A., & Llorens, S. (2006). Flow at work: Evidence for an upward spiral of personal and organizational resources. *Journal of Happiness Studies, 7,* 1-22.

Salanova, M., Schaufeli, W.B., Xanthoupoulou, D. & Bakker, A.B. (2010). Gain spirals of resources

Schaufeli, W. B. & Bakker, A. B. (2004). Job demands, job resources, and their relationship with burnout and engagement: a multi-sample study. *Journal of Organizational Behavior, 25,* 293-315.

Schaufeli, W. B., Bakker, A. B., & van Rhenen, W. (2009). How changes in job demands and resources predict burnout, work engagement, and sickness absenteeism. *Journal of Organizational Behavior, 30,* 893-917.

Schaufeli, W. B. & Salanova, M. (2011). Work engagement: On how to better catch a slippery concept. *European Journal of Work & Organizational Psychology, 20,* 39-46.

Schaufeli, W. B., Salanova, M., González-Roma, V. & Bakker, A. (2002). The measurement of engagement and burnout: A two-sample confirmatory factor analytic approach. *Journal of Happiness Studies, 3,* 71-92.

Schaufeli, W. B., Taris, T. W., & van Rhenen, W. (2008). Workaholism, burnout, and work engagement: Three of a kind or three different kinds of employee well-being? *Applied Psychology: An International Review, 57,* 173-203.

Shiffman, S. (2000). Real-time self-report of momentary states in the natural environment: Computerized ecological momentary assessment. In A.A. Stone, J.S. Turkkan, C.A. Bachrach, J.B. Jobe, H.S. Kurtzman, & V.S. Cain (Eds.), *The science of self-report: Implications for research and practice* (pp. 277-296). Mahwah, NJ: Lawrence Erlbaum Associates, Inc.

Siemsen, E., Roth, A. and Oliveira, P. (2010). Common method bias in regression models with linear, quadratic, and interaction effects. *Organizational Research Methods, 13,* 456-476.

Sonnentag, S., Dormann, C., & Demerouti, E. (2010). Not all days are created equal: The concept of state work engagement. In A. B. Bakker & M. Leiter (Eds.), *Work engagement: The essential in theory and research* (pp. 25–38). New York: Psychology Press..

Spector, P.E. (2006). Method variance in organizational research: Truth or urban legend. *Organizational Research Methods, 9,* 221-232.

Sy, T., Cote, S., & Saavedra, R. (2005). The contagious leader: Impact of the leader's mood on the mood of group members, group affective tone, and group processes. *Journal of Applied Psychology, 90,* 295-305.

Tims, M., Bakker, A.B., & Xanthopoulou, D. (2011). Do transformational leaders enhance their followers' daily work engagement? *The Leadership Quarterly, 22,* 121-131.

van Dierendonck, D., Haynes, C., Borril, C., & Stride, C. (2004). Leadership behavior and subordinate well-being. *Journal of Occupational Health Psychology, 9,* 165-175.

van Knippenberg, D. & Hogg, M.A. (2003). A social identity model of leadership effectiveness in organizations. *Research in Organizational Behavior, 25,* 243-295.

Weick, K. E., Sufcliffe, K. M., & Obstfeld, D. (2005). Organizing and the process of sensemaking. *Organization Science, 16,* 409-421.

West, M. (1996). Reflexivity and work group effectiveness: a conceptual integration. In M.A.West (Ed.), *Handbook of work group psychology* (1st ed., pp. 553-579). Chichester, UK: John Wiley & Sons.

West, M., Markiewicz, L., & Dawson, J.F. (2004). *TPI: The Team Performance Inventory: User guide.* Birmingham. Aston Organisation Development.

West, M. A., Brodbeck, F. C., & Richter, A. W. (2004). Does the 'romance of teams' exist? The effectiveness of teams in experimental and field settings. *Journal of Occupational & Organizational Psychology, 77,* 467-473.

Westman, M. (2001). Stress and strain crossover. *Human Relations, 54,* 717-751.

Wheeler, L., & Reiss, H.T. (1991). Self-recording of everyday life events: Origins, types and uses. *Journal of Personality, 59,* 339-354.

Xanthopoulou, D., Bakker, A. B., Demerouti, E., & Schaufeli, W. B. (2009a). Reciprocal relationships between job resources, personal resources, and work engagement. *Journal of Vocational Behavior, 74,* 235-244.

Xanthopoulou, D., Bakker, A. B., Demerouti, E., & Schaufeli, W. B. (2009b). Work engagement and financial returns: A diary study on the role of job and personal resources. *Journal of Occupational and Organizational Psychology, 82,* 183-200.

Xanthopoulou, D., Bakker, A. B., Heuven, E., Demerouti, E., & Schaufeli, W. B. (2008). Working in the sky: A diary study on work engagement among flight attendants. *Journal of Occupational Health Psychology, 13,* 345-356.

REVIEWED BY

Raymond Randall, Senior lecturer, Loughborough University, UK.

In: Perspectives in Leadership
Editor: Jerry D. VanVactor

ISBN: 978-1-62417-170-3
© 2013 Nova Science Publishers, Inc.

Chapter 4

LEADING IN A RESOURCE DEPENDENT ENVIRONMENT

Tracy L. Buchman[*]
Healthcare Emergency Management at HSS, Inc located in Denver, CO, US

Health-care organizations operate in a resource-dependent environment. The resource dependency and institutional theory paradigms have framed hospital strategies well. Both theories have an extensive history in health-care research (Balotsky, 2005; Dansky, 1996; Dunford, 1987; McNally, 2006; Pfeffer & Salancik, 1978; Zakus, 1998), have been extensively used, and imply greater explanatory power if considering perspectives in tandem rather than as mutually exclusive paradigms (Balotsky).

The resource dependence theory is one of several organizational theories used to describe organizational behavior. The aptitude to acquire and sustain resources predicts organizational survival (Pfeffer & Salancik, 1978). Organizations must acquire external resources as an essential tenet of their strategic and tactical management, and therefore organizations will respond to demands made by the external environment or they will try to minimize the dependence (Pfeffer & Salancik). According to Scott (2003), organizations could manage their resource dependence by either buffering or bridging. Buffering strategies might include increasing a company's tolerance for resource deficiency but increasing inventory over a limited period or by adjusting workflow to match forecasted resource availability (Scott). In contrast, bridging strategies might include trading autonomy by collaborating to share critical resources through a joint venture minimizing dependence on the external environment (Scott). Sheppard (1995) explained that the resource dependence theory detailed why organizations must enter into exchanges with others. Through the management of demands, these exchanges can affect the organization's survival (Pfeffer & Salancik).

---

[*] Dr. Tracy L. Buchman is the National Director of Healthcare Emergency Management at HSS, Inc located in Denver, CO and holds a doctorate in health administration from the University of Phoenix. Additionally, she holds several consultant and advisory positions with the Department of Homeland Security (DHS) and the Centers for Disease Control (CDC) and applies her expertise as a national level emergency preparedness site reviewer and an instructor for the FEMA Center for Domestic Preparedness course on *Hospital Emergency Response Training for Mass Casualty Incidents.*

Leaders of health-care organizations attempt to limit resource dependence and incorporate creative strategies to manage the numerous competitive pressures that affect how hospitals allocate scarce resources (Alexander & Morrisey, 1989; Tolbert, 1985). Consequently, health-care leaders must allocate resources to programs demanded by external customers and stakeholders providing the resources (Casciaro & Piskorski, 2005). Dunford (1987) and McNally (2006) noted that technology was a key component for health-care organizational survival in the overall competitive strategy. Dansky (1996) concluded that hospitals must have tight linkages with home health-care agencies to overcome the environmental pressures of federal reimbursement. Many organizations trade their autonomy by collaborating to share critical resources and maintain a clinical center for excellence, to encompass the best technology available for their patients, and to maintain their status as a technological leader in the community (Dunford; McNally).

Institutional theory involves focusing on the organization and limiting actions to structural conformity. Resource dependence theory and institutional theory both involve stressing the role of legitimacy in proving social worthiness in order to receive resources. An integrative relationship exists between the theories and "resource scarcity drives and institutional theory legitimizes the need for organizational change" (Balotsky, 2005, p. 338). Government fiat, societal rationalization, and professional requirements also legitimize an organization resulting in increased access to resources.

A reasonable test of resource dependency theory would be to investigate if the use of the theory can accurately predict the preparedness levels in health-care organizations. Recognition of the environmental pressures for resources resulted in making federal preparedness funding sources available to health-care organizations after fulfilling particular deliverables. Maldin et al. (2007) revealed that hospital leaders had concerns about the sustainability of the hospital preparedness program and that grant funds provided are not sufficient for all-hazards Emergency Preparedness (EP) planning. Consequently, federal preparedness funding is considered by the members of the U.S. Congress to be seed money and is not enough to accomplish expected preparedness outcomes. Therefore, consistent with resource dependency theory, the ability of health-care leaders to prepare for emergencies and sustain an acceptable level might hinge on the ability to procure critical resources from the external environment.

Systems theory emerged in the academic arena in the 1940s out of World War II operations research. Systems theory placed emphasis on system dynamics and a feedback loop (Bell, 2005). Bell noted "the most important task of system theory is to devise a process by which a diversity of perspectives can be brought together to define not the problem but the problem situation" (p. 473). The use of systems theory has helped researchers to comprehend an extensive array of political and social phenomena (Arthur & McMahon, 2005; Bell, 2005; Bernard et al., 2005; C. A. Brown, 2006; Schleicher & McConnell, 2005). As is true with any complex organization, hospitals are subsystems within the larger social, political, economic, and technical system, and the components of Academic Medical Centers (AMCs) add to this complexity. Academic medical centers consist of three related enterprises: (a) a medical school that trains physicians; (b) research activities involving laboratory science, clinical investigation, or both; and (c) a system for delivering health-care services that might include one or more hospitals, satellite clinics, and a physician office practice (Mallon, 2004). These semiautonomous enterprises, in a highly integrated system, consist of many interacting stakeholders who have intricate processes and multilevel collaboration at the federal, state, and local levels, often representing different and competing interests (Trochim, Cabrera, Milstein, Gallagher, & Leischow, 2006).

Similar to AMCs, public health preparedness is a complex system requiring multilevel collaboration with federal, state, and local entities (Williams, Lyalin & Wingo, 2005). The entities consist of first responders, physicians, nurses, emergency management, hospital administrators, public health administrators, and federal agencies who must integrate for maximum effectiveness and efficiency. The federal government's multifaceted approach to restructuring various regional and national public health and emergency management agencies and systems and their continued financial support reflects efforts to manage increasing the level of public health EP in a systems-oriented way.

To maintain effectiveness, the systems approach requires agents, who often have diverse and dynamic networks of monetary flows, to adapt to actions of others and to a changing environment (Trochim et al., 2006). Trochim summarized that issues of bureaucracy, jurisdictional conflicts among organizations, and factors in the academic environment might limit the adoption or use of the systems approach, consequently producing a negative ripple effect throughout the system. King (2006) concluded, "Perceptions, communications, interactions, and transactions ... in the interacting systems are critical in establishing mutual goals ... that lead to outcomes and cost-effectiveness" (p. 104). The systems approach facilitates the observation of health-care organizations in macro terms to detect problems and therefore offers a comprehensive organization approach to evaluating system-level EP (Bernard et al., 2005).

External sustainability, external funding, and internal resources are the most challenging factors that influence the ability of EP experts in AMCs to implement system-level strategies and achieve system-level goals. Federal spending related to bioterrorism preparedness prior to 1996 was nonexistent. Since that time, Congress enacted several pieces of legislation including the Nunn-Lugar-Domenici Domestic Preparedness Program, the Defense Against Weapons of Mass Destruction Act, the Public Health Threats and Emergencies Act, the Public Health Security and Bioterrorism Preparedness and Response Act, and the Pandemic and All-Hazards Preparedness Act that have allocated over $7 billion in funding to increase hospital preparedness. Many of the initiatives that have strengthened the level of preparedness are dependent on sustained federal funding for both bioterrorism preparedness and the public health infrastructure (DHHS, Office of the Inspector General, 2002; Levi et al., 2007).

The ability to generate adequate funds to support the hospital preparedness role is increasingly difficult to achieve. Hospital personnel currently use the just-in-time method of procuring durable commodities, equipment, and pharmaceuticals to meet immediate patient requirements, and adequate preparedness requires sustained, directed external funding sources with controls that promote true hospital preparedness (Barbera et al., 2002; Rubin, 2004). Health-care leaders must incorporate creative strategies to manage the numerous competitive pressures that affect how hospitals allocate scarce resources. Health-care organizations are part of the environment of social systems and widespread concern about resource dependence, sustainability of preparedness investments, and the lack of overall EP are problems that necessitate processing as a part of the overall national preparedness system (Gregory et al., 2005).

The ability of health-care organizational leaders to prepare for emergencies and sustain an acceptable level hinges on the ability to procure critical resources from the external environment. Current financial restraints limit adequate levels of hospital preparedness, and federal budget cuts and the current economic crisis will continue to present challenges to hospital leaders in sustaining existing levels of preparedness. Preparedness programs must be inclusive of a plan for the maintenance of systems, replacement of expired supplies and pharmaceuticals, and meeting new requirements with sustained federal funding. Without corrective action, preparedness levels will decrease and people in the United States will continue to face avoidable and inappropriately high levels of hazard and the potential to receive inadequate medical care during crises (Barbera et al., 2002; TFAH, 2006).

The leaders of AMCs with trauma center designation often face unique challenges (Aaron, 2000; Retchin & Clark, 2005; Sklar et al., 2007). Academic medical centers are university-supported facilities with a threefold mission of patient care, education, and research. Leaders of AMCs have struggled to redefine their special position in health-care delivery. Attributes of health-care delivery in the AMC represent both challenges and opportunities. Although reimbursement continues to decrease, the cost of doing business continues to increase. Organizational leaders must continue to procure new equipment and medications and maintain the facility, all of which have become progressively more costly (Barbera et al., 2002). Comfortable operating margins exist for few hospitals (Balotsky, 2005) and downsizing specialty services critical to disaster preparedness and response has been the result. Unlike law enforcement and fire services, explicit funding is not available to support the hospital standby role, and hospitals must incorporate preparedness into the overall cost structure of the hospital and support preparedness with revenues received from patient care (AHA, 2006; Barbera et al., 2002; Sklar et al.).

Reimbursement for hospitals after a disaster response is severely limited by the existing disaster assistance systems and result in financial losses (Matheny et al., 2007). Hospital personnel lose favorably reimbursed elective surgeries and diagnostic care to provide space and care for mass casualty victims and an expectation is that hospitals' uncompensated care will continue to rise (AHA, 2006), which makes the dependence on resources to support EP even more critical. A growing number of costly, unfunded, or underfunded regulatory mandates act have been identified as counterincentives to hospital preparedness preparation (Barbera et al., 2002; Rubin, 2004; TJC, 2003).

The current federal funding system has several redundancies and is fragmented, and contradictory to making preparedness progress (TFAH, 2005, 2007). The fact that federal preparedness funds are allocated annually and come from numerous sources and with various requirements complicated sustainability and funding concerns, making it difficult for hospital EP experts to pursue a comprehensive strategy. It is essential that preparedness and response activities occur at the state and local level. The current level of financial commitment toward preparedness allocated by members of the U.S. Congress only allowed the setup of infrastructure but was insufficient to support the successful development of comprehensive, sustainable preparedness programs. There are no apparent consequences for states whose leaders fail to comply with the maintenance of funding requirements. Leaders in the Federal Government allocate preparedness funding to the states. Federal Government leaders are responsible for policymaking and financing, but state and local governments have the authority to enact laws and regulations to ensure the health, safety, and welfare of their constituents, which might account for the geographical differences between the states.

External sustainability, external funding, and internal resources are the most challenging factors that influence the ability of EP experts in AMCs to implement system-level strategies and achieve system-level goals. Maldin et al. (2007) revealed that hospital leaders had concerns about the sustainability of hospital preparedness programs and that grant funds provided were not sufficient for all-hazards EP planning. Health-care leaders have become creative in allocating scarce resources and have continued to invest significant amounts of resources annually to develop and test disaster response plans, train staff, maintain and replace disaster response equipment and supplies, and enhance communication and surveillance capabilities, yet there is still an inadequate level of preparedness (TFAH, 2003, 2004, 2005, 2006, 2007). An adequate level of preparedness hinges on the ability to procure critical resources from the external environment consistent with the resource dependence and systems theories.

Health-care organizations are part of the environment of social systems. The widespread concern about resource dependence, sustainability of preparedness investments, and the lack of overall EP is a problem that needs processing as a part of the overall national preparedness system (Gregory et al., 2005). Political leaders should reevaluate current ineffective approaches utilizing hospital level EP experts to determine and evaluate strategies that have shown to be successful in achieving and sustaining strategic program goals in the social system environment.

The current federal funding system has several redundancies and is fragmented, which is contradictory to making preparedness progress (TFAH, 2005, 2007). The fact that leaders allocate federal preparedness funds annually. The numerous sources and various requirements make it difficult to pursue a comprehensive strategy. The goal of consolidating the federal funding agencies under the Public Health Security and Bioterrorism Preparedness and Response Act of 2002 was to clarify responsibilities and lines of authority within the Federal Government and improve the public health and hospital preparedness programs.

Variations in preparedness levels among the states signify that geographic location might still determine one's level of protection from vulnerabilities (TFAH, 2007). Government leaders must realize that multiple streams of preparedness funds and a lack of strategic direction on how to manage funds judiciously fosters planning in silos and duplication of efforts (TFAH, 2007) and execute changes that will generate a more effective and efficient comprehensive preparedness plan. Funding changes should reflect the individuality of each state or region and the particular challenges and risks associated with the geographic location and population of each state. Evaluating individual state challenges and risks might also allow for bundling of funds earmarked for specific strategic goals in the overall federal preparedness initiative.

Hospital preparedness is an essential component of the nation's preparedness against both intentional acts of terror and naturally occurring crises, and encompassing the perspectives of hospital-level EP experts as key stakeholders accountable for developing effective and sustainable hospital preparedness programs is important. Despite over $7 billion in federal spending, only modest gains have resulted in EP at the hospital level (TFAH, 2007, p. 94). Political leaders have always had an obligation to the country and to health-care organizations to ensure the necessary training, skills, tools, and flexibility to succeed by investing in the infrastructure to support, manage, and produce results in a sensible way (Public Health Foundation, 2005). Emergency preparedness system-wide strategies and goals are not consistent at the local, state, and federal levels, and the current federal preparedness funding system has several redundancies, is fragmented, and contradictory to making preparedness progress. It is the responsibility of political leaders to hold each state accountable for meeting intended preparedness goals by defining organizational outcomes at every level of government and addressing long-term preparedness strategies to strengthen leadership and accountability system-wide.

Political leaders should reevaluate current ineffective approaches utilizing hospital-level EP experts to determine and evaluate strategies that have been successful in achieving and sustaining strategic program goals. A multiyear funding process inclusive of health-care organizations as emergency responders needs evaluating to replace the annual allocation of preparedness funds to first responders and health-care organizations as separate components of the overall preparedness plan. A multiyear allocation of funds would also make it easier to collaborate with other emergency response partners and plan for the maintenance of systems, replacement of expired supplies and pharmaceuticals, and new requirements with sustained federal funding. There is a need to consider each region or state's unique circumstances, particularly around funding, and craft an EP strategy and funding solution that meets the needs of the region or state in question. Evaluating individual state challenges and risks might also allow for bundling of funds earmarked for specific strategic goals in the overall federal preparedness initiative.

The ability of hospitals to generate adequate funds to support the preparedness role has been increasingly more difficult to achieve. Health-care organizations are part of the environment of social systems. Therefore, the widespread concern about resource dependence, sustainability of preparedness investments, and the lack of overall EP is a problem that must be a part of the overall national preparedness system (Gregory et al., 2005). Resource dependence theory involves looking to external patterns for clarification of resource allocation (Balotsky, 2005), and the focus of institutional theory is the organization and limiting actions to structural conformity. Understanding that "resource scarcity drives and institutional theory legitimizes the need for organizational change" (Balotsky, p. 338) is paramount to successful change, and policy makers should strongly consider utilizing a resource dependence and institutional theory integrative approach to this change. Government fiat, societal rationalization, and professional requirements legitimize an organization, resulting in access to resources. This is true with the federal preparedness funding sources that have been available to health-care organizations fulfilling particular deliverables. Organizational leaders respond to this external force and evolve strategy to support stakeholder demands (Balotsky).

Hospitals are subsystems within the larger social, political, economic, and technical system. Hospital EP experts, hospital administrators, and government leaders should utilize the systems approach to addressing external sustainability and funding and internal resources associated with implementing system-level strategies and achieving system-level goals. Addressing external sustainability and funding and internal resources associated with implementing system-level strategies and achieving system-level goals facilitates the observation of organizations in macro terms.

The systems approach is the ongoing correlation involving elements or subsystems of the system and the modifications that transpire over time because of these ongoing relations (Arthur & McMahon, 2005). Utilizing the systems theory when evaluating change affords all leaders involved the ability to "examine the interconnections between internal and external variables that have an impact ... [and acts as] a theoretical lens for examining both a microanalysis of external influences on people's lives while also facilitating a microanalysis of factors that are relevant for development" (Arthur & McMahon, p. 209). The systems approach should involve a more useful perspective for improvements given that the practical goal of systems theory is to make systems more effective by detecting problems and focusing on organizational concerns (Bernard et al., 2005, p. 204).

Emergency preparedness experts and health-care leaders should take a proactive approach and champion significant reforms to existing preparedness funding processes before another crisis or event occurs. Government leaders have the power to alleviate preparedness challenges when given the necessary information to support change.

Community resources are an important contributor to health-care preparedness. Many organizational leaders might trade an organization's autonomy by collaborating to share critical preparedness resources and maintain a clinical center for excellence, encompass the best technology available for their patients, and maintain their status as a technological leader in the community (Dunford, 1987; McNally, 2006). Developing good working relationships and networking with other EP experts and health-care leaders in the same geographical area will facilitate the elimination of planning redundancies and can improve emergency response and recovery operations and ensure improved integration during future disasters.

REFERENCES

Aaron, H. J. (2000, May). The plight of academic medical centers. *Brookings Policy Brief, 59*, 1-8.

Alexander, J. A., & Morrisey, M. A. (1989). A resource-dependence model of hospital contract management. *Health Services Research, 24*, 259-284.

American Hospital Association. (2006, August). *Prepared to care: The 24/7 role of America's full service hospitals.* Retrieved December 16, 2007, from http://www.aha.org/ aha/content/2006/pdf/PreparedToCareFinal.pdf.

Arthur, N., & McMahon, M. (2005). Multicultural career counseling: Theoretical applications of the systems theory framework. *The Career Development Quarterly, 53*, 208-222.

Balotsky, E. R. (2005). Is it resources, habit or both: Interpreting twenty years of hospital strategic response to prospective payment. *Health Care Management Review, 30*, 337-347.

Barbera, J. A., Macintyre, A. G., & DeAtley, C. A. (2002, March). Ambulances to nowhere: America's critical shortfall in medical preparedness for catastrophic terrorism. *Journal of Homeland Security.* Retrieved September 15, 2007, from http://www.homelandsecurity. org/newjournal/articles/ambulancesbarbera.htm.

Bell, M. M. (2005). The vitality of difference: Systems theory, the environment, and the ghost of parsons. *Society and Natural Resources, 18*, 471-478.

Bernard, T. J., Paoline, E. A., & Pare, P. P. (2005). General systems theory and criminal justice. *Journal of Criminal Justice, 33*, 203-211.

Brown, C. A. (2006). The application of complex adaptive systems theory to clinical practice in rehabilitation. *Disability and Rehabilitation, 28*(9), 587-593.

Casciaro, T., & Piskorski, M. J. (2005). Power imbalance, mutual dependence, and constraint absorption: A closer look at resource dependence theory. *Administrative Science Quarterly, 50*, 167-199.

Dansky, K. H. (1996). Understanding hospital referrals to home health agencies. *Hospital & Health Services Administration, 41*, 331-342.

Dunford, R. (1987). The suppression of technology as a strategy for controlling resource dependence. *Administrative Science Quarterly, 32,* 512-525.

Gregory, J., Gibson, B., & Robinson, P. G. (2005). Variation and change in the meaning of oral health related quality of life: A grounded systems approach. *Social Science and Medicine, 60,* 1859-1868.

The Joint Commission. (2003). *Health care at the crossroads: Strategies for creating and sustaining community-wide emergency preparedness strategies.* Retrieved December 12, 2007, from http://www. usaprepare.com/ep3-12-03.pdf.

King, I. M. (2006). A systems approach in nursing administration. *Nursing Administration Quarterly, 30*(2), 100-104.

Levi, J., Juliano, C., & Richardson, M. (2007). Financing public health: Diminished funding for core needs and state-by-state variation in support. *Journal of Public Health Management and Practice, 13*(2), 97-102.

Maldin, B., Lam, C., Franco, C., Press, D., Waldhorn, R., & Toner, E., et al. (2007). Regional approaches to hospital preparedness. *Biosecurity and Bioterrorism: Biodefense Strategy, Practice, and Science, 5,* 43-53.

Mallon, W. T. (2004). *The handbook of academic medicine.* Washington, DC: Association of American Medical Colleges.

Matheny, J., Toner, E., & Waldhorn, R. (2007). Financial effects of an influenza pandemic on US hospitals. *Journal of Healthcare Finance, 34,* 58-63.

McNally, R. D. (2006). Acquiring new technology and surviving environmental pressures. *Radiologic Technology, 77,* 191-199.

Pfeffer, J., & Salancik, G. R. (1978). *The external control of organizations: A resource dependence perspective.* New York: Harper and Row.

Public Health Foundation. (2005, December 6). *Lack of performance tools and measures undermines preparedness efforts.* Retrieved September 5, 2006, from http://www.phf.org/performance-press-release.htm

Retchin, S. M., & Clark, R. R. (2005). Contemporary challenges and opportunities at academic health centers. *Journal of Healthcare Management, 50,* 121-135.

Rubin, J. N. (2004, January). Recurring pitfalls in hospital preparedness and response. *Journal of Homeland Security.* Retrieved August 2, 2006, from http://www. homelandsecurity.org/newjournal/articles/rubin.html.

Schleicher, D. J., & McConnell, A. R. (2005). The complexity of self-complexity: An associated systems theory approach. *Social Cognition, 23,* 387-416.

Scott, W. R. (2003). *Organizations: Rational, natural and open systems* (5th ed.). Upper Saddle River, NJ: Prentice Hall.

Sheppard, J. P. (1995). A resource dependence approach to organizational failure. *Social Science Research, 24,* 28-62.

Sklar, D. P., Richards, M., Shah, M., & Roth, P. (2007). Responding to disasters: Academic medical centers' responsibilities and opportunities. *Academic Medicine, 82,* 797-800.

Tolbert, P. S. (1985). Institutional environments and resource dependence: Sources of administrative structure in institutions of higher education. *Administrative Science Quarterly, 30,* 1-13.

Trochim, W. M., Cabrera, D. A., Milstein, B., Gallagher, R. S., & Leischow, S. J. (2006). Practical challenges of systems thinking and modeling in public health. *American Journal of Public Health, 96,* 538-546.

Trust for America's Health. (2003, December). *Ready or not? 2003 protecting the public's health in the age of bioterrorism.* Retrieved August 1, 2006, from http://healthyamericans.org/state/bioterror/Bioterror.pdf.

Trust for America's Health. (2004, December). *Ready or not? Protecting the public's health in the age of bioterrorism 2004.* Retrieved August 1, 2006, from http://healthyamericans.org/reports/bioterror04/Bioterror04Report. pdf.

Trust for America's Health. (2005, December). *Ready or not? Protecting the public's health from diseases, disasters, and bioterrorism, 2005.* Retrieved August 1, 2006, from http://healthyamericans.org/reports/bioterror05/ bioterror05Report.pdf.

Trust for America's Health. (2006, December). *Ready or not? Protecting the public's health from diseases, disasters, and bioterrorism, 2006.* Retrieved January 12, 2007, from http://healthyamericans.org/reports/bioterror06/ BioTerrorReport2006.pdf.

Trust for America's Health. (2007). *Ready or not? Protecting the public's health from diseases, disasters, and bioterrorism.* Retrieved December 18, 2007, from http://healthyamericans.org/reports/bioterror07/ BioTerrorReport2007.pdf.

U.S. Department of Health and Human Services, Office of the Inspector General. (2002). *State and local bioterrorism preparedness.* Retrieved August 1, 2006, from http://oig.hhs.gov/oei/reports/oei-02-01-00550.pdf.

Williams, W., Lyalin, D., & Wingo, P. A. (2005). Systems thinking: What business modeling can do for public health. *Journal of Public Health Management and Practice, 11*, 550-553.

Zakus, J. D. (1998). Resource dependency and community participation in primary health care. *Social Science & Medicine, 46*, 475-494.

In: Perspectives in Leadership
Editor: Jerry D. VanVactor

ISBN: 978-1-62417-170-3
© 2013 Nova Science Publishers, Inc.

Chapter 5

USING STRESS MANAGEMENT TRAINING TO ENHANCE LEADER PERFORMANCE AND THE UTILIZATION OF INTELLECTUAL ABILITIES DURING STRESSFUL MILITARY TRAINING: AN APPLICATION OF COGNITIVE RESOURCE THEORY

Roland S. Jacobs, Ronald E. Smith,
Fred E. Fiedler and Thomas G. Link
University of Washington
Seattle, Washington, US

ABSTRACT

Previous research has shown a surprisingly low correlation between leader intelligence and leader performance. Consistent with earlier reports, a recent meta-analysis yielded an average correlation of +.17 across 151 samples involving more than 40,000 leaders. One factor that contributes to the low overall correlation is that under conditions of high interpersonal stress, intelligent leaders seem unable to fully utilize their superior cognitive resources, often resulting in a null or negative correlation between intelligence and leader performance in highly-stressed leaders. In a 12-month field experiment that tested propositions derived from Cognitive Resource Theory at two National Guard Officer Candidate schools, Cognitive-Affective Stress Management Training (SMT) was administered to candidates (n = 51) in an attempt to counteract the deleterious effects of situational stress on performance and on the utilization of intellectual abilities. This empirically-supported manualized program teaches participants cognitive and somatic-relaxation coping skills that can be applied in stressful situations to dampen or prevent emotional arousal. A switching-replications quasi-experimental design was used. After a baseline assessment, one randomly selected school's candidates were trained during the first 3 months while the other school served as a no-treatment control. At Time 2, the SMT program was introduced to the second school while the first group began a 3-month follow up period. At Time 3, follow up measures were collected from the first group and post treatment measures from the second group. Following SMT, significant increases were found on candidate performance ratings made by instructors who were blind to the intervention and on a behavioral In-Basket measure of task performance. In accordance with cognitive resource theory, performance increments following SMT were greater for candidates who reported high boss stress than for low-stress candidates. In addition, SMT was related to changes in correlations between intelligence and In-Basket performance. For high-stress candidates, negative correlations between intelligence and performance were eliminated in one OCS group and became more positive in the other group following SMT. We conclude that although high situational stress is endemic to many leadership settings and cannot be easily reduced, interventions can be applied that are designed to help individuals within those settings be made more resilient in responding to the stressors. The results of this study suggest that structured coping skills training that enhances emotional self-regulatory skills can be an efficacious means for maximizing the ability of leaders to utilize their intellectual abilities and thereby perform at a higher level in stressful conditions.

INTRODUCTION

Because critical leadership functions such as planning, decision-making, problem solving and work coordinating are clearly intellectual in nature, it has long been assumed that intelligence is an important contributor to leadership effectiveness, as it is in many other performance domains (Kuncel, Hezlett, and Ones, 2004; Schmidt and Hunter, 2004). Somewhat surprisingly, however, empirical evidence has consistently failed to support the assumption that intelligence predicts leadership performance. Several hundred studies have yielded disappointingly small correlations between intellectual abilities and leadership performance. Stogdill (1948) reported median correlations of .22 to .28 in an early review of the literature, and similar findings were reported by Bass (1991), Ghiselli (1966), and Mann (1958). Fiedler (1995a) reported a median correlation of only .11 for 15 published and unpublished studies in his research program. More recently, a meta-analysis by Judge, Colbert, and Illies (2004) involving 151 intelligence-performance correlations and 40,652 leaders yielded an average correlation of .17.

What are we to make of this counterintuitive pattern of findings? One possible explanation is that some factor, or set of factors, serves to attenuate, or even reverse, the expected relation between intelligence and leadership performance. Research designed to test hypotheses derived from cognitive resource theory (Fiedler and Garcia, 1987; Fiedler, 2002) identified responses to work stressors, and in particular, stress created by interpersonal conflict or unreasonably high demands on the part of one's boss, as one significant factor. Fiedler and his associates (e.g., Fiedler, 1967; Fiedler and Garcia, 1987; Fiedler and Link, 1994; Potter and Fiedler, 1981) have demonstrated that so-called boss stress strongly moderates the correlations between leader intelligence and performance. Under low stress, leader intelligence test scores correlate quite highly with performance. However, as also shown in the Judge et al. (2004) meta-analysis, these correlations are either near zero or even negative when stress with one's boss is high. In particular, the contribution of fluid intelligence (the ability to respond productively to novel challenges) to performance is detrimentally affected by boss-generated stress. It appears, therefore, that stress interferes with leaders' ability to make effective use of their intellectual abilities, essentially negating the higher levels of performance we would expect from the more intelligent leaders.

The term stress is commonly used to refer either to situational conditions (stressors) that place excessive demands on an individual or to the individual's response to the stressor (Lazarus and Folkman, 1984). Reactions to situational stressors include cognitive, physiological, and behavioral responses that can interfere with behavioral efficiency. Especially disruptive in task situations that require reasoning, planning and decision-making are dysfunctional task-irrelevant cognitions that can interfere with information processing, memory, and problem solving (Sarason, Pierce, and Sarason, 1996). Such cognitions include unwarranted negative appraisals of the situation, oneself, one's abilities, and other people as well as preoccupation with anticipated negative consequences (Smith, 1996). To the extent that dysfunctional stress responses are evoked by work-related stressors (in particular, difficulties caused by a superior who has important fate control over the leader), we might expect precisely the pattern of results demonstrated in previous research: a dramatic reduction in the expected positive correlation between leader intelligence and performance as the stress interferes with the effective utilization of the leader's cognitive resources. Likewise, we might expect that if the interfering effects of stress could be reduced, either by reducing situational stressors or by increasing stress tolerance through the teaching of effective coping responses, the intelligence-performance correlations could be increased to a level approximating those seen under low-stress conditions.

The present study has both theoretical and practical implications. From a theoretical perspective, this study provides another test of cognitive resource theory's assertion that stress attenuates the relationship between leader intelligence and performance. To this point, evidence of a moderator effect of boss stress has been based entirely on correlational data. In contrast, this study provides a direct manipulation of stress through an empirically-supported intervention that is designed to affect the factor that is thought to mediate this pattern of results. While we cannot readily increase the leader's intellectual abilities, our approach is an attempt to increase the leader's effective use of intellectual abilities by reducing the effects of stress. From a practical perspective, the demonstration that stress reduction can reinstate the positive relation between leader intelligence found under low-stress conditions could have important implications for intervention. Most optimistically, it could provide organizations with a means of substantially increasing leadership performance at a very low cost.

Stress reduction can involve situational approaches, person-centered approaches, or a combination of both approaches. Situational approaches are directed at modifying the environment in order to reduce the stressful demands placed upon people. Person-centered approaches seek to make people more resistant to the impact of situational stressors by teaching them ways of coping with stress. Because situational stressors, including those produced by bosses, are often difficult or impossible to modify, we chose the latter approach. This consisted of a brief intervention known as cognitive-affective stress management training (Smith, 1980, 2010) that teaches emotional self-regulation coping skills for handling stressful situations. This structured program has proven effective when applied to a variety of populations, including test-anxious college students (Smith and Nye, 1989), students dealing with the stresses of medical and graduate school (Holtzworth-Munroe, Munroe, and Smith, 1985; Smith et al., 2011); elite athletes performing under stressful conditions (Crocker, 1989; Crocker, Alderman, and Smith, 1988), and individuals with stress-related drinking problems (Rohsenow, Smith, and Johnson, 1985). We predicted that stress management training could therefore (a) enhance leader performance, and (b) reduce the negative effects of stress on intellectual performance, thus increasing the expected positive correlation between leader intelligence and task performance. These effects were expected to apply in particular to leaders who reported high boss stress.

METHOD

Participants

The participants on which our results are based were 51 officer candidates (OCs) attending Army National Guard Officer Candidate Schools in the states of Washington ($n = 23$) and Oregon. ($n = 28$). The participants were drawn from the enlisted ranks of their respective state Guard units, and all had completed a minimum of two years of college. They ranged in age from 21 to 30. Four of the Washington and 5 of the Oregon participants were women. The candidates in this study were in their 7th month of officer training and were the survivors of a total group that totaled more than 130 candidates. Two other candidates were lost during the course of the study, one because of withdrawal from the OCS and the other because of withdrawal from stress management training.

Organizational Settings

The Washington and Oregon Military Academies conduct a deliberately stressful and rigorous training program in which Officer Candidate School (OCS) candidates are constantly evaluated in terms of their ability to lead their peers in formal and informal leadership situations. The primary evaluators are the Tactical Officers (TACs) who serve as supervisors, evaluators, and disciplinarians. They also are, by design, the primary source of stress in the candidates' lives, and their primary role is to candidates' ability to perform and lead under stress. This atmosphere thus provides the kind of boss-related stress that, on the basis of previous research, seems to be particularly deleterious to the effective utilization of cognitive resources by highly intelligent leaders (Fiedler, 2002).

Design

In order to make the intervention available to all officer candidates, we used a 2 (groups) X 3 (measurement times) quasi-experimental switching-replications design that provided a wait-list control condition, control for temporal factors in the administration of measures, replication of treatment effects, and a follow-up assessment in the group that received the training first (Cook, Campbell, and Peracchio, 1990).

This design initially involves a treatment group and a no-treatment control group to which baseline (pretreatment) dependent variable measures are administered concurrently. The treatment group then receives the intervention between Time 1 and Time 2, whereas the control group does not. At Time 2, another assessment occurs, which measures treatment effects in the experimental group and provides a second pretreatment assessment for the control condition.

Then, treatment is instituted between Times 2 and 3 for the former control group, whereas the former experimental group receives no further treatment. A Time 3 assessment provides follow up data for the initial experimental group and post treatment data for the former control group. This design strengthens causal inference by replicating the treatment effect at a later date within the group that initially served as a no-treatment control group, and it provides follow up data for one of the groups. In the present study, the Washington OCS candidates were randomly designated as the treatment group and the Oregon candidates as the control group.

The two groups were given the Time 1 pretreatment measures during the 4th month of OCS, Time 2 measures during the 9th month, and Time 3 measures in the 12th month of OCS training.

Both groups received the stress management training program from the same instructors, although at different times in the training cycle. The Washington OCS stress reduction training was administered during the 5th, 6th, and 7th months, and the post-training test in the 9th month, with the follow-up evaluation in the 12th month. Following their Time 1 and Time 2 assessments, the Oregon OCS candidates were given training during the 9th, 10th, and 11th month, and the post-training assessment during the 12th month. Thus, training for the Oregon cadets did not take place until the latter part of the OCS program, permitting us to assess the impact of stress management training at different program periods.

Measures

Stress and intelligence. All participants completed a background questionnaire at Time 1 which included the single item measure of perceived stress with their boss (e.g., their TACs) used in previous CRT studies (e.g. Bons, 1974, Gibson, 1990). This stress scale was also administered at Times 2 and 3. It asked the candidate to indicate on an 9-point scale (from no stress to extreme stress) " your overall feeling about the amount of stress your SENIOR tactical officer creates for you."

Previous research (e.g., Fiedler and Garcia, 1987; Frost, 1981; Gibson, 1990) has shown that boss stress measured in this fashion has a particularly strong effect on the utilization of fluid intelligence, which involves an individual's ability to see new relations, to be resourceful, and to solve new problems (Horn,1986). As in previous research, we used a well-validated brief fluid intelligence scale from Horn's Fluid and Crystallized Intelligence Sampler. The Letter Series test contains 15 items such as A, G, B:__?). It is designed to measure the abstract ability to detect the logical sequence underlying the series and to present the next letter in the series. It yields a score that can range from 0 to 15.

Leadership performance. Performance was measured in two ways to assess the impact of the stress management intervention on leader performance. The first method used a 14-item 5-point scale ranging from 1 (*poor*) to 5 (*outstanding*) for obtaining supervisor ratings of performance. This scale is routinely used by both officer candidate schools for assessment and counseling to evaluate such factors as soundness of judgment, ability to acquire knowledge and expertise, soundness of judgment, performance under stress, communication effectiveness, and ability to motivate and enhance the performance of subordinates. Ratings were obtained for each candidate from at least two of their Tactical Officers, all of whom had at least 10 years of experience. At each time point, the evaluators met as a group and assigned the candidates a score for each item by consensus. The item ratings were summed to yield a total performance score for each candidate. The officers were made unaware of the specifics of the training program and the experimental hypotheses in order to minimize potential sources of rating bias.

The second performance measure was the Army In-Basket Exercise developed by the Reserve Officer Training Corps (ROTC) to assess the ability of future officers to handle administrative, disciplinary, and training problems (Rogers, Lilley, Wellins, Fischl, and Burke, 1983). The series of tasks assess performance on 8 dimensions including problem analysis, judgment, and delegation. The items of the In-Basket exercise exhibit sufficiently satisfactory internal consistency to justify the creation of alternate forms of the tasks, and appropriately-designed alternate forms exhibit minimum practice effects, so that they are well-suited to measure performance changes over time.

For purposes of this study, we used three parallel forms of the In-Basket Exercise for evaluating each cadet at the three assessment periods. Candidates were given 30 minutes to deal with a packet of letters, memoranda, and directives that might be found in a newly assigned second lieutenant's in-basket. Different In-Basket problems were used on each administration to reduce potential practice effects and each of the dimensions of the In-Basket was represented by one or two items in each of the tests in order to develop parallel forms. Two trained judges rated each of the items, using the Army's scoring manual. The summed item scores yielded a total In-Basket performance score.

Stress Management Training Program

An adaptation of Smith's (1980, 2010) Cognitive-Affective Stress Management Training program was administered, using a structured training and resource manual (Smith, 2010). The training consisted of 3 sessions of approximately 2 hours duration conducted one month apart.

The stress management program is based on a cognitive-affective model of stress that contains four major components: (a) situational stressors, defined in terms of the balance between environmental demands and the individual's coping resources; (b) cognitive processes which involve perceptions of demands, resources, potential consequences, and the personal meaning of the consequences; (c) physiological arousal processes that are reciprocally related to the appraisal process; and (d) performance and coping responses. The program is aimed at modifying the appraisal and arousal components of the model. It is a structured psycho-educational intervention designed to teach participants an array of cognitive and physiological coping skills, such as cognitive self-assessment, cognitive restructuring to detect and change irrational self-statements that generate stress, self-instructional training to guide thinking and task performance in task-relevant ways, somatic (progressive muscle) relaxation, and Benson's (1976) cognitive relaxation (meditation or mindfulness) technique.

Trainees identified stress-producing cognitions through a daily self-monitoring procedure and developed alternate sets of self-statements that they could use in stressful situations to reduce or prevent emotional responses. They also learned to reduce and prevent dysfunctional somatic arousal quickly through progressive muscle relaxation and abdominal breathing exercises. Once acquired, these cognitive and somatic coping skills were rehearsed using an induced affect procedure in which trainees imagined stressful situations under instructions to experience as much emotional arousal as possible, then to using the coping skills to "turn off" the arousal (see Smith, 2010). The cognitive and relaxation skills were eventually combined into an "integrated coping response" that can be quickly applied in stressful situations in order to control dysfunctional cognitions and maladaptive emotional arousal. This coping response, tied into the breathing cycle, consists of a stress-reducing self-statement during the inhalation, followed by cue-produced voluntary relaxation during exhalation. The integrated coping response can be quickly and effectively applied within stressful situations without interfering with ongoing activities, and the rehearsal of these coping skills under conditions of induced affect fosters high levels of coping self-efficacy and the ability to control stress responses (Smith and Nye, 1989).

RESULTS

Two major sets of analyses were used to test the experimental hypotheses. First, we evaluated the effects of the stress management program on measures of leader performance as defined by the multidimensional performance ratings and the In-Basket task. Next, we assessed the relation between leader intelligence and In-Basket task performance in groups of candidates who rated themselves as either high or low in boss stress at each of the three measurement periods. This second set of analyses addressed hypotheses derived from cognitive resource theory relating to the effects of experienced boss stress on performance and, more specifically, the effects of the coping skills program on the relation between intelligence and leader performance.

Scale Reliabilities

All multi-item scales described above had high levels of internal consistency (Cronbach's alpha range = .91 to .97). In-Basket performance was scored by two trained raters on all but two dimensions (initiative and administrative control), which had unacceptably low interrater reliability and were therefore excluded from further analysis. Interrater reliability for the total score derived from the 6 reliable dimensions was .89 at Time 1, .85 at Time 2, and .81 at Time 3, indicating high rater agreement on this performance variable.

Table 1 displays overall means, standard deviations and intercorrelations among the intelligence, stress, and performance variables at Times 1, 2, and 3. Separate In-Basket totals were computed for the Washington and Oregon OCS for reasons discussed below.

Time 1 Group Equivalence

An initial analysis assessed the two groups of candidates for pre-intervention differences that might affect the interpretation of treatment effects (Cook, Campbell, and Perrachio,

Table 1. Descriptive Statistics and Intercorrelations of Variables

	1	2	3	4	5	6	7	8	9	10	11
M	10.62	5.46	5.18	4.45	-.73	-7.41	1.36	4.61	44.11	49.73	59.81
SD	2.61	1.87	1.50	1.81	10.42	9.74	8.89	9.24	9.73	10.72	9.10
1. Fluid IQ	---										
2. Boss stress (T1)	.19	---									
3. Boss stress (T2)	.22	.73	---								
4. Boss stress (T3)	-.10	.36	.40	---							
5. In-basket (T1 WA)	.21	.10	.00	-.02	---						
6. In-Basket (T1 OR)	.27	-.03	.11	.10	---	---					
7. In-Basket (T2)	.34	-.06	.01	-.22	.29	.59	---				
8. In-Basket (T3)	.24	.25	.21	-.02	.46	.55	.48	---			
9. Perform rating (T1)	.19	-.37	-.33	-.18	.33	.21	.34	.14	---		
10. Perform rating (T2)	.09	-.28	-.38	-.17	.34	-.16	.23	.14	.78	---	
11. Perform rating (T3)	-.11	-.27	-.16	.01	-.13	-.16	-.05	.06	.60	.74	---

Note. For all correlations except In-Basket Time 1, $r > .34$ is significant at $p < .05$, two-tailed; for Time 1 In-basket, $r > .47$ is significant at $p < .05$.

1990). With one exception (described below), no significant differences were found between the two groups of officer candidates at Time 1 on the variables in Table 1, supporting the assumption that all candidates came from the same OCS population.

The two groups also did not differ on the assessed background variables. The latter included self-reported civilian and family stress, leadership self-efficacy, self-esteem, military experience, civilian leadership experience, time in service, and gender composition (86% males in the Washington sample, 78% in the Oregon sample).

The only significant Time 1 group difference was a lower mean score for the Oregon group on the initial In-Basket task (Washington $M = -.73$, Oregon $M = -7.42$), $t(44)=2.26$, $p<.05$. The disparity in scores occurred because a major anxiety-producing barracks inspection was announced immediately before the test session. Because our assessment was not a required activity, candidates were free to leave the session, and a staff member who was substituting for the experimenter in administering the assessment because of unforeseen circumstances did not encourage the candidates to finish the tasks. As a result, many Oregon participants left early to prepare for the inspection and failed to complete all items. Given the amount of data lost and the diversity of tasks involved, we chose not to adjust the In-Basket scores for number of items completed so as to produce an estimated total score. The unfortunate loss of Time 1 In-Basket data for the Oregon group deprived us of the first pre-treatment baseline measure on this task. For this reason, the In-Basket scores for this session are presented separately by group in Table 1.

It is noteworthy, however, that despite lower Oregon mean scores, the groups exhibited similar Time 1 variability in scores (Washington SD = 9.74; Oregon SD = 10.42 (and variability similar to that exhibited at Times 2 and 3). Whereas the dissimilarity in means rendered the In-Basket task inappropriate for assessing performance changes over time using the Oregon Time 1 mean, the similarity in variance within the Washington and Oregon groups made the Time 1 In-Basket scores appropriate for assessing the pre-intervention correlations between intelligence and performance required by our second set of analyses that addressed differences between high and low boss-stress participants.

Effects of Stress Management Training on Performance

Mean performance ratings given to the total groups of Washington and Oregon participants (combined high and low boss stress) at the three measurement periods are shown in Table 1. The effects of stress management training on the performance ratings were assessed by means of a Groups X Time repeated measures ANOVA followed by a series of a priori planned contrasts. The repeated measures ANOVA yielded a non-significant groups effect and a significant effect for Time, $F(2,88) = 124.03$, $p<.001$. This main effect was qualified by a significant Groups X Time interaction, $F(2,88) = 10.27$, $p<.001$), indicating a differential amount of performance change over time depending on when the stress management training occurred.

To assess the nature of these changes, three planned contrasts were computed. The first contrast, assessing immediate treatment effects, compared the two training periods (Washington Time 1 to Time 2 and Oregon Time 2 to Time 3) to the control period (Oregon Time 1 to Time 2). The second contrast examined long term effects of the training by comparing the follow-up period (Washington Time 2 to Time 3) with the Oregon control period. The third contrast compared the training periods to the follow-up period to determine whether the long-term effects of the training were stronger than the immediate effects.

Since these combined-groups contrasts are not orthogonal, and thus are not independent, we used the Dunn-Sidak modification for *a priori* non-orthogonal contrasts (Kirk, 1995). This modification utilizes the more precise multiplicative experiment-wise error inequality rather than the more conservative additive inequality (Kirk, 1995). Similar to most adjustments that maintain an error rate of .05 for all tests taken as a group, Dunn-Sidak adjusts the critical *t*-value necessary for significance upward. In this case, the number of contrasts affected this adjustment. We chose to use focused interaction contrasts because we were comparing two change scores (for example, the change in performance for the group that was trained first from Time 1 to Time 2 compared with the control condition's performance change over the same period). Interaction contrasts require an additional assumption, namely, homogeneity of treatment variances, in order to use the pooled error term, i.e., mean square error of within-participant effects, or the Participants x Time interaction (Kirk, 1995). We tested this assumption by computing the variances of the change scores and found that they did not differ significantly. All of the variances in change scores across the three time periods ranged from 5.60 to 7.80, thus satisfying the assumption of treatment variance homogeneity.

Although both groups showed some improvement in performance following training, the first contrast, comparing the post-training means to the control mean, was not significant, $t(88) = 1.20$. However, the second contrast revealed a highly significant difference between the change during the follow-up period and that of the control period $t_{(88)} = 4.38$, $p < .01$, indicating that the performance of the Washington group, relative to Oregon, had continued to an even higher rate of improvement by Time 3. The expected incremental effects of the coping skills program over time was also confirmed by the third contrast, which revealed that the change during the follow-up period was significantly greater than the average amount of improvement shown immediately after training $t_{(88)} = 3.18$, $p < .01$. Thus, both the ANOVA interaction effect and the contrasts support the hypothesis that stress management training was associated with increased performance. The Groups X Time interaction suggests that Washington (trained first) was improving at a faster rate than Oregon (control first). This interaction is explained by the contrasts, which show that the greatest effect of the training for the Washington group was seen during the follow-up period. Indeed, at the Time 3 assessment, which occurred near the end of the OCS training programs, the mean performance ratings of the Washington candidates were one full standard deviation higher than those of the Oregon group that had just completed the SMT program. The groups had been virtually identical at the Time 1 baseline assessment, and the Time 3 scores of the Oregon group were very similar to the Washington group's post treatment Time 2 scores.

Because the Oregon Time 1 In-basket data were not usable for this analysis, the contrasts described above could not be computed. Instead, contrasts were computed separately for the two groups. For the Washington group, two planned contrasts were computed. The first, comparing pre-intervention In-basket scores at Time 1 with Time 2 post-treatment scores, was not significant, $t_{(19)} = 1.29$. The second contrast, comparing the Time 1 score with the Time 3 follow up score, yielded a significant contrast, $t_{(17)} = 2.22$, $p < .05$. For the Oregon group, only one contrast was computed because the Time 1 data were not comparable. This contrast assessed the performance improvement from the second pre-training assessment, whose Time 2 mean did not differ significantly from the Washington pre-training Time 1 mean, to the post training assessment at Time 3. A significant improvement was found, $t_{(22)} =$

2.61, p <.02. This pattern of results, while lacking the assessment of a non-treatment control interval, yielded a similar pattern of treatment and follow-up results found in the performance rating data for the Washington group, indicating a significant effect during the latter portion of the OCS training program.

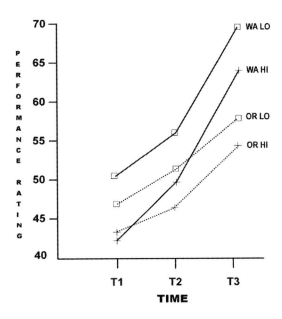

Figure 1. Mean Leadership Performance Ratings Obtained by Washington (trained first) and Oregon Officer Candidates with High or Low Boss Stress at the Three Assessment Periods.

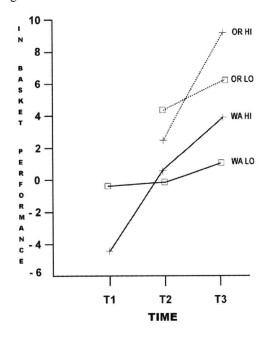

Figure 2. Mean In-Basket Performance Scores Obtained by Washington (trained first) and Oregon Officer Candidates with High or Low Boss Stress at the Three Assessment Periods.

Several additional findings indicated that the candidates who were high in reported boss stress were particularly responsive to the stress management intervention in terms of improved performance. Figures 1 and 2 present the performance means separately for the high- and low-stress groups (based on the median split) for the performance ratings and In-Basket performance measures, respectively.

A comparison of the Washington high stress group with the Oregon high stress participants during the first phase of the design (when the former group received the intervention and the latter did not) indicated a marked difference in improved performance ratings in favor of the Washington candidates, $t_{(22)} = 7.58$, $p < .001$. This effect was much larger than the effect for the combined high and low stress groups, which, as noted earlier, did not achieve significance. Second, we found that following the stress management intervention in the Oregon group, the highly stressed candidates showed a larger improvement in In-Basket performance than did those who reported low stress, $t_{(18)} = 2.56$, $p < .05$. Although a similar pattern of results occurred in the high- and low-stress Washington groups after training, the difference was not significant.

Stress, Intelligence and Performance

The second major hypothesis in this study was that relatively more intelligent leaders who experience high boss stress will be able to use their intellectual abilities more effectively than less intelligent leaders if they learn stress management coping skills. That is, we predicted that the stress reduction training would counteract the negative results of stress on the intelligence-performance relation. This hypothesis was tested by (a) dividing the candidates from each of the two OCS programs into those who fell above and below the median on the perceived stress scale at each time period, and (b) comparing correlation coefficients between fluid intelligence and performance at Times 1, 2, and 3. According to the hypothesis derived from cognitive resource theory, at high levels of stress the correlation between fluid intelligence and performance should be non-significant or negative, and the correlation should become more positive as a result of stress management training.

The results presented in Table 2 provide partial support for this hypothesis. At Time 1, prior to the intervention, the correlation between fluid intelligence and In-Basket performance in the combined Oregon and Washington groups was positive and significant, $r_{(14)} = .60$, $p < .05$, for candidates who reported low stress with their senior TAC, but a non-significant -.06 for the combined high stress candidates (and negative in the Oregon group). At Time 2, the correlation for the high stress Oregon group, which had not yet received stress management training, became even more strongly negative, whereas the low stress candidates continued to exhibit a positive correlation. Following the stress management intervention for the Washington group, the correlation for the highly stressed candidates became more positive, and the same occurred for the Oregon group in their post training assessment at Time 3, though neither positive correlation attained significance. Finally, it is worth noting that the large post training positive correlation seen in the Washington high-stress candidates at Time 2, though remaining positive in direction, was lower at the follow up Time 3 assessment, indicating a possible decrement in coping skills treatment effects on the intelligence-performance relation over time, a decrement that was not seen on the performance ratings of this group. Thus, the hypothesis that stress management training would significantly increase the correlation between intelligence and performance in highly-stressed leaders was only partially supported.

Table 2. Correlations Between Fluid Intelligence and In-Basket Performance for Trainees Reporting High and Low Boss Stress and Fisher z-values for Comparison of Low- and High-Stress Correlations in the Oregon and Washington Groups

	Assessment Period		
Correlations [a]	Time 1	Time 2	Time 3
Washington			
High Stress	.11 (13)	.59 (11)	.26 (11)
Low Stress	.56 (8)	.35 (7)	.17 (7)
Oregon			
High Stress	-.22 (12)	-.65* (13)	.06 (10)
Low Stress	.64 (8)	.67* (10)	.30 (8)
Fisher z tests [b]			
Washington			
High vs Low Stress	.95	-.51	-.15
Oregon			
High vs Low Stress	1.76*	3.22**	.43

Note. [a]Pearson correlations, *ns* in parentheses. [b]Fisher *z*-values for significance tests of differences between correlations obtained in high- and low-stress groups. * $p < .05$ ** $p < .01$.

On the other hand, at the time of the posttest, the relative performance of the cadets with high fluid intelligence was better than the performance of cadets with low fluid intelligence, suggesting that the stress reduction training enabled the more intelligent cadets to use their fluid intelligence more effectively.

CONCLUSION

Previous research has shown that stress, and especially interpersonal stress with one's superior, moderates the relationship between leader intelligence and performance. That is, the correlation between leader intelligence and performance is positive under low stress but negative or nonexistent under high stress. When boss stress is low, the more intelligent leaders perform better; if it is high, they tend to perform less well than do less intelligent leaders. Since leadership involves such intellectual functions as planning, decision making, and coordinating the work of others, we must assume that stress interfere with the effective use of intellectual skills in the performance of the leadership task. Dysfunctional task-irrelevant cognitions, as well as increased emotional arousal, may serve to negate the cognitive resources that should make intelligent leaders more effective. We cannot ordinarily make leaders more intelligent, nor can we decrease the stressful demands that are endemic to many leadership situations. What we can do, however, is decrease the interfering factor of subjective stress by teaching leaders stress management coping skills, thereby enabling them to make more effective use of their intelligence. This study was designed to assess the feasibility of such a strategy.

The data showed that for the combined OCS groups, stress management training was associated with increased performance ratings relative to the control period. later decreases in subjectively experienced stress (Table 1) and with an overall decrease in the apparent negative influence of stress on leader intelligence. There were also indications that both performance ratings and in-basket performance improved after the intervention, although the strongest increases in performance ratings occurred at the follow up. This might suggest that, as in other areas of skill acquisition, maximal utilization of skills sometimes requires a period of refinement and practice.

As in previous studies, our results indicated that stress had a more debilitating effect on the performance of relatively more intelligent leaders than was the case for relatively less intelligent leaders. At Time 1, prior to the intervention, an overall correlation of .60 was found for the combined low-stress candidates, whereas no significant relation was found for the high-stress candidates. When training was instituted for the Washington group, however, the correlation for the high-stress group increased to .59. This finding is tempered, however, by the fact that this high correlation was not maintained at follow up. Meanwhile, in the Oregon group, the negative correlation for the high-stress candidates increased in magnitude during the control period extending from Time 1 to Time 2, then became less negative (and essentially .00) following training. What we can conclude, therefore, is that for high-stress leaders, the intervention is associated with at least a decrease in the negative correlation between leader intelligence and performance. We have not demonstrated a consistent or a lasting ability to reinstate the expected positive correlation, but the results are sufficiently provocative to serve as a stimulus for future research.

One of the major strengths of this study is that it was conducted in one of the very few real-life situations in which the relationship between subordinates and superiors is made deliberately stressful. The degree of stress that exists in officer candidate schools clearly could not have been produced under present human subjects regulations in a highly controlled experiment. This fact enhances the ecological validity of the results. We should also note that the participants were fairly able survivors of a cohort that by the time of the study had lost over 60% of its members through elimination or attrition. Whether more of the eliminated candidates could have survived the training program has they been provided with stress management training early in training is open to speculation and is a worthy question for future research.

Our study does has a number of limitations, however. The study shares a problem all too common with other leadership field studies, namely, the small number of available cadets who served as participants. The switching replications design used in this study helped to ameliorate, but did not eliminate, this problem, and the staggered nature of the intervention application can confound the treatment with temporal factors, such as the phase of training. But perhaps the most important limitation of this study is the restricted range that existed on several critical participant dimensions. First, officer cadets are selected in part on the basis of having relatively high intelligence and motivation, and having completed at least two years of college. Second, at the time the stress reduction training began, these cadets had already completed approximately half of the OCS course. As noted, many candidates resign or are eliminated from the program during in the first three to four months of OCS, often because of stressful encounters with superiors. Thus, the candidates who remained in the program had already demonstrated an ability to withstand or handle a highly stressful environment. Many candidates informed us that they would have appreciated the stress training earlier in their program. It is possible, therefore, that the results of our study are highly conservative, and that they would have been more compelling in a less select sample.

It seems highly likely that two major differences in the administration of the study in the Washington and Oregon OCS affected the results. One, already mentioned, was the failure to obtain valid In-Basket measures on the pre-test for the Oregon cadets. As noted earlier, the Oregon pre-test, for reasons of time conflicts, had to be administered by the Oregon staff rather than one of the investigators. As we were later informed, in the face of an impending inspection, the Oregon administrator allowed cadets to leave without completing all pre-test In-Basket items. This invalidated the Oregon pre-test scores as a comparison measure for the Time 2 and 3 assessments. Although alternate sets of items were used for each In-Basket administration, we were, nevertheless, deprived of a control period (Time 1 to Time 2) that would have permitted us to evaluate the possibility of practice effects on the basic task itself. Therefore, despite assurances from the developers of the In-Basket task that practice effects are minimal when alternate forms are used, conclusions about In-Basket performance increments due to stress management training must be regarded as tentative. It is worth noting, however, that the mean performance level of the Oregon group at Time 2, before stress management training began, was not significantly different from the Washington group's pre-intervention mean at Time 1, supporting the conclusion that In-Basket practice effects are minimal when alternate items are used in repeated assessments. After stress management training, however, the Oregon group's In-Basket performance. like that of the Washington group, improved.

The second important issue derives from the research design that was adopted. The Oregon group received the stress reduction training 4 months after the Washington group. This delay provided the control required by the switching replications design. However, by the time the cadets were given stress reduction training, the Oregon group had been exposed to four additional months of stress and its detrimental effects without the benefit of stress-reduction training. While the delay may have provided an opportunity for some of the cadets to adapt better to their stressful environment, the delay may have increased the debilitating effects of stress on others. In any event, at this point the effect of this four-month delay remains unclear.

There was a marked improvement on both performance measures in the Washington cadets' performance between their post-training and follow-up evaluations. This suggests that a certain amount of time may be needed to integrate and successfully apply the coping skills taught in the stress management training program. While the Oregon group also showed a post-intervention increase in performance, the effects of the program on performance ratings were most clearly demonstrated at the follow-up assessment of the Washington cadets. Unfortunately, the ending of the OCS program did not permit a follow up assessment of the Oregon cadets to determine whether they would attain a similarly high level of performance 3 months after they finished stress management training.

In addition to acknowledgement of the study's limitations, several other points deserve comment. One of these concerns the nature of stress. As noted earlier, cognitive resource theory makes an important distinction between job stress and interpersonal stress. The former, by our definition, is created by such job characteristics as time pressure, the task's complexity, or physical danger. In contrast, stress with one's immediate superior or key subordinates is created by interpersonal conflicts. Most often it is generated by superiors who give frequent negative feedback, make unrealistic demands, or deliberately withhold resources and information needed to perform the task. Although job and boss stress frequently occur together, previous research has shown that boss stress is usually a much stronger moderator of the relation between cognitive abilities and performance than is job stress (e.g., Bons and Fiedler, 1976; Potter and Fiedler, 1981).

The officer candidates reported that both types of stress were present, but candidate reports as well as discussions with the training staff indicated that boss stress was the more salient one in this military setting. If this is indeed the case, the abilities of candidates to control stress responses evoked by aversive interactions with superiors would be particularly useful. The training provides such skills as the ability to control physiological arousal, to eliminate cognitions that could generate anxiety, anger, or dysphoria, and to avoid task-irrelevant and self-focused cognitions that can interfere with the ability of the leader to focus on the task at hand. Stress reduction should thus help to remove impediments to the exercise of task-relevant cognitive abilities. The results of this study, while hardly definitive, are sufficiently encouraging to justify additional research on the specific methods of intervention that are best suited for enabling the relatively more intelligent leaders to capitalize on their cognitive resources.

Another important question in this study, as well as for cognitive resource theory, is the mechanisms that underlie the detrimental effect of stress on the more rather than the less intelligent leaders. Several explanations have been advanced to account for this phenomenon. Fiedler (1995b, 2002) has suggested that the key to understanding this counterintuitive result may lie in the empirical finding that under low stress, experience tends to correlate negatively with performance, whereas under high stress, intelligence tends to correlate negatively with performance (Fiedler, Potter, and McGuire, 1990).

The interference becomes understandable if we make two assumptions. The first of these is that people use the tools they have. If you are highly intelligent, you will try to solve problems by logical and rational means. If you are highly experienced, you will rely on your experience in your search for solutions. Second, we can define experience as overlearned behavior or automatically processed cognitions. If stress is low, there is usually sufficient time to weigh and consider alternative actions, a process that favors the highly intelligent leader. On the other hand, if there is an emergency or if interpersonal stress is high enough to be creating task-irrelevant cognitions, it is probably most adaptive to fall back on previously acquired responses. This coping mode would favor the highly experienced leader who can engage in relatively automatic processing. In contrast, the inexperienced but highly intelligent leader may be unable to effectively use his or her cognitive resources, and rumination about uncertain and random outcomes may delay action and lead to poorer performance. The interference arises because we cannot simultaneously react on the basis of hunch and intuition while trying to find logical answers or weigh alternative options.

In summary, this study suggests three conclusions that address important issues in leader selection and training. First, it provides evidence that the deleterious effects of stress on the use of intelligence can be counteracted. In so doing, the study indicates that intelligence can be an important factor in leadership performance and supports the continued use of intelligence tests as a selection tool to assess abilities that can contribute to leader performance. Second, we find that the stress management program seems to benefit primarily the relatively more intelligent persons who report experiencing high levels of stress. Finally, this study extends the positive results found for the cognitive-affective stress management program in other populations (e.g., medical students and elite athletes) to a military population, further indicating that the coping skills taught in the program are applicable within a wide range of stressful performance situations. However, it leaves unanswered questions about when and how the stress management program would be most effectively applied in this setting. Would training at the very beginning of OCS result in lower attrition and elimination rates than the more than 60% rate found in the schools that participated in this study? Would briefer, more frequent training sessions result in better application of coping skills? Are booster sessions needed to maintain and enhance training effects? Can the Cognitive-Affective Stress Management program be adapted in ways that will make it more effective in this military setting? It is our hope that the encouraging results obtained in this study will stimulate additional research on these practical questions.

AUTHOR NOTE

Roland S. Jacobs is now at the U.S. Fish and Wildlife Service, National Conservation Training Center, 698 Conservation Way, Shepherdstown, WV 25443. Ronald E. Smith, Fred E. Fiedler, and Thomas G. Link are at the Department of Psychology, University of Washington, Seattle, WA 98195-1525.

This research was in part supported by Contract MDA-903-89-K-0183 with the U. S. Army Research Institute, Alexandria, VA (Fred E. Fiedler, Principal Investigator). The views and conclusions expressed here do not necessarily reflect those of Army Institute for Research or the Department of Defense.

Correspondence concerning this article should be addressed to Ronald E. Smith, Department of Psychology, Box 351525, University of Washington, Seattle, WA 98195-1525. Electronic mail may be addressed to <resmith@uw.edu>.

REFERENCES

Bass, B. M. (1991). *Handboook of leadership: Theory, research, and managerial application.* New York: The Free Press.

Benson, H. (1976). The relaxation response. New York: Avon.

Blades, J. W. and Fiedler, F. E. (1973). Participative management, member intelligence, and group performance. Technical Report 73-40. Seattle, WA: Organizational Research Group, University of Washington.

Bons, P. (1974). The effects of changes in leadership environment on the behavior of relationship and task-motivated leaders. Unpublished doctoral dissertation, University of Washington, Seattle, WA.

Cook, T., Campbell, D., and Peracchio, L. (1990). Quasi-experimentation. In M. Dunnette and L. Hough (Eds.) Handbook of Industrial and Organizational Psychology, (pp. 491-576). Palo Alto, CA: Consulting Psychologists Press.

Crocker, P. R. E. (1989). A follow-up of cognitive-affective stress management training. *Journal of Sport and Exercise Psychology*, 11, 236-242.

Crocker, P. R. E., Alderman, R. B., and Smith, F. M. R. (1988). Cognitive-affective stress management training with high performance youth volleyball players: Effects on affect, cognition, and performance. *Journal of Sport and Exercise Psychology*, 10, 448-460.

Fiedler, F. E. (1967). A theory of leadership effectiveness. New York: McGraw-Hill.

Fiedler, F. E. (1995a). Cognitive resources and leadership performance. Applied Psychology: *An International Journal,* 44, 5-28.

Fiedler, F. E. (1995b). Cognitive resources and leadership performance: A rejoinder. Applied Psychology: *An International Journal*, 44, 50-56.

Fiedler, F. E. (2002). The curious role of cognitive resources in leadership. In R. E. Riggio, S. E. Murphy, and F.J. Pirozzolo (Eds.), Multiple intelligences and leadership (pp. 91-104). Mahwah, NJ: Erlbaum.

Fiedler, F. E., and Garcia, J. (1987). Leadership: Cognitive resources and performance. New York: Wiley.

Fiedler, F. E., and Link, T. G. (1994). Leader intelligence, interpersonal stress, and task performance. In R. J. Sternberg and R. K. Wagner (Eds.), Mind in context: Interactionist perspectives on human intelligence (pp. 152-167). New York: Cambridge University Press.

Fiedler, F. E., Potter, E. H., and McGuire, M. (1990). The utilization of staff member intelligence and experience under high and low stress. *Academy of Management Journal*, 24, 362-276.

Frost, D. (1983). Role perceptions and behavior of the immediate superior: Moderating effects on the prediction of leadership effectiveness. *Organizational Behavior and Human Performance*, 31, 123-142.

Ghiselli, E. (1966). The validity of occupational aptitude tests. New York: Wiley.

Gibson, F.W. (1990). Leader cognitive abilities, leader stress, group behaviors, and group performance. Unpublished doctoral dissertation, University of Washington.

Holzworth-Munroe, A., Munroe, M., and Smith, R. (1985). Effects of a stress management training program on first- and second-year medical students. *Journal of Medical Education*, 60, 417-419.

Horn, J. (1986). Remodeling old models of intelligence. In B.B. Wolman (Ed.) Handbook of intelligence (pp. 223-267). New York: Wiley.

Judge, T. A., Colbert, A. E., and Illies, R. (2004). Intelligence and leadership: A quantitative review and test of theoretical propositions. *Journal of Applied Psychology*, 89, 542-552.

Kirk, (1995). Experimental design (3rd ed.). Belmont, CA: Brooks-Cole.

Kuncel, N. P., Hezlett, S. A., and Ones, D. S. (2004). Academic performance, career potential, and job performance: Can one construct predict them all? *Journal of Personality and Social Psychology*, 86, 148-161.

Lazarus, R. S., and Folkman, S. (1984). Stress, appraisal, and coping. New York: Wiley.

Mann, R. (1959). A review of the relationship between personality and performance in small groups. *Psychological Bulletin*, 56, 241-270.

Potter, E. H., III, and Fiedler, F. E. (1981). The utilization of staff member intelligence and experience under high and low stress. *Academy of Management Journal,* 24, 361-376.

Rogers, R., Lilley, L, Wellins, R., Fischl, M., and Burke, W. (1983). Development of the precommissioning leadership assessment program. *ARI Technical Report* 560.

Rohsenow, D. J., Smith, R. E., and Johnson, S. (1985). Stress management training as a prevention program for heavy social drinkers: Cognitions, affect, drinking, and individual differences. *Addictive Behaviors*, 10, 45-54.

Sarason, I. G., Pierce, G. R., and Sarason, B. R. (Eds.) (1996). Cognitive interference: *Theories, methods, and findings*. Hillsdale, N. J.: Erlbaum.

Schmidt, F. L., and Hunter, J. (2004). General mental ability in the world of work: Occupational attainment and job performance. *Journal of Personality and Social Psychology*, 86, 162-173.

Smith, R. E. (1980). Development of an integrated coping response through cognitive-affective stress management training. In I. G. Sarason and C. D. Spielberger (Eds.) Stress and anxiety (Vol 7, pp. 265-280). Washington, D.C.: Hemisphere.

Smith, R. E. (1996). Performance anxiety, cognitive interference, and concentration enhancement strategies in sports. In I. G. Sarason, G. A. Pierce, and B. R. Sarason (Eds.) (1996). Cognitive interference: Theories, methods, and findings (pp. 261-284). Hillsdale, N. J.: Erlbaum.

Smith, R. E. (2010). Cognitive-affective stress management training: A treatment and resource manual (Revised ed.). Unpublished document, Department of Psychology, University of Washington, Seattle, WA USA.

Smith, R. E, and Nye, S. L. (1989). Comparison of induced affect and covert rehearsal in the acquisition of stress management coping skills. *Journal of Counseling Psychology*, 36, 17-23.

Smith, R. E., Fagan, C., Wilson, N. L., Chen, J., Corona, M., Nguyen, H., Racz, S., and Shoda, Y. (2011). Internet-based approaches to collaborative therapeutic assessment: new opportunities for professional psychologists. *Professional Psychology: Research and Practice. Advance online publication.* doi: 10.1037/a0025393.

Stogdill, R. (1948). Personal factors associated with leadership: A survey of the literature. *Journal of Psychology*, 24, 35-71.

In: Perspectives in Leadership
Editor: Jerry D. VanVactor

ISBN: 978-1-62417-170-3
© 2013 Nova Science Publishers, Inc.

Chapter 6

THE INFLUENCE OF SPIRITUALITY UPON LEADERSHIP AND THE WORKPLACE

James Michael Lewis
Retired US Army Chaplain, US

ABSTRACT

Leadership, though variously defined, is a process that always involves at least two persons, a leader and one being led. With this human dimension in mind, let us approach the subject of "leadership" as something quite distinct from "management." While a person in charge of an organization or some aspect of its operation may exercise both leadership and managerial responsibilities, leading and managing involve two distinct processes. Though frequently used as interchangeable terms, they are not synonymous.

UNDERSTANDING LEADERSHIP AS RELATIONSHIP

First of all, leadership, unlike management, is built upon a relationship between people. Martin Buber wrote that the attitude of man is twofold and these are revealed with the two basic words or word pairs he can speak. These two word-pairs are "I-Thou" (ich-du) and "I-It (ich-es). He further illustrates the idea by declaring "love is reciprocity of an I for a Thou." (Buber, 1970)

Building upon this basic concept, we understand that one may work with an object (an "It") through the process of management but one relates to a subject (a "Thou") through the dynamics of personal leadership. Management is an activity appropriately directed toward non-personal entities, such as plans, agendas, programs, schedules, reports, projects, budgets, records, inventories, etc. These "things" do not require motivation, only systematic organization and functional handling. Managers are concerned with control, problem-solving and taking corrective action. (Ricketts, 2009) However, the "things" they manage have no life, no self-awareness or consciousness. They do not reason or feel or wonder. They can neither be inspired nor demoralized. In short, "things" cannot be led because they lack the ability to respond to any leader. They simply function according to their design and are "managed" by their assigned handlers. Leadership takes place within the dynamics of human relations.

To further contrast their workplace functions, leaders establish a relationship of multi-directional influence while managers exercise unidirectional authority. Leadership involves providing direction and clarifying the big picture. It focuses on aligning people, communicating goals, seeking commitment, and team building. While leadership is about motivating, inspiring, energizing, and empowering followers, management is about the co-ordination, support and monitoring of organizational activities. (Ricketts, 2009) Leadership is about having a vision and articulating it. It is about ordering priorities, persuading others to go with you and constantly reviewing what you are doing. Leadership is about holding on to things you value. Management is about the functions, procedures and systems by which you realize the vision. (Day & Harris, n.d)

SOME TRADITIONAL THEORIES OF LEADERSHIP

Fairholm suggests that when a theory of leadership does not address higher human values including sense and meaning, obligation, morality, and self sacrifice, the theory becomes defective. By omitting these kinds of values, leaders within organizations will tend to focus upon controlling people, managing them as objects. (Fairholm, 1998, 2001 as cited in Bonner 2007) Both those who lead and those who follow share the common qualities of humanness. Both leader and follower think, reason, imagine, and are consciously, self-aware. They wonder about things; they ask questions, explore, and experiment. They both desire things. They both possess complex dimensions of mind and personality including that most hard-to-define quality, spirituality. These human qualities connect leader and follower, enabling them to develop a workplace culture characterized by shared vision, values, and principles. When people are managed, they are assigned the role of "subordinates". People who lead do not have subordinates, they have followers. Followers are people who have responded to a leader's motivation and vision. Following is always a voluntary activity. (Changing Minds, 2012)

McGregor applied Maslow's hierarchy of needs to describe leadership styles. Theory X or Transactional Leadership is focused on maintaining the status quo through top-down control. (Marzano, Waters, & McNulty, 2005 as cited in Bonner, 2007) The manager's authority over subordinates is vested in him or her by the organization. The manager requires the subordinate to perform certain work and offers a reward for compliance, at minimum a paycheck. (Changing Minds, 2012) The manager-subordinate transaction is often the simple formula, "a day's work for a day's pay, no more and no less". The management, following the Theory X model, seeks to maintain control over people by engaging them on the lowest level of the hierarchy of needs as described by Maslow. Because these lower level survival needs are their primary focus and that maintaining economic livelihood is their motivation, managers control subordinates through reward and punishment, sometimes called the "stick and carrot". McGregor's Theory X is based upon certain assumptions about human nature. It presumes that these coercive controls are necessary because people are lazy, self-centered, indifferent to organizational needs, resistant to change, lacking in ambition, disliking responsibility and would prefer to be told what to do. Essentially people are not very bright! Consequently, managers must motivate subordinates by applying the "stick and carrot". (McGregor, n.d.) However the theory is self perpetuating. While it promotes superficial harmony it actually produces apathy and indifference. By appealing only to their lower level needs, managers will tend to motivate subordinates at less than optimum level. They are motivated to offer minimum required performance to complete the transaction, keep their jobs, and maintain the status quo. A low level of performance is then offered as clear evidence that people are naturally apathetic and need to be controlled, thus validating the existing management model. (McGregor, 1960 as cited in Bonner 2007)

The coercive, transactional approach has been widely employed in the United States in industry and has even influenced public education. It persists because it carries an image of efficiency and effectiveness that may be traced back to a classic and successful military model, the Prussian Army. Their success was due to machine-age thinking. They introduced standardization and drill training for the sake of efficiency and uniformity. (Gatto 2003; Miller, 1997; Senge 2000, as cited in Bonner 2007) Soldiers were trained to do small repetitive tasks that could be replicated by other soldiers. As the products of this training regimen, soldiers became replicable parts. This machine-like Prussian army became the standard for military forces of its day. During the early industrial age, factories created the modern techniques of assembly-line production. With increased production, factories needed larger numbers, of workers, who, like an army, had to be controlled. Industry successfully applied this military model to its workers who, like Prussian soldiers, were expected to be obedient, uniform, and efficient. (Senge, 2000 as cited in Bonner 2007)

McGregor described another leadership style, sometimes called the Humanistic model or Theory Y. Unlike those operating from Theory X, Theory Y leaders believe that people are not lazy and un-ambitious, but they can become so as a result of their experience in organizations. The core principal of Theory Y leadership is integration of personal and organizational goals. McGregor believes the motivation, the potential for development, the capacity for assuming responsibility and the readiness to direct behavior toward organizational goals are all present in people. Leaders create conditions that enable the members of the organization to achieve their own goals by directing them toward achieving the organization's objectives. (McGregor, n.d.). Argyris (1957, 1964 as cited in Bonner) recognized the same conflict between organizations and people. He believed institutionalized systems often treat people like children rather than mature adults leading to psychological failure. As with Theory X, the institutionalized system creates what it believes it is preventing. Theory Y leaders are aware that under the conditions of industrial life, the intellect, creativity, and imagination of humans are only partially utilized. However, while self-actualization is a motivational goal, the success of the business is still the main goal. These leaders, while not subscribing to the assumptions of Theory X, cannot yet be what Maslow called called "Transcenders" or spiritual leaders because they are not inclined to change the existing power base of institutionalized systems.

Theory Y leaders bring assumptions about human nature to the workplace. They assume that their expenditure of physical and mental effort in work is as natural as play or rest. They believe the average human does not dislike work. They assume that work can be a source of satisfaction or a source of punishment. They are more optimistic in their assessment of human potential, recognizing that external control and punishment are not the only means of motivating people towards organizational objectives. Rather, they assume that, with commitment, people can be self-directed and self-controlled. However, commitment to achieving those objectives is still a function of the rewards associated with their achievement. (Bonner, 2007)

SPIRITUAL MODELS FOR LEADERSHIP

Fairholm (1998, 2001 as cited in Bonner 2007) wrote that some current management styles, masked as leadership styles, have emphasized a leader's ability to apply rationality and objectivity. Self interest, individuality and detachment were desirable traits. While some of these are valid characteristics of leadership, higher levels of human needs such as membership in a group, the ability to create sense and meaning, a sense of intrinsic morality, of duty, and of self-sacrifice are not addressed as equally important values in the workplace. (Sergiovanni, 1992 as cited in Bonner 2007)

In order to lead people effectively, to inspire followership, the leader must be able to apply his or her own higher level personal qualities including focus, passion, wisdom, field independence, courage, and integrity. These are not second-hand techniques taught by leadership theory but are all "rooted in faith and soul" (Bolman &Deal, 2002 as cited in Bohnner 2007) By applying their higher values, leaders may redefine workplace relationships. Instead of seeking to achieve machinelike obedience and lockstep performance, the leader would be free to approach followers as humans recognizing their various levels of needs. This motivates people of the workforce to function at a level above that of basic survival. They are encouraged to develop a sense of personal investment in the organization and to perform their work from intrinsic motivation rather than external coercion. A dimension of leadership that involves personal character and the application of sacred or transcendent values is the"Spirituality" of the leader.

Following upon discussions of theories X and Y, Bohnner describes Spiritual Leadership or Theory Z . Expressed in terms of Maslow's hierarchy of needs, this type of leader has both met deficiency needs and self-actualization needs and is pursuing a connection with transcendent needs. Theory X perpetually engages people at their lowest level of motivation, simple survival; Theory Z, spiritual leadership,attempts to connect with them at a point higher on the pyramid of human needs and thereby stimulate their intrinsic motivation. Maslow describes Spiritual Leaders as "Transcending Self-Actualizers". Transcenders find that peak or transcendent experiences are the most important, precious aspects of life. They can converse in the language of "mystics, seers, and profoundly religious men". They tend to perceive life unitively, sacredly, and holistically under the aspect of eternity. Spiritual leaders tend to view their own work as a sort of "calling", living in relationship with the transcendent. They also encourage followers to meet their own transcendent needs within the workplace. Leaders who do not reflect a spiritual orientation view their work only in terms of cost-effectiveness. (Maslow 1943, 1981, 1971 as cited in Bonner 2007) One traditional definition of "spirit" describes it as the vital principle or animating force within living beings, thus relating to the deeper sense, meaning, or significance of something. Combining the two terms, spiritual and leadership, suggest that the leader seeks to follow a holistic approach to encourage a higher sense of significance and interconnectedness among followers in the workplace. (Barnett, 2012) Without the spiritual component, Fairholm claims, the "caricature of the leader offered by contemporary leadership theory will become more and more the operational truth." That being the case, leadership theory will be no more than management theory (Fairholm, 2001; Barth, 2001 as cited in Bonner 2007)

Spirituality, like religion, is often treated as a "hot button" subject. It is regarded as a highly personal and totally internal matter for individuals. One may ask, does something as personal as spirituality have a place within corporate life? If one accepts the premise that all people, simply by virtue of being human, possess some sort of "spirituality" in their lives, neither the leader nor the follower cease to be spiritual beings simply because they report to work. Fairholm was one of the first scholars to put the terms spiritual and leadership together in the context of the workplace. (Fairholm 1966, 1998 as cited in Dent, Higgins, & Wharff 2005) Spiritual values seek expression in the workplace as naturally as they would in any other setting. The leader's ability to articulate and demonstrate these values and facilitate their expression by others may transform the culture of the workplace.

Presuming that profit-driven, no nonsense thinking characterizes the world of business and commerce, one might expect its leaders to regard any discussion of workplace spirituality as an unwelcomed distraction. However, far from being dismissed or marginalized, the interest in workplace spirituality has steadily grown.

There have been many attempts to develop and define practical models that integrate spiritual leadership into the workplace. They employ a variety of descriptive language in an effort to capture the rather abstract qualities they are advocating, and to formulate these into teachable leadership models. Some of these models do not explicitly apply the term "spiritual" but they describe many of the same concerns and characteristics.

Greenleaf advocates a model he calls Servant Leadership. The servant-leader begins with the natural feeling that one wants to serve, and to serve first. Later on, through conscious choice, one may aspire to lead. The servant-first individual is sharply differentiated from one who has sought to be a leader first, motivated by any number of personal reasons. These may choose to serve later on, after having already established themselves as leaders. The leader-first and the servant-first are two extreme types, between which are shadings and blends that reflect the infinite variety within human nature. Greenleaf holds that the primary purpose of business should be to create a positive impact on its employees and community. The Servant Leaders brings together service and meaning. The servant leader is attuned to basic spiritual values and by serving those values, will serve colleagues, the organization and society. (Greenleaf, 1977)

Covey refers to "Principle-Centered Leaders" who, like Greenleaf's "Servant Leaders", willingly try to live in "calling" to others. They seek to promote harmony with natural laws and universal principles. Rather than remaining abstract ideas, Principle-Centered Leaders put principles into action within a wide range of relationships at the personal, interpersonal, managerial, and organizational levels. The goal is to unleash the creativity, talent and energy of employees whose jobs have not previously rewarded the use of such resources. Value-Based Leadership is predicated on shared, strongly internalized values that are advocated and acted on by the leader (Bass & Avollio, 1994; House, 1996; House and Shamir, 1993 as cited in Fry 2003)

SPIRITUAL LEADERS

How then should we describe and characterize the term "Spiritual Leader"? To whom may it be applied? It describes a leader who addresses values of sense and meaning by asking, "Why should a leader conduct himself with a sense of obligation, morality, sacrifice, and a willingness to seek guidance from the divine?" (Brubaker and Coble, 2005; Covey, 2004; Hoyle, 2002; Housaton and Sokolow, 2006; Mitroff and Denton, 1999; Senge et al., 2004 as cited in Bonner 2007). A Spiritual Leader must, first of all, know what it means to be a follower. He or she has a sense of calling and relationship, choosing to be a follower of something larger than self . Spiritual leaders acknowledge the reality of a transcendence in the universe that can be tapped to make a leader more effective. (Brubaker and Coble, 2004 as cited in Bonner 2007).

American business leaders and managers often recognize the reality of these needs and are quite open to applying Spiritual Leadership principles. Recent polls found that managers and leaders want a deeper sense of meaning and fulfillment on the job-even more than they want money and time off. A major change is also taking place in the personal and professional lives of leaders as many of them more deeply integrate their spirituality and their work. Most would agree that this integration is leading to very positive changes in their relationships and their effectiveness (Neal, 2001 as cited in Fry 2003)

If we assume that every person has spiritual qualities and some level of spiritual awareness, it does not necessarily follow that everyone is able to articulate these or understand their applications in daily life. The leader's own personal spirituality, in whatever form it takes, must be authentic, not contrived. Some form of individual spiritual "awakening" or "calling" may or may not be indicated. However it comes about, the leader must have a relationship with someone or something larger than self and actively following this source of spiritual authority. Benito advised leaders "rely on a power greater than yourself to guide your vision." He added "I believe that the deeper we go into the exploration of leadership, the more we need to deal with the spiritual dimensions of sense-making, connection-building, choice-making, vision-inspiration, reality-creating roles of leaders" (Benito, 2000 as cited in Bonner 2007) Theories about spirituality and models for its application may be taught, but the leader's spirituality itself cannot be acquired second-hand through a leadership seminar.

The personal spirituality of the leader is manifested through his or her core values. Values become the criteria for all decision-making within the organization. Harvey states that, after meeting with chief executive officers and other high ranking executives, they reported that many decisions at the highest levels of all kinds of organizations are made on the basis of prayer. He also notes that leaders "of significant stature and influence" care deeply about the spiritual side of their leadership roles and are starved for opportunities to discuss it (Harvey, 2001 as cited in Dent, Higgins, & Wharff 2005)

SPIRITUALITY IN THE WORKPLACE

To discuss spirituality in the workplace may seem absurdly idealistic for some hard-nosed number-crunching managers responsible for the organization's success as measured by output and profitability. But spirituality is not about the "fluffy clouds" of obscure concepts that float above our heads. Rather, it is the solid foundation under our feet, the indispensable bedrock upon which life is built.

There appears to be considerable overlap between workplace spirituality and motivation-based theories of leadership. Both address intrinsic motivation. They both speak to the concept of spiritual survival through a sense of meaning, calling, and membership. (Pfeiffer, 2003 as cited in Fry 2003) It is the leaders who are instrumental in the process of integrating workplace spirituality at the individual, team, and organizational level. Leaders who bring their own spirituality to work may transform organizations from impersonal mechanical routines limited to mission driven activities into places where individual and collective spirituality are encouraged and integrated into the day to day work life (Konz & Ryan, 1999 as cited in Dent, Higgins, & Wharff 2005)

Workplace spirituality may be understood as a framework of organizational values that, collectively, are evidenced in the culture. It promotes the employees' experience of transcendence through the work process. It facilitates their sense of being connected to others in a way that provides feelings of completeness and joy. (Giacalone &Jurkeiewicz, 2003 as cited in Dent, Higgins, & Wharff 2005) Many writers noted that spiritually empowered employees are more creative, more honest, stronger, more resilient, and more compassionate human beings (Bento, 1944 as cited in Dent Higgins & Wharff 2005) Cacioppe (2000 as cited in Dent, Higgins, & Wharff 2005) concludes that spirituality in the workplace is not just good for business, it is the only way leaders and organizations can succeed. Organizational leaders who are more willing to use their personal spiritual values to make business decisions and transform organizations instill values that become the standard. Such organizations are believed to be more profitable and perform better (Biberman & Whitty, 1997 ; Biberman et al, 1999; Bierly et al,. 2000; Burack, 1999; Cacioppe, 2000; Dehler & Welsh, 1994; Delbecq, 1999; Konz & Ryan, 1999; Korac-Kakabadse & 1997, 2002; Kriger & Hanson 1999; Mitroff & Denton, 1999; Poth, McCall & Bausch, 1999; Sass, 2000; Strack et al , 2002 as cited in Dent, Higgins & Wharff, 2005)

However, relating workplace spirituality to increased productivity or profitability presents an ethical problem for many who note that spirituality is, by definition, antithetical to materialism. This raises concerns that efforts to apply spiritual leadership theory in the workplace, might be no more than cynical efforts to harness the language of high-minded idealism to serve the economic bottom line. Historically, the Puritan concepts of spirituality were perfectly suited to production-minded people. They valued the behaviors of "self denial, self-discipline, glorification of work, the subordination of the present to the future and of oneself to the larger whole. The Puritan work ethic was rooted in Calvinist theology which taught that material success is evidence that one is numbered among God's "elect". (Hill, 1999). This work ethic originated in a pre-industrial setting, but its principles served to fuel the 19th century's industrial development. In time, however, the ethic was no longer directed in obedience and service to a Puritan God but to serve the goals of industrial production (Quigley, 1966 as cited in Bonner 2007) This concern may be legitimate, but we must take care not to presume that true spirituality floats above the material world and only exists in some pure form. To do so would suggest that no truly spiritual qualities can be applied to the workplace in practical terms or linked to accomplishing workplace missions lest their work result in production and profit. By this reasoning, any material accomplishment and commercial success would be, by definition, unspiritual, exploitive, and somehow tainted.

This thinking would effectively isolate the workplace from spiritual influence and offer no alternative to the coercive top-down management style. At the same time we should note that while increased spirituality and ethical awareness would presumably prohibit individuals from performing certain kinds of work, it is quite likely that the spiritually healthy person will be more effective in performing any kind of work that is consistent with his or her spiritual principles. (Dent, Higgins, & Wharff 2005)

An internally motivated, ethical person who lives with a sense that every aspect of life is something sacred, is likely to function at a higher level of motivation on and off the job than one who lacks those qualities. It should not be surprising to us when an increased level of effectiveness and productivity on the job becomes one of its byproducts. We should remember that spirituality as experienced within the workplace should not be compared to that practiced by an ascetic monk in a cloister.

Spirituality in the workplace has gained significant attention in recent popular literature. A number of best-selling books on leadership and management include "spirit" or some comparable word in the title. The concept is also beginning to be incorporated into organizational behavior textbooks (Robbins, 2003 as cited in Dent, Higgins, & Wharff 2005) For some researchers, the surge in this type of literature raises the red flag that this may simply be the newest management fad.

Bonner suggests that "Society is at an evolutionary place and time where spirituality is emerging across a wide range of venues: biology, physics, game theory, evolutionary psychology, business management, adult education, popular books, magazines, and educational leadership theory. (Fullan, 2001; Ridley, 1996; Sober and Wilson, 1998; Wright, 1998 as cited in Bonner 2007) Posner (1999 as cited in Bonner 2007) observes that the "workplace spirituality movement is gaining momentum and beginning to penetrate the conscience of the world's corporations". Companies as diverse as Taco Bell, Pizza Hut, BioGenenex, Aetna International, Big Six accounting's Deloitte and Touche, and Law firms such as New York's Kay Scholer, Fierman, Hays' and Haroller have extolled lessons usually doled out in churches, temples, and mosques (Mitroff & Denton, 1999 cited in Fry 2003)

What inspires a renewed interest in this subject? Perhaps it is in response to a working environment that is increasingly insecure and demoralizing. In many cases the workplace may be described as "tense". Many organizations are going through downsizing, reengineering, restructuring, outsourcing, and layoffs. Jobs may be threatened and the workloads of those who remain may have increased with the requirement to do more with less. People find themselves spending more and more time at work. It is not uncommon for people to eat, exercise, date, drop their kids and even nap at the workplace. Lacking continuity and connection in so many other settings they may look to their organizations as a communal center (Mirvus, 1997 as cited in Fry 2003). While spirituality is closely linked to relationships, fewer people are now firmly connected to stabilizing and spiritually nourishing institutions such as extended families, churches, neighborhoods, and civic groups. These traditionally served to meet spiritually based needs and to provide a sense of belonging, connectedness, and contribution. Some now look to the workplace as a substitute for those traditional institutions. (Ashmos Duchon (2000) and Brandt, 1996; Donger, 1994 as cited in Dent, Higgins, & Wharff 2005) Almost universally, people have the intrinsic drive and motivation to learn and find meaning in their work. They want connectedness, to be members of a group in which they feel valued for their contribution to that group's performance.

(Giacalone & Jurkiewicz, 2003 cited in Fry 2003) The organization, through its leadership, may tap into this natural drive or utterly stifle it.

ACADEMIC INTEREST IN SPIRITUALITY

The subject has steadily gained legitimacy in academic circles, having been incorporated into many graduate and undergraduate business programs. The Academy of Management has even created a new Management, Spirituality, and Religion special interest group, (Academy of Management, 2004 as cited in Dent, Higgins, & Wharff 2005) Scholarly articles on workplace spirituality have appeared in the Journal of Management Inquiry, the Journal of Managerial Psychology, the Journal of Organizational Change Management, and the Leadership and Organizational Development Journal. (Dent, Higgins & Wharff 2005

Having been established as a legitimate field of study, spirituality has become the subject of much scholarly research. Those academics who attempt to examine the phenomenon are often frustrated by a lack of consensus as to what should be encompassed by the term "spiritual". While literature abounds, it is reasonable to ask whether or not the various studies are even talking about the same thing. Strack et. al. (2001 as cited in Dent, Higgins&Wharff 2005) contends that a research agenda linking spirituality and leadership is a conceptual quagmire because each construct can be defined in hundreds of ways. Assumptions brought to the discussion are often highly subjective when determining what falls within the parameters of this study. It is by nature a "highly personal, subjectively understood construct" and lacks a clear definition. (Freshman, 1999 as cited in Dent, Higgins,& Wharff 2005). While spirituality, as a matter of interest to humans, is almost universal, it has been observed that "there are more definitions for spirituality than there are authors/researchers to write about it". (Mohammed, Hassan, and Wisnieski, 2001)as cited in Dent, Higgins, & Wharff 2005)

A study of spiritual leadership can be viewed as a field of inquiry within the broader context of workplace spirituality. Both are areas of research in the early stage of development and therefore lack a strong body of theory and research findings. Most organizational theory offered in this area comes from the fields of Western religious theology and practice and from leadership ethics and values (Blackaby and Blackaby, 2001; McNeal, 2000; Northouse, 2001; Sanders, 1986 as cited in Fry 2003)

SPIRITUALITY, REASON, AND SCIENCE

How relevant is the concept and practice of spirituality is in our age, one that is dominated by empirically based science and cold, calculating reason? Spirituality will be summarily dismissed by many as utterly irrelevant because it does not conform to the assumptions and categories of these dominant schools of thought. Historically, Cartesian skepticism and Lockean empiricism emphasized the idea that man and the universe could be explained by critical reason alone. (Fairholm, 1998; Polanyi, 1946; Senge 2000 as cited in Bonner) This train of thought would imply that the universe was rational and could be "calculated and controlled" and those irrational elements of religion would be eliminated. (Tillilch, 1967) The role of religion and spirituality in western culture was increasingly diminished as radical skepticism and empiricism became the accepted models for understanding the world around us and within us. Spirituality, as a way of "knowing", has no place in their epistemological framework. While these methods were instrumental in the birth and growth of the modern industrial age, it was also instrumental in eliminating traditional belief systems that had long served to provide purpose and meaning to human existence (Franks, 1952; MacIntyre, 1984; Polanyi, 1946 as cited in Bonner 2007). Peterson and Nodding lament this loss of the ethical and aesthetic in that it removes passion and relationality from "reason". (Peterson, 2002 and Nodding, 1998 as cited in Bonner 2007) Reason and observation are a valid method for apprehending "facts" within the world around us. However, they seem ill-equipped and inadequate to explore something called "truth" which belongs to the spiritual dimension of life. Ultimate Truth is something that is encountered, experienced, or intuitively discerned through an "I-Thou" relationship rather than defined as an "I-It" calculation. However, the resurgence of interest in the spiritual perspectives on life suggests that pure rationality may be losing whatever monopoly it may have enjoyed within our culture as the sole method available in the search for both facts and truth. One of Gibbons' characteristics of post modern spirituality is to deny that rationality is the sole source of knowledge. (Gibbons, 1999 as cited in Bonner).

A rigidly exclusive dichotomy may not be necessary. Another view sees the scientific and spiritual perspectives as complimentary. Shermer argues that humans as pattern-seeking animals need to believe there are two ways of knowing. The first he calls "logos" which is the scientifically provable. The second he terms "mythos" referring to that which is faith based and is improvable. (Shermer, 2000 as cited in Vos & Barker 2007) The problem is that modern people often fail to see the "spiritual world" as the "real world". Rather, we only see the logos with its physical, tangibility as "real". However, we cannot deny the reality of either. We operate within logos while still being drawn by mythos toward a higher reality. Nevertheless, the playing field for this mythos experience or spirituality is still the solid logos world in which we life. The workplace is a specific logos reality in which mythos spirituality may be lived out and expressed. Reality does not follow an either-or view in which the physical and spiritual are mutually exclusive or antagonistic. There is a holistic inter-connectedness in the process of knowing. (Voss & Barker 2007)

Theologian Paul Tillich (1967as cited in Bonner2007) believes that spirituality may itself be described as a form of reason. He proposes four aspects of reason: Universal, Critical, Intuitive, and Technical. The first, Universal Reason, corresponds to what many have called the spiritual aspect of knowing. It is characterized by belief in the Divine mind, knowledge, ethical awareness or conscience, and aesthetic intuition. He presents this as a legitimate way of reasoning, an alternative to the analytical Technical Reason primarily being used today.

Spirituality, as a way of knowing things has also been described as a category of intelligence. Zohar and Marshall (2011 as cited in Bonner 2007) describe three aspects of intelligence. The first is the intellectual or rational intelligence expressed as the IQ. This category of intelligence is used "to solve logical or strategic problems" The second is emotional intelligence expressed as EQ and characterized as, a "basic requirement for the effective use of IQ" The third is spiritual intelligence or SQ which is the "necessary foundation for the effective functioning of both IQ and EQ". Spiritual intelligence is what we may also describe as "conscience" (Zohar and Marshall, 2001 as cited in Bonner 2007) Conscience is represented as the central and fundamental intelligence that guides all the other expressions of intelligence. When leaders live by their spiritual intelligence or conscience, "their behavior echoes in everyone's souls. People instinctively feel trust and confidence toward them" (Covey, cited in Greenleaf, 2002 as cited in Bonner 2007) How can we describe this intangible quality? Covey describes four dimensions of conscience. First, conscience involves sacrifice. Second, it inspires us to become part of a cause worthy of commitment. Third, it teaches us that ends and means are inseparable. Fourth, conscience introduces us into the world of relationships. Covey (2004 cited in Greenleaf, 2002, cited in Bonner) believes that, when listening to conscience, it is the quiet voice of God that is heard. (Covey cited in Greenleaf, 2002, cited in Bonner 2007)

Although sometimes presented as two irreconcilable and competing worldviews, the empirically-based field of science and the realm of spirituality are not antithetical. For the scientific community, spirituality is not a new topic and, historically, has not been automatically dismissed. Charles Darwin ends his seminal work "On the Origin of Species" with the statement" "There is grandeur in this view of life' with its several powers having been originally breathed by the Creator into a few forms or into one". (Darwin, 1909) Collins, the Director of the Human Genome Project is open about his convictions on religion and spirituality, describing his beliefs as "intellectually inescapable". Gatto, 2001 cited in Bonner 2007)

Historically it was the "holy men" of the community to whom the common people looked as the "keepers of the secrets". In modern times that mantle has been claimed by the scientists, physicians, and psychologists who, to ordinary people, also seem to deal in mysteriously esoteric knowledge. Religion, the ancient authority, and science, the new authority, are often at odds. Within the discipline of psychology, itself dealing with intangible aspects of the human mind, Freud set the tone when he described religion as the "Universal obsessional neurosis." (Freud, 1964). Elkins (1999) notes that back when it was a new science, psychology tried to distance itself from theological explanations of behavior and to discover its own truths through scientific inquiry. Since that time, many within that discipline have regarded spirituality and religion as something that is pathological. While clinical experience has pointed to evidence that Freud was at least partly correct, in some cases religion can indeed become neurotic, many psychologists recognize a therapeutic quality in personal spirituality even when expressed through religious language and practice. Many psychologists now feel more comfortable referring clients who are struggling with spiritual issues to a priest, pastor, or rabbi. Spirituality and religion are able to offer people some things that science cannot. These include a sense of hope, a sense of forgiveness, redemption, reconciliation, and purpose for living that is linked to something larger than self. Some of the most respected individuals in the history of psychology, William James, Gordon Alport, Erich Fromm, Viktor Frankl, Abraham Maslow, and Rollo May, to name a few, have made spirituality a major focus in their work. Jung states that spirituality was such an essential ingredient in psychological health that he could only heal those middle-aged people who embraced a spiritual or religious perspective toward life. Psychologists today are not of one mind in their approach toward religion. Some still view it as an obstacle to mental well-being or even a cause directly related to mental disorders. However, others suggest that, in many cases, spirituality and religious faith can also play an important role in promoting the mental health of their patients. (Elkins, 1999)

SPIRITUALITY AND RELIGION

A major point of disagreement revolves around the distinction between religion and spirituality. In researching theories of leadership and management practice, questions of workplace spirituality are often excluded, possibly as a result of this confusion. (Fry, 2003) The question is this, does promoting workplace spirituality mean promoting religious practices? Because sectarian religious passions are easily aroused in the form of doctrinal disagreement, some may fear that it has the potential to introduce a divisive factor into the workplace.

Simply put, are religion and spirituality essentially the same? Can they be separated? Are they qualitatively different? Is one a category of the other or are they two entirely different experiences? Can one be spiritual without religion or religious without being spiritual? If we can presume that all people have some kind of spiritual nature, have formed assumptions about spiritual things, or have been exposed to some form of religion, objectivity will be difficult . Personal experience and assumptions will likely color the discussion.

One position voiced by Cash & Gray (2000 as cited in Dent Higgins and Wharf, 2005) suggests spirituality, religion, and "sincerely held beliefs" should be regarded as essentially the same thing. Others see them as related but not synonymous. Spirituality is described as something that is essentially moral and emotional in nature. It involves an understanding and appreciation of one's position in the universe, ones soul, and the role of a God. The rituals, routines, ceremonies, and practices of organized religion would not be viewed as an end in themselves, but they serve as a vehicle for seeking and achieving spirituality. At the same time one could be functionally religious, faithfully observing these rituals and activities, without automatically achieving a personal sense of spirituality. (Bierly et al. 2000 as cited in Dent Higgins &Wharff 2005)

Religion is easier to describe, analyze, and critique than spirituality because the former is observable through its practices and activities. As organized institutional bodies, religious communities must define themselves, their beliefs, practices, and purposes. They establish their orthodoxy in the form of theology, dogma, and prescribed ritual. Any religion, established as a particular faith group, denomination or sect, must define and elaborate upon that which distinguishes it from other groups. This is necessary to establish for its followers and potential converts how their organization, belief system, and practices are different from other groups and why they believe theirs' the proper form. Spirituality, on the other hand, may have aspects so ephemeral that they cannot be clearly identified, let alone measured. People with a largely negative view toward organized and established institutions of religion may be more favorably inclined toward "spirituality" because its vagueness requires no clear accountability outside of one's self and may be more subjectively defined to suit the individual. It can mean virtually whatever they decide it means. Fornaciari & Dean (2001 cited in Dent, Higgins & Wharff 2005) contend that it is not possible to measure spirituality, one's relationship to the sacred. For this reason, religion and spirituality cannot be subjected to the same criteria of examination.

Studies have shown that Americans want spirituality in their lives, but not necessarily in a traditional religious form. During the 1960s and 70s participation in denominational religious practices dropped significantly with an 84% drop among Jews, 69% among mainline Protestants, 61% of conservative Protestants, and 67% of Catholics. Elkins suggests that the drop did not indicate a loss of interest in spirituality, only that many people were finding their traditional expressions of religion inadequate to meet their higher needs. By the 1990s there was evidence that Americans were becoming more expressive in terms of spirituality. National polls reported that 9 out of 10 Americans still believed in God and considered religion important in their lives. This rekindling of spiritual awareness has not been limited to a return to traditional religion. Among baby boomers an estimated 32 million remain denominationally unaffiliated but many have turned to other expressions including Eastern practices, new age philosophies, Twelve Step Programs, Greek mythology, Jungian psychology, shamanic practices, massage, yoga, and a host of other traditions and practices. Others report finding spiritual fulfillment in music, poetry, literature, art, nature, and intimate relationships. (Elkins, 1999)

Spirituality is usually described as something much broader than any single formal or organized religion as defined by its prescribed tenets, dogma and doctrines (Zellers & Perrewe, 2003 as cited in Fry 2003) For example, spirituality may be described as a "Source" that a person seeks to achieve a "spiritual survival" which would encompass finding meaning in life and achieving a sense of inter-connectedness with other beings (Zinnbauer, Pargament & Scott, 1999 as cited in Fry 2003) It is also defined as a "Process" through which people seek to discover their potential, an ultimate purpose, and a personal relationship with a higher power or being . That power/being may or may not be called God. (Tart, 1975; Wuff, 1996 as cited in Fry 2003). This relationship to the higher power may occur with or without affiliation or connection to formal religious organizations. While spirituality is important for religion, religion is not essential for all spiritual experience. Following this understanding, workplace spirituality and spiritual leadership can be inclusive or exclusive of religious theory and practice. One set of paradigms sets the concept of spirituality apart from that of religion by linking it to such pursuits as personal self-actualization, forming purpose and meaning in life, and seeking health and wellness as outcomes. These pursuits may be consistent within some religious thought but are not necessarily theistic concepts. (Goertzen & Barbuto, 2001 as cited in Dent, Higgins, & Wharff 2005)

Other writers make less of a distinction between religion and spirituality. Mohammed et. al. (2001 cited in Dent Higgins Wharf 2005) argue that there is no significant difference between religion and spirituality despite the fact that many see the prior as negative and the latter as positive. Gibbons (2000 cited in Dent, Higgins, & Wharff 2005) says that spirituality cannot be separated from ancient religious traditions because of its obvious importance to so many people. He cites reports that 95% of Americans believe in God, there are1.5 billion Buddhists in the world, and that Western Europe is estimated to be 80% Christian. Hicks (2002, as cited in Dent, Higgins &Wharff 2005) critically examined the religion-spirituality dichotomy. He suggests that scholars have too broadly defined spirituality, narrowly defined religion, and failed to acknowledge the factor of religious diversity. He contends that scholars invoke the religion-spirituality dichotomy to argue that if a practice or belief is controversial, it is probably religious and not spiritual, and thus conflict is defined away. Moch and Bartunek also contend that spirituality and religion cannot be separated and illustrate how religion interprets spirituality and how religion and business have co-evolved over the last 3 centuries. They observe how some authors, in promoting a distinction between spirituality and religion in their articles, write as if there is no belief system that accompanies someone's spirituality. Theory development should recognize that any form of spirituality also includes practices and beliefs which also happens to be one of the descriptions of religion. (Moch &

Bartunek submitted for publication, as cited in Dent, Higgins & Wharf, 2005) While highly subjective and lacking the kind of historical and institutional authority doctrine provides for a religion, individually held beliefs or "personal religion" are an important element of how someone's spirituality will be manifested in his or her leadership.

Spirituality may be pursued through a variety of modes and methods. Institutionalists or traditionalists may encounter God in the context of the time honored beliefs and practices of their church or religious community. Rationalists may find God through hard study and reflective thought. Mystics may approach God through silent, intuitive contemplation. Moralists may serve God thorough active obedience to duty. In each case, through different methods, we find someone actively seeking a relationship with God. In each case, we find a spiritual quest for an ideal source of help and object of devotion. (Horton, 1950 as cited in Fry 2003)

Horton observes the variety of ways in which personal conceptions of God as Higher Power may be understood. On one end of the continuum he places absolute atheism with its assumption that there is no God coupled with a nihilistic view that one has no sense of calling or membership and that all is evil, hopeless, and rooted in sorrow, distress, despair, and calamity. Further down the scale is humanism. On the far end end he places complete pantheism which assumes everything is God and that all is good and rooted in joy, peace, and serenity. Somewhere around the middle of this continuum he places ethical monotheism, primarily expressed through established, historical religions such as Judaism, Christianity, and Islam. Ethical monotheism, often called theism for short, differs from pantheism and humanism in that it thinks neither nature nor humanity is the measure of all things. Rather, both are understood as being dependent on God their creator. Ethical monotheism thinks of God as engaged in purposive combat with evil tendencies in the world. Horton noted that some who call themselves atheists or agnostics still operate from faith assumptions. While denying belief in a Supreme Being and life after death, they may place their trust and faith in science and technology. Practically speaking, he concludes, they are effectively worshipping an objective or nature-based pantheistic god. (Horton, 1950 as cited in Fry 2003)

Ashmos and Duchon (2000 cited in Dent Higgins and Wharff 2005) argue that workplace spirituality is neither about religion nor about getting people to accept a specific belief system. Rather it is about employees who understand themselves as spiritual beings at work whose souls need nourishment, a sense of purpose and meaning, and a sense of connectedness to one another and to their workplace community.

MYTHOLOGY AND THE LIMITS OF LANGUAGE

Definitions of spirituality tend to elude us because we lack an adequate language for an aspect of reality we are trying to capture in words and concepts. When speaking of spiritual things, the language of empirical science and philosophical reason is unsatisfactory. Transcendent or sacred things are difficult or impossible to capture within the finitude of language. Therefore whenever we seek to express an experience with "God" we rely upon the language of the ancients, the media of symbol, myth, and ritual. Myth is a term whose popular usage suggests something that is not real, a false belief, a whimsical fairy tale. Actually "mythopoeic thought" is simply the pre-philosophical, pre-scientific mode for connecting with and understanding life and the world around us. Myth does not employ our commonly applied techniques of rationality, logic, or cause and effect thinking to address "truth" or the transcendent. Through mythology, truth was conveyed in the form of storytelling in which natural phenomena, not yet understood scientifically, were personified. Through mythology, the ancients explained why things were the way they were. They told myths instead of presenting an analysis or conclusions. However, the imagery of myth is by no means allegory. It is nothing less than a carefully chosen cloak for abstract thought. Through mythology, one operates through the relationship of an "I" to a "Thou" rather than the scientific approach in which we observe the the world as an "I" looking at an "It". Sometimes the myths, sacred stories if you prefer, are not simply recounted as stories containing information. They are also frequently dramatized, acknowledging in them a special virtue which could be activated by recital. In the Christian faith, Holy Communion is such a dramatization, activating a special connection with the divine through the drama of Christ's self-sacrifice for the redemption of humanity. Through the ceremony, the participant becomes an "I" in relationship to God as a "Thou". Spirituality does not have to be defined in the conventional manner in order for one to encounter, experience or participate in it. (Frankfort, Frankfort, Wilson & Jacobsen, 1971)

In Hebrew scripture, the attempts to capture and possess God in the form of an image are prohibited by the second commandment. It is called idolatry, creating something less than God and venerating it as though the object was God. Language that presumes to do more than hint at or point toward ultimate things may also become a form of idolatry. Once fully captured in concept and definition, it is diminished, no longer transcendent. In Christian scripture Jesus consistently employed the medium of storytelling and specifically the "parable" to teach spiritual truth through practical imagery quite familiar to his listeners. The parable (παραβαλλο) means to "throw alongside" or to offer a sort of illustrative comparison. (Bauer, Arndt, & Gingrich, 1957) He is saying "Think along these lines and you will grasp what I am talking about". A parable has often been characterized as "an earthly story with heavenly meaning" (Buttrick, 1977) While this was a vehicle for cognitive instruction for the listeners, it was also an " I-Thou" moment, an opportunity to meet God on his own terms, opening self to enlightenment.

Far from being dependent upon literalism, or a smug satisfaction of having "captured the truth", a spiritual seeker must approach the transcendent with a sense of reverence, awe, and humility. The seeker must open self to receive spiritual insight from its source rather than attempting to seize, define, and force it into a conceptual mold in order to validate one's existing opinion, ideology or dogma. The story of Moses encountering God in the burning bush on Sinai is instructive. Rudolph Otto describes an encounter with this overwhelming presence of the divine as "mysterium tremendum" or the great mystery that fascinates (Otto, 1968). This may well describe what Moses stood before. The manifestation of God himself was something that Moses did not discover; rather, he was called by it. It was an "I-Thou" moment; the establishment of a relationship. When given a mission to go back to Egypt and free the slaves, Moses asked "What is your name"? To us this may seem like innocent curiosity. In mythopoieic thought, the coalescence of a symbol and the thing it stands for means treating a person's name as an essential part of him-as if it were identical with him. (Frankfort, Frankfort, Wilson & Jacobsen, 1971) This appears to be an effort by Moses to "capture" God, the great mystery. To know his "name" is to know all about him, to possess him. However this would make that which he now possessed and fully understood something less than God, i.e. and idol. The only answer Moses received was "I am that I am. To paraphrase, "I am who I am and there is nothing I can tell you that will make it clearer than that." He was telling Moses "You have to meet me on my own terms." This suggests that our efforts to describe spirituality will, at best, be feeble because we have nothing adequate in our experience or language to which we can compare it. So spirituality is not known through precise definitions that would allow us to assign "a name" to the great mystery. Rather it is known through an encounter with the one who "is", meeting God on God's terms. This produces change in the lives of the people who experience it. Though unable to develop a definition of spirit, we may still observe and describe the results of a person's relationship with it.

FRUIT OF THE SPIRIT AND AUTHENTICITY

In Christian theology, the term "spiritual" is employed in a more specific way, usually referring to the purposeful workings and influence of the Holy Spirit of God in and through a relationship with the follower. In his Biblical letter to the Galatians the apostle Paul describes certain personal attributes and behaviors that are the recognizable signatures of a relationship with God. He calls it "Fruit of the Spirit." It is the external evidence of inner character created by the influence of the Holy Spirit. In Galatians 5:22, he characterizes this spiritual fruit as "love, joy, peace, patience, kindness, goodness, and faithfulness" (The Bible NIV,1984) All of these are attitudes and behaviors that are recognizable and they naturally grow from a relationship with the omnipresent spirit of God. Given the limitations of language, this analogy of "fruit" may be the most effective way through which one can catch a glimpse into the nature of spirituality. We do not presume to fully define spirit, but can describe its signature, its footprint, its characteristic effects upon the lives of people. Spirituality motivates ethical, values-based attitudes and behavior as its fruit.

Fruit is something that is natural, authentic, and is consistent with the nature of the tree that bears it. "A tree is known by its fruit", Jesus declares in Matthew 7:16 when addressing the subject of inauthentic people or "false prophets". A leader cannot successfully "fake" spirituality any more than a pine tree can grow apples. Before a leader presumes to lead others, he or she would do well to examine the "fruit" they produce as a consequence of their own spiritual relationship with the divine and that which they would bring into the workplace. The spiritual dimensions of leadership require personal authenticity more than technique. A leader cannot encourage the spirituality of others until he or she is in touch with the spirit that powers his or her own life, both on and off the job.

CONCLUSION

Spirituality is about a relationship with something larger than self. What we call it and how we find ourselves in this relationship is intensely personal and hard to define. We may point toward its reality within the limits of human language, we may speculate about its essence within the limits of our imagination. It is not about explaining a phenomenon but about acknowledging an experience. In the end, personal spirituality is recognized by its signature, the identifying imprints this relationship leaves upon us. These prints are the values, behaviors, attitudes, and choices by which we live and are known to others. These remind us of the tangible characteristics that the Bible calls "Fruit of the Spirit". (Galatians 5:22)

Leadership is also about a relationship. It is about one's purposeful influence upon the lives of others. It is about recognizing the spiritual nature and potential that is part of every person whom we presume to lead. It is about recognizing their higher level needs including belonging, esteem, and self-actualization; characteristics that are often suppressed in the workplace culture. It is about enabling followers to realize and tap into their own transcendent source of power for living. It is about transforming the workplace by correlating the goals of the organization with the higher aspirations of the individuals. It is about enabling them to find a sense of belonging within the workplace; choosing to be a contributor rather than a passive cog in a machine. Spiritual leadership is not about technique but relationship. It is about the spiritual authenticity of the leader producing "fruit" that is recognizable to those who follow. It is that which enables them to move from passive compliance toward intrinsic motivation. Collectively, even the workplace, affected by the spirituality of its people, may begin to produce a sort of "fruit" that is the essence of organizational transformation.

REFERENCES

Barnett, T. (2012). Spirituality in leadership. *Enclclopedia of Business* (2 ed.). Advameg, Inc. Retrieved from http://www.referenceforbusiness.com/ management/Sc-Str/Spirituality-in-Leadership.html.

Bauer, W., Arndt, W., & Gingrich, F. (1957). *A greek-english lexicon of the new testament and other early christian literature* (14 ed. pp. 616-617). Chicago: University of Chicago Press.

Bonner, C. (2007). *From coercive to spiritual: what style of leadership is prevalent in k-12 public schools.* (Unpublished doctoral dissertation, Drexel University), Available from Proquest. (1317336221)Retrieved from http://proquest.umi.com/pqdlink?did= 1317336221&Fmt=7&clientI d=79356&RQT=309&VName=PQD.

Buber, M. (1970). *I and thou.* New York, NY: Charles Schribner's Sons.

Buttrick, G. (1977). *The parables of jesus.* (pp. xv-xxx). Grand Rapids, MI: Baker Book House.

Changing Minds.org. (2012). *Leadership vs. management.* Retrieved from http://changingminds.org/disciplines/leadership/articles/manager_leader.htm.

Darwin, C. (1909). *The foundation of the origin of species, a sketch written in 1842.* Cambridge: The University Press. Retrieved from http://darwin-online.org.uk/pdf/ 1909_Foundations_F1555.pdf.

Day, C., & Harris, A. (n.d.). *Effective school leadership.* Retrieved from National College for School Leadership http://www. nationalcollege.org.uk/media/416/99/effective-school-leadership.pdf.

Dent, E. B., Higgins, M. E., & Wharff, D. (2005). Spirituality and leadership: an empirical review of definitions, distinctions, and embedded asumptions. *The Leadership Quarterly, 16,* 625-653. Retrieved from www.uncp.edu/home/dente/LQaspublished.pdf.

Elkins, D. (1999, September 01). Spirituality. *Psychology Today*, Retrieved from http://www.psychologytoday.com/articles/199909/spirituality.

Frankfort, H., Frankfort, H. A., Wilson, J., & Jacobsen, T. (1971). *Before philosophy*. Baltimore, MD: Penguin Books.

Freud, S. (1964). *The future of an illusion*. Garden City, NY: Doubleday and Company.

Fry, Louis W. (2003). Toward a Theory of Spiritual Leadership. *The Leadership Quarterly*, 693-727. Retrieved from www.tarleton.edu/ ~fry/SLTTheory.pdf.

Greenleaf, R. (1977). *Servant leadership*. Mahwah, NJ: Paulist Press.

Hill, R. (1999). *History of work ethic*. University of Georgia. Retrieved from http://www.coe.uga.edu/~rhill/workethic/hist.htm.

McGregor, D. (n.d.). The human enterprise. *Reflections*, *2*(1), Retrieved from http://resource. udallas.edu/132/humansideofenterprise.pdf.

Otto, R. (1968). *The idea of the holy*. New York, NY: Oxford University Press.

Ricketts, K. (2009, February). *Leadership vs. management*. Retrieved from http://www.ca. uky.edu/ agc/pubs/elk1/elk1103/elk1103.pdf.

The Bible New International Version. (1984) Colorado Springs, CO : The International Bible Society.

Tillich, P. (1968). *A history of christian thought*. New York, NY: Simon and Schuster.

Vos, E., & Barker, J. (2007). Wealth mazimization, self-realization, and the spiritually susatainable enterprise. *Journal of Management, Spirituality and Religion*, *4*(3), 355-383. Retrieved from http://wms-soros.mngt.waikato.ac.nz/NR/Personal/EdVos/includes/ publications/pdf/ Vos and Barker forthcoming.pdf.

In: Perspectives in Leadership
Editor: Jerry D. VanVactor

Chapter 7

ETHICS: AN INGREDIENT IN EFFECTIVE LEADERSHIP

Jerry D. VanVactor[*]
United States Army, Fairbanks, Alaska

ABSTRACT

What determines an act to be ethical and how does an organization define right from wrong? Who defines the criteria for ethically appropriate behavior? How do ethical considerations vary among levels of leadership responsibility? These questions remain foremost throughout this chapter and relate to the potential impact ethical considerations may have on decision-making processes and organizational planning. In an applied sense, this manuscript provides managers among a broad spectrum of industries with concepts related to effective, ethically grounded leadership.

Leadership is a generalized skill set inculcated among supervisors and managers at various levels of organizational operations and processes and is not specific to any job title, rank or role. Ethically driven behaviors affect everyone throughout an organization and are likely to be a valuable consideration in any decision-making scenario. Leaders have an inherent responsibility to develop and plan tactics, operational templates and strategy based upon a strong ethical foundation. Arguably, a critical path to success involves a contiguous consideration of the implications that misdirected ethics may have on organizational outcomes.

---

[*] Dr. Jerry D. VanVactor, FAHRMM is a native of Hopkinsville, Kentucky and an active duty medical service corps officer in the United States Army where he is a health care logistics manager. He began his military career in 1989 as an enlisted man and later earned his commission through the U.S. Army officer candidacy program. He has been involved in a variety of leadership roles since entering the military. His education includes a Doctor of Health Administration from the University of Phoenix, Masters in Healthcare Management from Trident University, and Bachelor of Science in Health Science degrees with an undergraduate minor in Procurement and Acquisitions Management from Athens State University. He is a Certified Materials & Resource Professional and a Fellow of the Association for Healthcare Resource and Materials Management of the American Hospital Association. Dr. VanVactor is the recipient of numerous individual military awards and decorations for demonstrated professionalism and leadership excellence.

The need for an ethical approach to organizational leadership has become all the more acute with some of the recent ethical difficulties experienced among large corporations such as Enron, WorldCom, Tyco, AIG, Citibank, Lehman Brothers, Bear Stearns and more (Bhal & Dhadich, 2011; Groves, 2011; Woods & Lamond, 2011). Ethics, whether analyzed as a term or a concept, is not foreign to managers among contemporary organizations. In fact, one need investigate no further than a search on Amazon.com to discover over 75,000 titles related to the subject. Additionally, academicians can leverage a search of online peer-reviewed journal databases, such as ProQuest or EBSCOHost, to discover another 246,000 and 144,000 titles related to the subject respectively.

Are industry leaders being held accountable for identified corporate failings? What are the criteria for ethically grounded behavior? Who determines the variance between right and wrong? Are concepts such as ones associated with determinations of right and wrong universally accepted or acceptable across a wide continuum of businesses and industries? Where in any of these concepts is a thread of leadership that should be included in any corporate strategy development?

One of the pervading problems associated with ethics is that the word can be defined in many ways; there is truly no one right answer concerning ethics' inclusion among business operations. Taking into account the various interpretations and differing values for the term among a wide array of work groups, an absolute value or universally accepted definition for ethics is potentially not possible (Woods & Lamond, 2011). Perhaps ambiguity associated with defining ethics leads to a potential improper employment and misalignment of organizational processes in some instances (Woods & Lamond, 2011). The purpose of this work is to provide readers with a better understanding of ethics' involvement in leadership decision-making processes. In an applied sense, this manuscript provides managers, among a broad spectrum of industries, with concepts related to ethically grounded leadership.

With the amalgam of separate entities involved in contemporary business decision-making among an ever-flattening world (Friedman, 2005), ethics may prove a challenging concept to overcome. One of the first steps in comprehensive leadership may be related to understanding ethics as a concept, but this too may be a challenge for some corporate decision-makers. While there are many ethical models from which organizations can draw concepts for socially acceptable behavior; a model related to ethical behavior and upheld by one culture may be very different from the one upheld by another in a similar set of circumstances (Harrison, 2010). More importantly, what is deemed ethically appropriate for one culture may be egregiously immoral or entirely unacceptable by another (Ledlow & Coppola, 2011). One question that may persist within academic and organizational literature relates to examining how cultural values and ethical ideations inform, influence, and frame an individual's image of an ideal manager, leader, or organization.

Ethics involves an array of widespread worldwide variations whose preoccupations may be just as foreign to each other as they are within a singular organization. Ethical concerns are often very real to individuals and are nested among disparate backgrounds, cultures, and ideals. There exists, according to Dumouchel (2008) a widespread tendency to see ethics as intertwined within various business studies and not as a distinctly separate discipline or a stand-alone concept. The challenge for leadership scholars, as opined by Groves (2011), is to understand how ethical value is linked to specific behavioral and leadership styles and how styles, in turn, engender ethically and socially responsible attitudes and behavior among organizations. Simplistically defined, ethics is an element of many individualized mental models concerning the normative power of morals based within categorical imperatives and a contemporary ideation of implied neutrality or deviance from perceived right and wrong (Galavielle, 2004).

Some research suggests that individual managers and organizational entities apply standards differently depending on the characteristics, or moral intensity, of the issue involved (Barsky, 2011; Frey 2000; Jones 1991; May and Pauli 2002; Reynolds 2006; Singhapakdi et al. 1996). Ethics and ethically grounded behavior are moral philosophies that focus on concepts of right and wrong behavior as they are linked to resource allocation. Associated philosophies also deal with values related to human conduct concerning perceptions of goodness and badness among motives (Ledlow & Coppola, 2011

In contemporary organizational constructs, there is an underlying perception that perhaps people, in general, may be subject to a desensitization of ethical issues and this, in turn, is contributing to a void in moralistic thinking among corporate leaders. Ethics, perceptibly having become an invisible and silent trauma within society, may be inadvertently leading to organizational and systemic failings within corporate America, individually and collectively, by cloaking work environments in suspicion and mistrust thereby contributing to decreased productivity, regulation, and solution set development (Ivanov, 2011). Among some of the more prominent concerns within contemporary society involves organizations that are routinely perceived as treating employees like commodities, generating general suspicion and mistrust, undermining [employee and corporate] self-esteem, and generating conflict over compensation among interpersonal relationships (Ivanov, 2011).

Within a corporate setting, personnel should examine the importance applied to corporate and individual values. The two must converge at some point along employee - employer axes (Swayne, Duncan, & Ginter, 2008). When people choose to act in accordance with established values, they do so to uphold a desired reputation in the eyes of family, colleagues, friends, the public, and, potentially, a religious ideal (Nye, 1986). Reflections of an inner being include virtues such as truthfulness, benevolence, trustworthiness - each is a perceived element of what constitutes a worthy person. Individuals develop ideations of moral standards (values) over time. Adherence to such values tends to reflect the engendered self-conscious behaviors demonstrated by managers, staff, and other corporate stakeholders.

If such values or mental models cannot be conveyed definitively, and if they change from one culture to the next, how can society be so sure that ethics have been violated or that an organization has acted unethically? Attempting to address the seemingly unrelenting waves of ethical violations in the corporate sector, business schools have responded with programs to infuse ethics across their curricula (Smith, 2011). Many organizations, as well, have developed internal training programs to reinforce ethics among employees. The challenge becomes teaching people with an espoused corporate aptitude or attitude, who are potentially culturally disparate, to act in accordance with an established collective (foundation) of beliefs in situations of great pressure and when equally favorable choices are present (Nye, 1986).

Theoretical Underpinnings

Ethics are the fundamental principles upon which organizations and people stand and by which processes are often designed - ethical considerations make each organization unique in a variety of ways (Swayne, Duncan, & Ginter, 2008). Ethics are often steeped within individual perspectives and moral reasoning that can be both personal and learned throughout a person's life. Research in leadership theory posits that subordinate's self-concepts are comprised of self-views, current goals, and possible selves that interact across multifaceted individual, interpersonal, and group levels of identity. By developing a basic understanding of such concepts, leaders engender a level of appreciable emotional intelligence concerning the interactivity between seniors and subordinates and may improve the organization's ethical climate. How effectively information is communicated may be influenced by the dominant ethical theory underlying the existent work climates (Weber & Gerde, 2011).

Ethical ideologies generally manifest between two focal priorities: (1) principles (corporate and individual) and (2) consequences (Smith, 2011). Ultimately, these priorities, according to Smith (2011) can be associated with divergent ideologies related to relativism and idealizations of right and wrong behaviors. While ethical questions need to be analyzed on a case-to-case basis, owing to the great differences in value systems worldwide, there is a need for a general theoretical framework within which such cases involving an exchange of information or knowledge can be analyzed (Chen & Choi, 2005).

Relativism involves conceptions of truth and moral values that are not absolute but are relative to personal or group idiosyncrasies. Ethical relativism inherently allows for some variance (elasticity) in judging the moral objectives associated with a leadership climate (Smith, 2011). Idealized thinking, on the other hand, generally leads people to make decisions based upon general perceptual accounts of natural phenomena that ignore factual elements that may prove too difficult to accommodate within an established theory. Ethical idealism generally leads people toward the highest level of morality where outcomes never produce harm for involved stakeholders (Smith, 2011). Ethical idealism reflects an inclination that would favor consistency in decision standards and desired outcomes articulated by leadership. Neither of these concepts is always based on fact.

Social Exchange Theory

Social exchange theory, according to Cropanzano and Mitchell (2005), is among the most influential conceptual paradigms for understanding workplace behavior; however, the core ideas that comprise the theory have not been adequately articulated and integrated into contemporary literature. Social exchange theory assumes a form of agreement between two or more parties in a social exchange system and is applicable to many fields of study to examine issues ranging from non-monetary exchanges to perceptions of equity within groups (Chen & Choi, 2005). Viewing ethics through a lens of social exchange theory lends a perspective concerning the importance of social structures in ethical debates (Chen & Choi, 2005). There is an inherent need for ongoing leader - subordinate interaction and social exchange among relationships and an implied obligatory reciprocation on the part of subordinate for high quality extra-role behavior (Bhal & Dadhich, 2011).

Ethical and social responsibilities are extremely important aspects of corporate behavior and managers should remain cognizant of how employees perceive each as they occur (Swayne, Duncan, & Ginter, 2008). Perceptions related to ethical behavior provide insight and instruction about how individuals acknowledge, respond to, and evaluate one another during a manager-subordinate exchange (Smith, 2011). A variety of entities may view culture, ethics, and leadership as collectively reinforcing concepts; however, each of these concepts may tend to reflect the norms by which individual behavior is portrayed. Consequently, different levels and types of manager must remain cognizant of employees bearing their own sets of individualized beliefs concerning acceptable leadership behavior (Smith, 2011).

Ethics Position Theory

Ethics position theory states that individuals possess personal moral philosophies that guide their judgments, actions, and reactions in various contexts based upon psychological schemas defined by culture, background, ethnicity, and so forth (Forsyth, 1980; Smith, 2011). Ethics, values, and beliefs are guiding principles that provide focus and parameters for organizational and individual expectations. In a corporate setting, this inherently individualized belief structure provides a means for determining the essential aspects of what must be accomplished as part of a relationship between two people (Swayne, Duncan, & Ginter, 2008).

Mental models related to moralistic, ethically grounded philosophies may have a significant influence upon an individual's evaluation of different people, relationships, encounters, or situations. While there are generally accepted consensus (in most cases) concerning interpretations of immorality, unethical behavior, and other types of inappropriate acts, there are still many more which may quickly elude moral classification (Smith, 2011). Managers, in this regard, have a stake in learning how intangible factors affect individual perceptions of social exchanges among relationships (Smith, 2011).

Cognitive Dissonance Theory

Festinger posits that within each person's mental framework are mechanisms for creating feelings of discomfort or dissonance (lack of harmony) when inconsistencies among valued attitudes, beliefs, and items of knowledge associated with models related to believed right and wrong occur (Wong, 2009). Two cognitions (acquired knowledge) are said to be dissonant if one follows from the opposite of another or if, considering either element alone, the obverse of one would follow from the other. In other words, two equally valued propositions confront a manager and a choice must be made between the two; albeit, either choice may be right or wrong. In theory, if an individual experiences cognitive dissonance when an unpleasant mental state results from two equally uncomfortable choices, the individual is motivated to reduce one or both outcomes as quickly as possible.

Ethical dilemmas (a form of cognitive dissonance) tend to originate from professional or values-based conflicts of interest within a social exchange. Two individuals, with similar sets of moral standards and when experiencing similar sets of circumstances producing a perceptible ethical dilemma, may respond quite differently depending on the selective activation or disengagement of self-sanctions (Barsky, 2011). The presence of dissonance is assumed, in most cases, to cause psychological or sociological discomfort concerning what the individual feels most motivated about reducing or eliminating (Badaracco, Jr., 1998).

IMPLICATIONS FOR LEADERS

Ethics could be defined as central to leadership and critical in the engagement of followers for developing a sense of need toward the accomplishment of mutual goals that is perceptibly consistent with organizational values (Harrison, 2010). Depending upon a leader's perspective of management and the permissions, rights, and entitlements therein, a significantly varied understanding of treatment of subordinates could be applied. Each individual leader employs a framework of ethical decision-making based on a foundation of principles for moral guidance. Some leaders may take their own decision-making from a vein of superiority in dealing with a defined class of ethical problems while others may take a universal approach and look for a convergence of judgment among alternative solution sets (Dunfee, Smith, & Ross, 1999). If leaders want to engender a positive impact on individuals, teams, and organizations, according to Raja and Palanichamy (2011), leadership paradigms (e.g., directive versus participative, consideration versus initiating structure, autocratic versus democratic, and so forth) may, in some cases, need to be re-evaluated and established parameters broadened.

From a managerial perspective, ethics refers to moral principles applicable to necessary management practice (Woods & Lamond, 2011). Leadership and ethical values are fundamentally inseparable from decision-making regarding how to influence others in a contemporary business operation (Smith, 2011). There may often be no clearly defined opportunity or right of refusal regarding wrong business practices within an organizational setting. There also may not always be an easily understood right or wrong answer and processes may have to be adapted to a given set of circumstances. To understand ethics means a manager focuses on the moral issues associated with how a person interacts with others within personally or professionally defined guiding principles and beliefs (Woods & Lamond, 2011).

Each individual leader must wrestle with an established set of values, ideals, principles, and so forth and each must resolve inherent internal chords of dissonance (Kouzes & Posner, 2007). There may be recognizable issues related to specific sets of norms being somewhat divisive if not adequately understood by all (Millar & Choi, 2009). An introspective (in many cases) understanding of such knowledge can help leaders to be more effective in how they communicate information, train, and construct organizational change for employees throughout an organization (Weber & Gerde, 2011). Within a business setting, there may be identified norms that are an essential aspect of knowledge transfers and social exchanges and alternatively continue to support such knowledge transfers at additional sub-network level. Bering (2011) relates that the most successful organizations are those that are not set among encrusted ritualistic methods behind processes or stuck in antiquated ways of doing business.

Ethical Work Climate

Research into environmental work conditions seems to convey the need for leadership scholars and practitioners to place more emphasis on an examination of relationships among dynamic leader and followers while accounting for contextual influences from an established environment in which a trade is plied (Groves, 2011). Groves (2011) advocates research that assesses the multiple contextual influences related to inter- and intrapersonal aspects of leadership such as experience levels, personality, gender, and cultural orientation. Other influences that can affect leadership styles and processes may include external contingencies (i.e., environmental stability, social context, and industry type) and internal contingencies (i.e., task characteristics, nature of goals and performance criteria, cultural context, organizational structure, and social/physical distance).

Seemingly, a fundamental precursor to socially responsible behavior is the degree to which leaders believe that such actions are necessary for organizational effectiveness (Groves, 2011). All employees throughout an organization need to be motivated, guided, and directed through effective communication and by permitting them a sense of belonging within organizational processes. People, including leaders throughout an organization, may behave differently when they have a sense of where they fit into a vision of the future and to what effect their actions may have on others (Atchison & Bujak, 2001). Everyone's values and ethics are not equal, however, and some personnel will have to have ethical decision criteria established for them before effective decisions can be made (Swayne, Duncan, & Ginter, 2008). This could become a challenge in the contemporary multi-ethnicity and multicultural business environment in which such decisions are being made. Practices and perceptions are grounded within a larger social, cultural, task, and interpersonal environment (Groves, 2011).

An ethical work climate is a culmination of an organization's culture that influences each member's ability to recognize a problem, make decision, and determine how to act appropriately within the construct of established norms (Weber & Gerde, 2011). People want to work for an organization that is led by someone who is perceptibly ethically grounded - says what they are going to do, does it, shares the recognition, and provides an articulate concept concerning what they are going to do next (Atchison & Bujak, 2001). Leaders must be able to articulate what is right - clearly communicate and demonstrate the criteria for expected compliance with standards of ethics and performance as well as why these are important (Kolenda, 2001).

Leaders should engender a culture of trust, creativity, and learning throughout an organization and among multiple layers of management and direct supervision (Kolenda, 2001). To develop a culture of trust, and a more inspiring layer of motivation for employees, leaders must acculturate an environment that inspires meaning and challenge in a subordinate's work and encourages employees to envision appealing future states for work units and organizations. Employees should be challenged intellectually through leader emphasized behaviors that encourages them to be innovative and creative - questioning assumptions, reframing problems, and approaching old problems in new ways (Groves, 2011). A leader establishes a culture of innovation and independence by aligning expected performance results with healthy, shared, ethics-based values (Kolenda, 2001).

Employees seek guidance from leaders who can elucidate expectations related to standards of conduct. Those employees who perceive that leaders adhere to high standards may be more willing to report problems to their superiors and recommend changes for ill-designed processes (Barsky, 2011). The leader, of course, must uphold an environment of open communications, demonstrate a willingness to accept ideas, be open to change, and does not minimize subordinates based on their assumed position of inferiority. Honest mistakes can, and often do, enhance an organizational learning process and should not be the catalyst for punishment or castigation of an employee who is trying to achieve organizational goals as defined by corporate leadership. If the expectation by individual employees concerning mistakes involves automatic punishment then initiative and independent thought could become hindered and progress invariably stymied.

The opposite of this concept involves a climate of mistrust that will inherently lead to employees' unwillingness to aid the organization in progressive thought or innovation. When people feel they cannot work or contribute to organizational processes productively, there may be endemic feelings of demoralization and wastefulness. Employees may even start to feel that the organization does not value or care for them individually and may become less than fully engaged, innovative, or productive (Ivanov, 2011). In a less than healthy environment, presenteeism, absenteeism, and multifaceted transition will increase and organizational productivity will most certainly decrease. There could inevitably be a loss of collective will to make the organization successful. Failure, in this sense, is usually a function of poor design in a process, not the quality of the personnel involved; however, employees will not readily believe processes to be the problem if managers encourage and support a climate that seems to indicate subordinates as a problem that must be repaired (Atchison & Bujak, 2001).

Emotional Intelligence

Emotional intelligence consists of an ability demonstrated by a manager to perceive, appraise, and express emotion accurately and adaptively. Based on a variety of viewpoints, however, definitions of organizational commitment may differ concerning emotional intelligence (Raja & Palanichamy, 2011). Through this engendering of adaptive cognizance, leaders develop within employees an ability to self-regulate emotions and inculcate a more productive emotive state among internal and external stakeholders – if the environment throughout the organization supports such ideations (Khosravi, Manafi, Hojabri, Aghapour, & Gheshmi, 2011).

Most scholars recognize that organizational commitment can be understood as an ascribed loyalty to one's organization (Weber & Gerde, 2011). Organizational commitment is an intervening variable that can affect a member's value, attitude, and behavior within an organization. These factors, in no particular order of precedence, may influence a person's knowledge of himself and accordingly knowledge of associated feelings and emotions toward others in developing communications that are more effective and relationships among colleagues throughout the workplace (Khosravi, Manafi, Hojabri, Aghapour, & Gheshmi, 2011).

Successful leaders within an organization are able to use a variety of tools and methods to create functionally dynamic environments among staff members to create aesthetically appealing relationships among positions (Khosravi, Manafi, Hojabri, Aghapour, & Gheshmi, 2011). By permitting a participative voice in organizational decision-making and corporate goal-setting, corporate value (in terms of collaboratively communicating ethical norms) instills individual value throughout a firm. If an employee observes even a perceptible failure by their supervisors to follow prescribed standards and rules when making decisions about outcomes, an incongruent message is sent regarding the values and expectations for honorable work practices (Barsky, 2011). From word choice to implementation, policy (related to established norms) can be more effective when people observe leadership supporting the very norms being communicated to subordinate staff members.

Locus of Control

Many managers suffer from a form of ethical myopia wherein they believe that an entire group of people will view a situation through the same lens and social filters as they do (Badaracco, 1998). In general, an ethical work climate contributes to influence over a variety of individuals, groups, or organizations - in turn, they too, influence the organizational entities as well (Weber & Gerde, 2011). Differences in idiosyncratic factors such as background, religion, ethnicity, and levels in education can collectively create challenges for multiple people viewing a situation similarly (Badaracco, 1998). As can be easily discerned from this concept, managers who force views on others could create an array of ethical challenges for an organization.

The locus of control ranges, depending on the capability of the manager involved, from individual to organizational and cosmopolitan (or societal). Ethical criterion dimensions range a continuum as well - from egoism (focus on consequences to the self), to benevolence (focus on consequences to others), to principle (application of ethical standards) (Weber & Gerde, 2011). Often, organizational construct has much to do with this type of management. Hierarchical relationships within formalized organizational constructs are phenomenon of interests to an array of business academicians and practitioners. These relationships constitute phenomenon that need to be explained by organizational behaviorists and theorists concerned with organizational structure and information and process management (Mahoney, 1979).

Senior-level managers influence the processes of subordinates directly thereby creating a dynamic wherein subordinates, out of realized or unrealized fear, submit to senior manager influence and process non-value added work (Ivanov, 2011). Herein rests a form of ethical dilemma in that while the employee wants to finish a process effectively, they feel they must yield to the senior manager's requests and fulfill an obligation to the senior due to a perceived lack of oversight and influence by middle managers acting as a buffer for unnecessary workflow. Managers and subordinates do not work effectively because the manager does not add value to the work of the subordinate. In a compressed organization, the manager and subordinate are often required by the organization to work within the same stratum (Ivanov, 2011).

Many of these issues could be resolved at a middle-management level of responsibility, yet because the senior manager engages subordinate level employees directly, the subordinate's attention will invariably be directed to "what the boss wants" and take priority over what needs to be done as a part of day to day processes and productivity. Work varies in terms of its underlying complexity from level to level; ergo, middle managers are aligned with work processes to ensure a continued effective and efficient flow of goods and services. When this construct is compressed, as previously described, productivity and processes are often disrupted and problems arise. Eventually compressed organizational designs can lead to stagnation and increase the potential for organizational failure.

MANAGERIAL CONSIDERATIONS

Decision-Making Processes

Managers make decisions throughout the day within organizations and at every leadership level. Decisions are most profound for an organization when they occur at senior levels - when incorrect, ineffective, or laced with unethical or bad judgment decisions potentially lead the organization from one crisis to the next (Ivanov, 2011). Sometimes answers will seem very clear while at others, complexity will enter into a process and decisions will not be so easily made (Swayne, Duncan, & Ginter, 2008). One thing that must be considered within a corporate setting, when a member of a senior leadership team of a large corporation makes a decision (good or bad), the effects are often not clear for years from when the decision was made (Ivanov, 2011) (see Figure 1). The environment in which an organization operates also can produce a tremendous impact on outcomes as well.

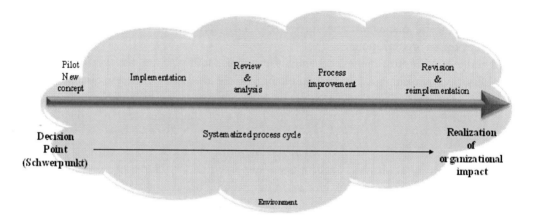

Figure 1. Implications concerning time and decision-making.

Whether the end state involves ethically or unethically grounded choices, individuals move through a series of sequentially ordered steps during the course of making a decision (Barsky, 2011). Ethical decisions involve choosing between two options, one of which is believed to be right, the other believed to be wrong (Badaracco, 1998). Some of the complexities involved in multi-stage ethical decision-making include such elements as moral awareness, moral judgment, moral motivation, and individually defined moralistic behavior (Barsky, 2011).

Individually and organizationally, there may be conflict among any of these. Individuals may depart from impartiality with respect to the ethical dilemmas they face, and employ cognitive strategies and tactics that enable them to rationalize or legitimatize the pursuit of self-serving behaviors at the cost of group interests or ethical conduct (Barsky, 2011). A true defining moment of ethical decision-making is being able to choose between two ideals in which a person truly believes - such options rarely have one right choice (Badaracco, 1998).

Managers need not feel alone or unique in ethical struggles related to decision-making. The struggle to regulate one's ethical conduct in managing others has left, according to Woods and Lamond (2011), a rich legacy of consequences and decision pathways from which others may learn. Participation by multiple parties in decision-making, especially when equally favorable options exist, can lead to the development of better-defined strategies for accomplishing organizational tasks.

Involvement in organizational decision-making processes allows individuals to think more strategically about options when an objective is specified, thus increasing the likelihood that alternate criteria will be considered and shifts in paradigms may potentially occur (Barsky, 2011). Participation by others is defined as joint decision-making or as an opportunity to share influence between hierarchical superiors and their subordinates. Theoretically, researchers have argued that allowing subordinates to participate in organizational decision-making and setting corporate goals affects performance by enhancing employee commitment to, and satisfaction with, organizational performance (Barsky, 2011).

Transactional vs. Transformational Leadership

The definitions of transformational and transactional leadership styles are often built upon prior classifications of leadership behaviors concerning such elements as relations-oriented versus task-oriented and directive versus participative styles (Raja & Palanichamy, 2011). Transactional leadership is defined as leadership that supports the established status quo through individualistic, singularly focused leader and follower self-interests (Groves, 2011). This type of leader is often primarily concerned, according to Groves (2011), with managing outcomes and seeking behavioral compliance with practices that will maximize the mutual interests of both parties - not in a collective sense, but as idiosyncratically defined measures for success.

Transactional leadership. Transactional leadership is based primarily upon practical values and reciprocity norms, which are, according to Groves (2011), unlikely to generate strong beliefs among stakeholder perspectives concerning corporate social responsibility. Groves (2011) continues this discourse by relating that transactional leaders rely heavily on the power, rewards, and sanctions afforded through an official position to influence subordinates to demonstrate requisite performance. Such leaders are often perceived as serving self-centered (personal) interests by getting others to exhibit compliant behaviors. Concerning ethical decision-making, the leadership dynamic between managers and subordinates depends upon whether what (ways) is being done complements how (means) decisions are being made and how information is being employed to achieve (ends) a morally legitimate outcome and if the legitimacy of others' moral interests are being respected.

Transactional leaders influence subordinates by believing they can and attempting to control behavior, rewarding agreed-upon relational behaviors, and eliminating performance problems through established (at times) corrective transactions between leader and followers (Groves, 2011). Transactional leadership, according to Raja and Palanichamy (2011), motivates individuals primarily through contingent reward exchanges and active management by exception. Transactional leaders will sometimes set goals, communicate agreements regarding acceptable behavioral and performance-based expectations, and will often reward or recognize mostly individual achievements.

If subordinates do not know what is being expected of them, though, how can the right decisions be made in a more effective manner without the proper guidance and direction from a senior leader? Without direction, whether morally sufficient, ethically based, or principally sound, initiative will orient an employees' course and the manager will be left with the fallout. Throughout a manager-subordinate exchange, subordinates should be provided with constructive feedback concerning how to stay on task and a collaborative exchange concerning ethical direction must ensue.

Transformational leadership on the other hand, while it may complement transactional leadership in some regards, often supplements transactional leadership with implicit argument related to the view that leadership activities must be built on a foundation of transactional exchanges (Raja & Palanichamy, 2011). Transformational leaders are often more likely to use universal principles of reasoning in decision-making rather than emphasizing set objectives related to obedience, escape from punishment, self-interest, or laws and rules as a way of regulating behavior and interacting with others (Groves, 2011).

Transformational leadership. Transformational leadership is often defined as charismatic, inspirational, intellectually stimulating, and individually considerate (Avolio, Bass, & Jung, 1999). Leaders who exhibit the aforementioned characteristics often help individuals transcend self-interests in efforts to achieve the larger vision of the firm. Transformational leaders believe in people, and they are driven by a strong set of values such as loyalty, trust, and personal attention to employees, something that could positively influence organizational commitment (Raja & Palanichamy, 2011) and result in outcomes that are more positive. This type of leader tends to follow, and is perceived as doing so, a sense of ethically bound duty by performing critical leadership responsibilities regardless of the consequences of their responsibilities. This type of leader treats followers as a critical component in an achievable outcome (ends) and never as merely a step (means) in achieving an outcome. Transformational leaders tend to influence subordinates through a collective appreciation of established value that, in turn, drive socially responsible changes in work units, organizations, and communities.

Transformational leaders denounce a perceptible isolationist behavior and exclusivity in the pursuit of self-interest and adopt a concept of self that is strongly connected to friends, family, colleagues, and the community in which they serve. This type of behavior can be easily interpreted as incorporating all of the interests deemed critically important in a leadership process. Groves (2011) indicates that a transformational leadership process tends to influence followers through the development of a collaborative vision that clearly delineates the importance of multiple stakeholders' involvement while inspiring multiple parties to look beyond their own self-interests in the improvement of an organization or community as a whole.

Transformational leadership can be strongly associated with altruistic beliefs, universal rights, and principles that lay the groundwork for enacting key motivational and inspirational behaviors that can drive positive leadership outcomes within organizations (Groves, 2011). This type of leader employs visionary messages that sometimes include explicit references to values, moral justifications, and a sense of collective purpose, which translate into motivational effects on subordinate's self-regulating attitudes and behaviors. By influencing subordinates through an inculcation of collective vision that inspires behavior or decision-making beyond self-interests, transformational leaders articulate the collective importance of multiple stakeholders in determining organizational goal and vision attainment (Groves, 2011).

Linear vs. Shared Leadership

For a process to qualify as inclusive (or shared) leadership there must be judgments concerning the quality of outcomes. Leaders should have a desire to include others in decision-making processes so that proper judgments concerning leadership can be produced. There is a need for other individuals, who are members of a team, to take some responsibility for leadership rather than perpetuating a belief that a singular entity with some vast array of leadership capabilities can lead an organization to a successful end state. Shared leadership does not abdicate a formal leader's level of ownership in a process or accountability for inappropriate decisions, but the implication is that one person will not be responsible if other members of a team share in the associated responsibility of organizational outcomes.

Organizations tend to be structured for optimal performance, however, improper structure can often prevent organizations from succeeding by collapsing decision-making ability and stagnating organizational processes between crises (Ivanov, 2011). There is emerging evidence via business-focused research that organizations should be understood as open systems - specifically as complex and self-adapting (French, Kouzmin, & Kelly, 2011). Linear thinking has limited value in the complexity of a contemporary business environment. An organizational system of this design is based on scientific stratification related to what was once determined as value-adding manager-subordinate relationships wherein managers could control organizational behaviors and attitudes. Each level of managerial oversight does add, however, value in organizational processes. The effectiveness of decision-making across organizational lines can be mutually supportable given the effectiveness of various levels of leadership. Through an effective management construct, the organization can work more effectively to support decision-making by leaders at the highest levels (Ivanov, 2011).

Organizational design embeds trust among employees at a variety of levels throughout an organization because managers and subordinates work together closely to achieve common organizational goals potentially freeing the organization of perceptible absurdity and discord (Ivanov, 2011). Theoretically, according to Ivanov (2011), this design drastically boosts organizational productivity systemically because it eliminates non-value added steps that could potentially degrade work productivity. Unfortunately, many organizations resolve conflict of this nature by developing additional, duplicative, management structures, or eliminating necessary supervisorial chains that compresses the organizational work levels further (Ivanov, 2011).

Such mental models should be consigned to the history books as antiquated approaches to management as contemporary work environments tend to not lend themselves to this style of leadership (French, Kouzmin, & Kelly, 2011). One consideration for contemporary managers or leaders relates to abilities and skills that may be better used when developed and set among new strategies and guidelines for teams. By involving other staff among the organization in collective decision-making, other people's skills and abilities grow as well. This can potentially help engender a learning environment for future instances of similar projects or problem solving opportunities. When managers delegate tasks to other staff members thereby inculcating more confidence and passion among subordinates, minimal supervision may be required as projects progress (Khosravi, Manafi, Hojabri, Aghapour, & Gheshmi, 2011).

Collaboration

Leadership is regarded as a critical factor in the initiation and implementation of the transformations among contemporary organizations (Raja & Palanichamy, 2011). In recent years organizations have gone through some dramatic changes wherein the norm includes a continual flattening and loosening of controls among organizational structure, downsizing, and horizontal approaches to the flow of information (Raja & Palanichamy, 2011). Managers need to cooperate and collaborate effectively with staff in a workplace to ensure continued success.

Collaboration reflects a common culture bound by a common vision, values and business purpose. Collaborating effectively also promotes integration and interdependency among staffs who may have not been accustomed to working under such conditions previously as well. In order to collaborate effectively, there must be trust among employees concerning senior leaders throughout an organization (Atchison & Bujak, 2001). Studies related to communication within complex environments highlight a need for collaborative communications for enhanced organizational strategy and tactics. A variety of task interdependencies and integration may influence communication behaviors (Weber & Gerde, 2011). Collegiality, inculcated via collaboration among multiple layers of an organization, celebrates differences and promotes autonomy and independence (Atchison & Bujak, 2001).

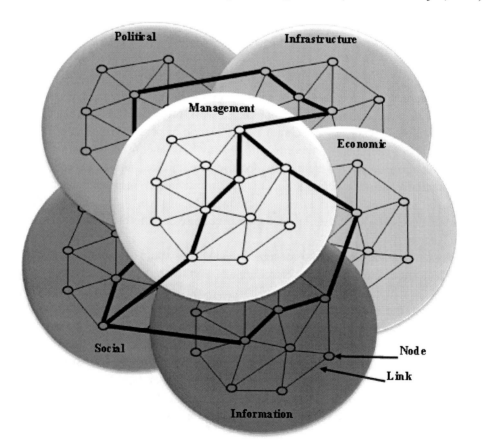

Figure 2. Interconnectivity of the operational environment (Adapted from US DoD, JP 3-0).

A system is a functionally related group of elements that form a complex whole. A systems perspective relates to management and managerial processes wherein leaders develop and provide an understanding of multifaceted, interrelated systems that influence each other (see Figure 2). A variety of factors will invariably affect the fidelity of employee perspectives concerning perceptible ethically grounded right and wrong behaviors. Understanding organizational processes (from a systems perspective), the inherent interactivities among various stakeholders, and changes in relationships over time will increase a manager's knowledge of how actions within a system can affect other system components. This may allow leaders and support staffs to consider a broader set of options among process designs to focus limited resources, create desired effects, avoid undesired effects, and achieve objectives.

When evaluating a complicated system, one would be able to divide and analyze individual parts; in a complex system, the interaction between multi-disciplined parts is so intricate that it would be impossible to understand a system by focusing merely on individual subcomponents (Khanfar, 2007). Systems are often comprised of many nonlinear parts that interact without control or perpetual oversight through many data points that converge in organizational processes and practices (Styhre, 2002). As a result, systematized processes are often emerging from a number of sources and the undercurrent of informal communiqués may produce results that may or may not be seen by managers. For this reason, Richardson (2008) advocates that organizations be viewed as a collection of interacting departments rather than a collection of individual parts (people).

Within a contemporary corporate environment, a manager cannot oversee every decision being made. Leaders have to establish expectations and the organizational culture that will influence subordinates to make ethical decisions without direct intervention of the leader (Weber & Gerde, 2011). How would a manager account for the unseen, informal lines of communication that proliferate organizational processes; or, the productivity that is not accounted for in managerial decision-making? While it may be necessary to consider the entire system as a communal entity, every individual element will have an influence on the output generated by the organization. Each element of output, as a whole, must be considered in the overall characteristics of a system.

CONCLUSION

The purpose of this chapter has been to provide readers with a better understanding of ethics' involvement in leadership decision-making processes. Readers have been provided some of the theoretical underpinnings for ethical decision-making and have been provided implications for why this is important in the development of a leadership approach. The chapter closed with some considerations concerning the importance for including corporate ethics and personal values in decisions and how such concepts apply to different types of organizational design. This discourse is purposefully not all-inclusive as there is no way one author could cover the wide gamut of ethics or navigate the intricacies of every scenario to which such concepts might apply.

This information is presented in the hope of providing managers, among a broad spectrum of industries, with concepts related to ethically grounded leadership and knowledge of why such concepts may be important in the conduct of professional affairs. From a managerial perspective, ethics refers to often individually developed moral principles applicable to critical management practice. Leadership and ethical values, however, are fundamentally inseparable from decision-making regarding how to influence others in a contemporary business operation.

One of the pervading problems associated with a study of ethics is that the term can be defined in so many ways. While ethics could be defined as central to leadership and critical in the engagement of followers for developing a sense of need toward the accomplishment of mutual goals, there is, at times, a seemed disconnect related to perceptible consistency among individual and organizational values. Depending upon a leader's perspective of management and the permissions, rights, and entitlements therein, a significantly varied understanding of treatment of subordinates could be applied.

An organization cannot protect itself from environmental affects if leaders are divorced from their values or some version of moral creed to which they subscribe. The critical takeaway is that leadership practices, of their own rite, are not amoral per se - leaders themselves, however, can be deemed moral or immoral. This determination, unfortunately and due to the varied degrees in which terms such as values and ethics are defined, can be incredibly subjective. Within a professional business setting, there may be identified norms that are an essential aspect of knowledge transfers and social exchanges. While such transfers of knowledge may be valuable and professionally critical, correct information must be conveyed for the right values to become part of the environment in which managers lead and render decisions.

REFERENCES

Atchison & Bujak. (2001). *Leading transformational change: The physician-executive partnership.* Health Administration Press: Chicago, IL.

Badaracco, Jr., J. L. (1998). The discipline of building character. *In Business leadership* (pp. 307-329). Jossey-Bass, San Francisco, CA.

Barsky, A. (2011, Nov) Investigating the effects of moral disengagement and participation on unethical work behavior. *Journal of Business Ethics,* 104(1), 59–75.

Bering, H. (2011). The perfect officer. *Policy Review,* 168, 51-68.

Chen, T. (2005) Towards an ethics of knowledge. *MELUS,* 30(2), 157-174.

Chen, S. & Choi, C. J. (2005) A social exchange perspective on business ethics: An application to knowledge exchange. *Journal of Business Ethics,* 62(1), 1-11.

Cropozano, R. & Mitchell, M. S. (2005) Social exchange theory: An interdisciplinary review. *Journal of Management,* 31(6), 874-900.

Cunningham, J. (2006). Back to supply chain basics. *Materials Management in Healthcare,* 15(7), 32-38.

Galavielle, J. P. (2004). Business ethics is a matter of good conduct and of good conscience. *Journal of Business Ethics,* 53(1-2), 9-16.

Groves, K. S. & LaRocca, M. A. (2011) An empirical study of leader ethical values, transformational and transactional leadership, and follower attitudes toward corporate social responsibility. *Journal of Business Ethics,* 103(4), 511–528.

Harrison, J. P. (2010). *Essentials of strategic planning in healthcare.* Health Administration Press, Chicago, IL.

Ireland, R. K. & Crum, C. (2005). *Supply chain collaboration: How to implement CPFR and other best collaborative practices.* Boca Raton: J. Ross Publishing, Inc.

Isaacson, W. (2010). *Profiles in leadership: Historians on the elusive quality of greatness.* New York, NY: W. W. Norton & Company.

Ivanov, S. (2011, Summer) Why organizations fail: A conversation about American competitiveness. International *Journal of Organizational Innovation,* 4(1), 94-110.

Khanfar, M. (2007, December). *Visionary approaches to management of corporate communication strategy and its implications.* The Business Review, Cambridge, 8(2), 198-207.

Khosravi, B. G., Manafi, M., Hojabri, R., Aghapour, A. H., & Gheshmi, R. (2011). The relationship between emotional intelligence and effective delegation. *International Journal of Business and Social Science,* 2(19), 223-235.

Kolenda, C. D. (2001). *Leadership: The warrior's art.* The Army War College Foundation Press: Carlisle, PA.

Kouzes, J. M., & Posner, B. Z. (2007). *The leadership challenge* (4th ed.). John Wiley & Sons: San Francisco, CA.

Ledlow, G. R., & Coppola, M. N. (2011). *Leadership for health professionals: Theory, skills, and applications.* Jones & Bartlett Learning: Sudbury, MA.

Mahoney, T. A. (1979). Organizational hierarchy and position worth. *The Academy of Management Journal,* 22(4), 726-737.

Nye, R. H. (1986). *The challenge of command.* Avery Publishing Group, Inc.: Wayne, NJ.

Raja, A. S. & Palanichamy, P. (2011) Leadership styles and its impact on organizational commitment. *Journal of Commerce,* 3(4), 15-23.

Schutt, J. H. (2004). *Directing the flow of product: A guide to improving supply chain planning.* Ft. Lauderdale: J. Ross Publishing, Inc.

Smith, B. (2011). Who shall lead us? How cultural values and ethical ideologies guide young marketers' evaluations of the transformational manager–leader. *Journal of Business Ethics,* 100(4), 633–645.

Swayne, L. E., Duncan, W. J., & Ginter, P. M. (2008). *Strategic management of health care organizations* (6th ed.). West Sussex, UK: Jossey-Bass.

Wong, Andrew. (2009). Cognitive dissonance: A comprehensive review amongst interdependent and independent cultures. *The Journal of Educational Thought,* 43(3), 245-257.

Woods, P. R. & Lamond, D. A. (2011). What would Confucius do? – Confucian ethics and self-regulation in management. *Journal of Business Ethics,* 102(4), 669–683.

In: Perspectives in Leadership
Editor: Jerry D. VanVactor

ISBN: 978-1-62417-170-3
© 2013 Nova Science Publishers, Inc.

Chapter 8

POLITICAL LEADERSHIP FROM A GENDER PERSPECTIVE

Chiara Rollero, Filippo Rutto and Norma De Piccoli*

Department of Psychology, University of Turin, Italy

ABSTRACT

Although women have gained increased access to leadership positions, they often remain in second to men in competitions for top executive roles. Even in most industrialized societies, women are still suffering disadvantage in access to major leadership posts. There are fewer women members of national Parliaments than men in all European member states and in thirteen member states women account for less than 20% of members of Parliament (Eurostat, 2008). The gender composition of national Parliaments is reflected in the representation of women in national governments; except for Austria, there was no EU member state in 2006 where women held more than 40% of ministerial posts, in either ministries responsible for basic functions or those responsible for the economy (Eurostat, 2008). In the United States, women account for 17% of U.S. senators, hold 24.3% of the state legislator seats, 22.1% of the state senate seats, and 25.1% of the state house seats (Center for the American Women and Politics, 2009).

Several theories have been formulated to explain the sparse representation of women in leadership roles. Studies of men and women in position of leadership reveal no thorough evidence of male superiority (Eagly, Karau, & Makhijani, 1995), but evaluative and perceptual biases among group members (Eagly, Makhijani & Klonsky, 1992). Female leaders are perceived as less dominant than males and receive lower evaluations and fewer promotions than men even when actual performance or behaviors are held constant (Heilman, Block, & Martell, 1995; Geis, Boston & Hoffmann, 1985).

Concerning the political domain, gender differences are pervasive and impactful. According to Social Role Theory (Eagly, 1983, 1987), gender differences in political attitudes can be understood by attending to the social roles of men and women (Eagly & Diekman, 2006).

When judging women as actual or potential leaders, prejudice can arise in perceivers because of inconsistency between the predominantly communal qualities they associate

---

* Corresponding author: Chiara Rollero (chiara.rollero@unito.it); Tel +39 011 6702055. Fax +39 0116702061; Department of Psychology – University of Turin, Via Verdi, 10, 10124 Torino (Italy).

with women and the predominantly agentic qualities they believe are required to be a successful leader (Eagly & Karau, 2002).

Another key factor affecting gender prejudice is sexism. As Glick and Fiske (2001) argued, sexist attitudes encompass considerable ambivalence on the part of each sex toward the other. More specifically, these attitudes combine both subjective negative and positive feelings, which they define as "ambivalent sexism" (Glick & Fiske, 1996; 1999).

Here we present a study aimed at investigating the role of sexism in affecting prejudice toward male and female political leaders. Male and female University students participated in the study.

Keywords: Gender, leadership, politics, ambivalent sexism

INTRODUCTION

During human history, men have always played a predominant role in most fields of society, particularly in power control, while most societies have relegated women in a spectator's role, powerless, so that no room for permitting them express their opinions and ideals was allowed.

In European dynasties, heritage was transmitted via masculine lineage, with just a few exceptions and even in these cases it was subordinated to the absence of a male heir of throne.

Nevertheless, the few queens Europe has seen were always surrounded by male ministers and advisors. Even with the advent of modern democracies, women were still excluded from voting.

Only after XIX century Western societies witnessed a major change, represented by women suffrage opening up the political world and power rooms to women which is still an ongoing process as, even if no formal impeachments exist to women to assume predominant roles in politics and government, a significant issue regarding gender gaps persists.

At present (March 2010) women are only 18.9% of all members of Parliament in the world, starting from Scandinavian Countries with 42.1% ending with the Arabian States with 9.7%. Italy is 56th out of 140 countries, 21,3% at the Lower Chamber and only 18.3% at the Senate (Francescato & Mebane, 2011) and no female Prime Minister has ever been appointed insofar.

In short, in both Western and Eastern culture a gender gap in leadership positions exists in all the institutional domains: both in the public one and in the private one, in economics, in politics, in organizations and so on (for specific data see Catalyst, 2009; Center for the American Women and Politics, 2009; Eurostat, 2008).

There are several theoretical approaches which address the question of this gender gap. Ayman and Korabik (2010) consider that the three most common theoretical positions underling the study of gender and leadership are: intrapsychic, social structural, and interpersonal perspectives. Even if all of them are of interest in gender studies, we ground the present research specifically on a social psychological point of view. Therefore in the present work we will refer to the social structural perspective and particularly to some recent theories about gender differences in the leadership domain. Then, we will describe a study aimed at investigating the role of sexism in affecting the choice of a potential political leader.

Gender and Leadership: The Role Congruity Theory

Psychosocial perspective considers gender differences especially in studies on stereotypes and prejudices. On this basis, some interesting theories about this issue have been developed.

In their meta-analysis, Eagly and Johnson (1990) reviewed different classes of leadership studies, concluding that sex differences appeared in all of them, and they interpreted these findings according to a Social Role Theory of sex differences of social behaviour. Eagly, Makhijani and Konsky (1992) pointed out that bias exists against female leaders and such a tendency is more evident when women adopt a masculine leadership style and when evaluators are men. Besides, women tend to adopt a more democratic leadership style than men, consistent with stereotypic expectations (Eagly & Johnson, 1990).

Furthermore, studies of men and women in position of leadership reveal no thoroughly evidence of male superiority (Eagly, Karau, & Makhijani, 1995), but evaluative and perceptual biases among group members (Eagly, Makhijani, & Klonsky, 1992; Shackelford, Wood, & Worchel, 1996). Female leaders are perceived as less dominant than males and receive lower evaluations and fewer promotions than men even when actual performance or behaviours are held constant (Geis, Boston, & Hoffmann, 1985; Heilman, Block, & Martell, 1995).

Empirical research has largely demonstrated that people link management ability with being male and possessing masculine characteristics (Johanson, 2008; Powell, Butterfield, & Parent, 2002; Schein, 2001). Individuals associate power holders with stereotypically masculine qualities and link feminine characteristics to people who hold less power (Lips, 2001). In their experimental studies, carried out enrolling Canadian University students, Scott and Brown (2006) demonstrated that perceivers had difficulty encoding leadership behaviors into their underlying prototypical leadership traits when the behavior implied an agentic trait and was enacted by a female.

For women to be considered as competent as men, perceivers must be given clear evidence of women's superior performance compared to their male counterparts (Biernat & Kobrynowicz, 1997; Foschi, 1996). In particular, as a study conducted in the US with both college students and common people showed, for female leaders to be perceived as effective as men they need to demonstrate both sensitivity and strength, whereas male leaders only need to demonstrate strength (Johnson et al., 2008). Women in leadership positions are often evaluated more harshly or at least viewed with less tolerance than their male counterparts (Rudman & Glick, 2001).

Many recent studies – carried out with both European and US college student samples - show that not only men but also women still endorse sexist beliefs (e.g. Barreto & Ellemers, 2005; Swim et al., 2005). Duehr and Bono (2006) compared gender and leadership stereotypes in the US early in the 21st century to those evident 15 and 30 years ago. Their results suggest that stereotypes about women may be changing. Male managers, in particular, characterize women as less passive and submissive and more confident and assertive. However, male students today hold gender stereotypes that are surprisingly similar to those of male managers 15 years ago (Duehr & Bono, 2006; Sczesny, 2003). Similarly, in her study on the "think manager, think male" phenomenon across five countries (United States, United Kingdom, Germany, China, and Japan), Schein (2001) found that the view of women as less likely to possess requisite management characteristics is a common belief among male management students around the world. Another research testing the "think manager, think male" hypothesis has demonstrated a shift away from this ideology at least among US young women (Jackson et al., 2007).

The Role Congruity Theory (RCT) (Eagly & Karau, 2002) is a fruitful theory to explain prejudice toward female leaders. According the RCT such prejudice stems from a perceived conflict between leadership roles and women's gender roles (for further details see here Rollero and De Piccoli "The gendered image of power: How male and female leader are perceived"). Recently Rudman, Moss-Racusin, Phelan, and Nauts (2012) consider the RCT limitations because this theory does not explain why agentic women suffer backlash even when they are not in leadership positions. "By exhibiting masculine competencies, agentic women undermine the presumed differences between the genders, and discredit the system in which men have more access to power and resources for ostensibly legitimate reasons. That is, agentic women should incur penalties because they threaten the gender hierarchy. As a result, women's perceived status violations should account for backlash effects" (Rudman et al., 2012, p. 167).

According to the Status Incongruity Hypothesis (SIH), women that possess or pursue power are de facto status incongruent, but particularly when their behaviour violates status expectations. The incongruence arises when a woman act agentically, both in a leadership and not in a leadership position (Rudman et al., 2012).

Gender and Politics

Also in politics, stereotype plays a significant role and is a potent barrier to women's advancement to positions of leadership (De Piccoli & Rollero, 2010; Koenig, Eagly, Mitchell, & Ristikari, 2011). Social Role Theory (Eagly, 1983, 1987) states that gender differences in political attitudes can be understood by attending to the social roles of men and women (Eagly & Diekman, 2006).

Other theoretical approaches have tried to explain women's under-representation in politics. Apart from the more classical institutional and structural theories that focused on women's inferior levels of social involvement (lower educational levels, inferior support by electorate, lower financial backing and scarce familiar support) the most relevant theories entail:

- Situational theories focused on difficulties women have to face in reconciling political and family commitments as shown by research (Thomas, 2002). A more recent study by IPU (2008) highlighted that domestic responsibilities and lack of support on the site of their families are respectively the first and third barrier for women engaged in political activities, whereas they are eleventh and eighth for men;
- Gatekeeping theories maintain that men hold more important positions in institutions and they play the role of gatekeepers, those prevent women to enter power rooms (Matland & Montgomery, 2003). Very often political parties are perceived as major gatekeepers (Norris, 2003), even if left wing parties show a larger number of female MPs;

- Sex or gender differences theories pointed out how different cultures may reinforce or lessen gender stereotypes viewing men as more suitable to political commitment. (Conway, Steuernagel, & Ahern, 2005), so that male chauvinist society characterized by predominant gender stereotypes and biases normally show few female candidates and MPs.

Moreover, research on voters has shown gender stereotypes according to which female candidates are perceived as more compassionate and gentle, while ideal men candidates are strong ambitious and assertive (Huddy & Terkildsen, 1993). Often women tend to adjust their behaviours and leadership styles according to the agreed-upon political context, generally based on masculine rules: formal, hierarchical, authoritative and competitive (Eagly & Johnson, 1990).

Two experiments (Lammers, Gordijn, & Otten, 2009) investigated the effect of a candidate gender and gender prototypicality on judgment of the suitability of this candidate in elections. Both experiments demonstrated that voters use gender stereotypes when judging political candidates. Some other studies have demonstrated how masculine qualities are more and more necessary while candidates climb up their political career (Huddy & Terkildsen, 1993).

Several others underline the role of mass media in promoting political candidates (Mazzoleni & Sfardini, 2009) in emphasizing political candidates' individual characteristics, personality traits and values but also how they are perceived. Other authors (Dolan, Dieckman, & Swears, 2006) maintain that women candidates are both less present in the media and less favourably represented.

The effects of gender stereotypes are thought so relevant to compel researchers exclude female candidates in experiments testing such first impressions, thus once more underlining the usefulness of exploring stereotypes and attitudes towards women in politics (Rule, Ambady, & Adams, 2010).

A new perspective might therefore fruitfully enhance understanding of female exclusion from leading political roles: investigating if and to what extent sexist attitudes affect the choice of women versus men candidate. Research shows that, in deciding who to vote for, people tend to use impression of competence solely gained from facial appearance (Todorov et al., 2005), contrary to the common notions that they use rational strategies under such circumstances. Moreover, first impressions are often reinforced by cultural consensus thus turning judgment from faces a good predictor of political success (Rule & Ambady, 2010).

The experiment conducted by Chiao, Bowman, and Gill (2008) by means of a series of pairs of political candidate showed that the gender of both voter and candidate affects the kinds of facials impressions that predict voting behaviour. However female candidates appearing more attractive are more likely to be chosen, as are men who look competent.

Ambivalent Sexism

Another key factor affecting gender prejudice is sexism, which may negatively affect the degree of both participation and election of women (Glick et al., 2000).

The uniqueness of the relationship between men and women as social groups is due to its long last, characterizing status inequality, and close physical and psychological intimacy.

Because of the basic structure of traditional male-female relationships, in which a power differentiation coexists with a strong interdependence between the groups, sexist attitudes encompass considerable ambivalence on the part of each sex toward the other (Glick & Fiske, 2001). Glick and Fiske (1996, 1999) suggest that these attitudes combine both subjective negative and positive feelings, which they define as "ambivalent sexism". In respect to women, hostile sexism (HS) is an adversarial view of gender relations in which women are perceived as seeking to control men and usurping men's power. On the contrary, benevolent sexism (BS) elicits a positive affective tone. However, since it idealizes women as pure creatures who ought to be protected, supported and whose love is necessary to make a man complete, it implies that women are weak and best suited for conventional gender roles. As the authors claimed (Glick & Fiske, 2011), HS and BS are two sides of a sexist coin.

Similarly, sexist attitudes toward men include both hostility toward men (HM) and benevolence toward men (BM). The first dimension refers to the expression of hostility in response to power inequalities; men's arrogance; cultural attitudes that portray men as superior; and the ways in which men exert control within intimate relationships. Benevolence toward men represents overtly positive attitudes and is based on a set of beliefs holding that, just as women are dependent on men, so are men dependent on women. Experiencing positive feelings of protectiveness and intimate connection with men represents benevolence toward men (Glick & Fiske, 1999).

Ambivalent sexism forms a coordinated ideological system that justifies and maintains gender inequality (Glick et al., 2000; 2004; Rollero & Fedi, 2012). As Jackman (1994) has suggested, engaging in stereotypic differentiation treats each gender group as well-suited to occupy the positions and roles that are prescribed for them by society. Moreover, ambivalent sexism prevents women from withdrawing totally from the system of gender relations in a societal context in which men's competence is assumed and women's is not (Glick & Fiske, 2001). As well as hostile attitudes, also benevolence toward women, although positive in tone, pacifies women's resistance to gender subordination by masking gender inequality with the cloak of chivalry (Burn & Busso, 2005). Indeed, in respect to women, benevolent sexism is used to reward those who embrace traditional gender roles, while hostile sexism punishes women who try to change the status quo. This combination of rewards and punishment is particularly effective in maintaining gender inequality (Glick & Fiske, 2001). Empirical research gives evidence of the negative correlation between ambivalent sexism toward women and national indices of gender equality (Glick et al., 2000). In their cross-cultural study, Glick and colleagues (2000) considered two United Nations indices: (a) the Gender Empowerment Measure (GEM), which reflects women's representation in powerful occupational roles and government and (b) the Gender Development Index (GDI), which focuses on women's life expectancy, literacy rates, education and other standards of living. It was found that both BS and HS were negatively correlated with GEM and GDI (Glick et al., 2000). Similar results were obtained when considering ambivalence toward men: in a large-scale study of 16 nations, Glick et al. (2004) showed that hostile and benevolent attitudes toward men correlated with the national indices of gender inequality. As the authors claim, on the one hand, BM paints a positive picture of men as suited for high-status roles outside the home, on the other, HM, even if does not justify men's power as morally correct, reinforces the notion that male dominance is inevitable. Overall, these findings are consistent with the notion that HM, BM, HS and BS are a complementary set of gender-traditional beliefs which reinforce the status quo (Glick et al., 2004).

THE CURRENT STUDY

Grounded on these findings, the present research aims at investigating the effect of gender and ambivalent sexism on the choice of potential political leaders. Following the above described literature, it was predicted that:

- Women choose female candidates more than men (Jackson et al., 2007);
- Benevolent Sexism does not affect the choice of a political candidate (Sibley & Perry, 2010);
- Individuals with high Hostile Sexism prefer a male candidate, being HS an expression of overt prejudice toward women (Masser & Abrams, 2004);
- Benevolence toward Men, expressing a positive representation of men as suited of high-status roles (Glick et al., 2004), favors the choice of a male candidate;
- Hostility toward Men does not affect the choice of the candidate. Although it expresses hostility to power inequalities (that is to say, men as superior), it is not *per se* sufficient to justify a preference for a woman (Heilman & Okimoto, 2007; Rudman et al., 2012).

Method

Participants were 204 undergraduates attending the University of Turin, in the north west of Italy. 33.87% of participants were male. Age ranged from 18 to 38 years, with a mean age of 22.95 (SD = 4.86).

Data were gathered by a self-reported questionnaire which took about 20 minutes to be filled in, divided into three sections.

1. In the first section participants completed a hypothetical voting task (Chiao et al., 2008). They saw 15 pairs of grayscale photographs of Italian members of Parliament. All photos were obtained from the Italian Ministry of Interior website. Participants were asked to decide which of the two candidates they would vote for in the Primaries of their party. Order of presentation of faces was randomized. In 8 out of the 15 pairs of photographs, a male and a female politicians were shown, whereas in the other pairs same sex candidates were shown.
2. The second section comprised the following measures:

   Ambivalent Sexism Inventory (ASI; Glick & Fiske, 1996). It is a 22-item self-report measure of sexist attitudes composed of BS and HS subscales. Respondents indicated their agreement or disagreement with each statement on a 1 (= strongly disagree) to 5 (= strongly agree) scale. The Italian version was used (Manganelli Rattazzi, Volpato & Canova, 2008). Cronbach's alphas for BS and HS were .80 and .89 respectively.

   Attitudes toward Men Inventory (AMI; Glick & Fiske, 1999). It is a 20-item self-report measure of attitudes toward men composed of two subscales: BM and HM. Participants indicated their agreement or disagreement with each statement on a 0 (= strongly disagree) to 5 (= strongly agree) scale. The Italian version was used

(Manganelli Rattazzi et al., 2008). Alphas for BM and HM were .84 and .82 respectively.

3. The final section of the questionnaire included questions on demographic characteristics.

Table 1. Gender differences on the choice of the candidate

	Men: $M(SD)$	Women: $M(SD)$	T value	Sig.
Number of preferred women (range 0 – 8)	3.82 (1.86)	5.80 (1.38)	-.8.41	<.001

Table 2. Gender differences on ambivalent sexism

	Men: $M(SD)$	Women: $M(SD)$	T value	Sig.
BS	2.57 (.68)	2.65 (.74)	-.75	n.s.
HS	2.97 (.87)	.21 (.67)	6.90	<.001
BM	2.66 (.80)	2.14 (.66)	4.87	<.001
HM	2.64 (.69)	3.07 (.73)	4.06	<.001

Results

First, we tested the effect of gender on the choice of the candidate. Women were significantly more likely to vote for female candidates, whereas male voters preferred male politicians (Table 1). Gender played a significant role also on ambivalent sexism toward both men and women (Table 2).

Men show higher levels of HS and outscore women on BM, whereas women report higher levels of HM.

Finally, a multiple regression analysis was performed, in which the number of preferred female candidates was regressed onto gender of the voter and each dimension of ambivalent sexism (BS, HS, BM, HM). As presented in Table 3, the model accounted for a large proportion of variance in number of preferred female candidates (adj. R^2 = .35). Gender of participant was the most significant predictor (β=.33): in respect to men, female voters were more likely to choose a female politician. However, also ambivalent sexism accounted for a large proportion of variance. Specifically, both hostility toward women (β=-.23) and benevolence toward men (β=-.20) decreased the likelihood to vote for a woman.

Table 3. Multiple regression analysis predicting number of preferred female candidates

Predictor	β	t	p
Gender (0 = male)	.33	4.66	<.001
BS	.13	1.81	n.s.
HS	-.23	-3.05	<.01
BM	-.20	-2.48	<.05
HM	.06	.75	n.s.

R^2 adj. = .35.
F (5, 195) = 21.91 p<.001.

DISCUSSION

The present study aimed at investigating the gender gap in relation to the choice of a potential political leader. Specifically, the main goal was testing how ingroup favouritism (i.e. women vote for women and men prefer men) and ambivalent sexism lead individuals to choose a male or a female politician, following the methodology used by Chiao and colleagues (2008). Results confirm the hypothesized ingroup favouritism, as women tend to choose a female candidate more often than do men. Our data show also that both hostile sexism toward women and benevolent sexism toward men lead people to prefer a male politician.

The present findings are in line with those obtained in other countries: it is noteworthy the fact that also in this study ambivalent sexism is shared even by high-educated (undergraduates) and young subjects (mean age = 22.95 years). There is a clear ingroup effect, showing boys higher hostility toward women, higher benevolence toward men, and lower hostility toward men in respect to girls. Instead, benevolence toward women does not differ according to gender. This means that both men and women positively evaluate women that follow the traditional gender roles, and consider them weaker, and needing for male protection (Glick & Fiske, 2011).

Considering the specific role of each dimension of ambivalent sexism our hypotheses have been confirmed. Benevolence toward women does not contribute to make females suited for political roles, which are not, actually, traditional female roles. Hostility toward women, on the contrary, leads individuals to prefer a male candidate: if women behave in an unexpected way, i.e., trying to achieve political positions, they have to be "punished" (see backlash effect; Heilman & Okimoto, 2007). Similarly, benevolence toward men predicts the choice of a male candidate, reinforcing the idea that male traits are well suited for leadership roles.

The Role Congruity Theory states that, because gender roles are differently played in the social context (i.e. women work in social, educational and care domains, whereas men are occupied in business, economical and power domains), people consider that men and women are suited for specific activities and not for others. This explains why both men and women are involved in actions and roles considered suitable for a sex and not for the other. This is a vicious circle: if one gender is underrepresented, it is more difficult to change stereotypes also because the scarce presence of this gender.

Thus, the choice of a political candidate is "also" a question of gender. Why a man or a woman chose a male or a female candidate when both represent the same ideological point of view and same values? Probably, when people choose a candidate, different mental schemata might be activated, according to the politician's gender. Further research might develop this hypothesis. Qualitative instruments could help to better understand the cognitive patterns arising when a citizen chose his/her candidate.

We are aware that other aspects must be taken into account. Contextual elements, for example, play a significant role (see the Think Crisis – Think Female effect; Ryan, Hersby, & Bongiorno, 2011), as well as the specific political issues, being men and women evaluated differently according to specific domains (De Piccoli & Rollero, 2010; Norris, 2003).

Beaman and colleagues (2009) show that reservation policies, improving women's access to political office and, consequently, augmenting their visibility, not always help women gain seats: an higher presence of female leaders can help to show that women too can be competent. We agree with their conclusion: quotes are not sufficient to modify a deep cultural stereotype. The challenge is to develop a culture of difference, in which both agentic and communal characteristics are valued, regardless individuals' gender.

According to Diekman & Schneider, (2010) a deeper understanding of gender gaps is necessary because gender differences in the political realm are both pervasive and impactful.

REFERENCES

Ayman, R., & Korabik, K. (2010). Leadership. Way Gender and Culture Matter. *American Psychologist*, 65, 3, 157-170.

Alozie, N.O., Simon, J. & Merrill, B.D. (2003). Gender and political orientation in childhood. *The Social Science Journal*, 40, 1-18.

Barreto, M., & Ellemers, N. (2005). The burden of benevolent sexism: How it contributes to the maintenance of gender inequalities. *European Journal of Social Psychology, 35,* 633-642.

Beaman, L., Chattopadhyay, R., Duflo, E., Pande, R., & Topalova, P. (2009). Can political affirmative action for women reduce gender bias? *Vox.* http://www.voxeu.org

Biernat, M., & Kobrynowicz, D. (1997). Gender- and race-based standards of competence: Lower minimum standards but higher ability standards for devalued groups. *Journal of Personality and Social Psychology, 72,* 544-557.

Burn, S.M., & Busso, J. (2005). Ambivalent sexism, scriptural literalism, and religiosity. *Psychology of Women Quarterly*, 29, 412–418.

Catalyst. (2009). *2009 Catalyst Census: Fortune 500 Women Executive Officers and Top Earners. New York: Catalyst.*

Center for the American Women and Politics (2009). *Fact sheet.* http://www.cawp.rutgers. edu/ index.php.

Chiao, J. Y., Bowman, N. E., & Gill, H. (2008). The Political Gender Gap: Gender Bias in Facial Inferences that Predict Voting Behavior. *Plus One, 3* (10).

Conway, M., Steuernagel, G., & Ahern, D. (2005). *Women and Political Partecipation. Cultural Change in the Political Arena.* Washington: CQ Press.

De Piccoli, N., & Rollero, C. (2010). Public involvement in social and political participation processes: A gender perspective. *Journal of Community & Applied Social Psychology*, *20*,167-183. Doi: 10.1002/casp.1027.

Diekman, A. B., & Schneider, M. C. (2010). A social role theory perspective on gender gaps in political attitudes. *Psychology of women quarterly*, *34*, 486-497.

Dolan, J.A., Dieckman, M.M., Swears, M.L. (2006). *Women and Politics: Path to power and political influence.* Upper Saddle River: Pearson Prentice Hall.

Duehr, E. E., & Bono, J. E. (2006). Men, women, and managers: Are stereotypes finally changing? *Personnel Psychology, 59,* 815-846.

Eagly, A. H. (1983). Gender and social influence: a social psychological analysis. *American Psychologist, 38,* 971-981.

Eagly, A. H. (1987). *Sex differences in social behavio: a social role interpretation.* Hillsdale: Erlbaum Publischer.

Eagly, A. H., & Diekman, A. B. (2006). Examining the gap in political attitudes: It's not Mars and Venus. *Feminism & Psychology, 16*, 26-34.

Eagly, A. H., & Johnson, B. T. (1990). Gender and Leadership Style: A Meta-Analysis. *Psychological Bulletin, 108* (2), 233-256.

Eagly, A. H., & Karau, S. J. (2002). Role congruity theory of prejudice toward female leaders. *Psychological Review, 109*, 573-598.

Eagly, A. H., Karau, S. J., & Makhijani, M. G. (1995). Gender and the Effectiveness of Leaders: A Meta-Analysis. *Psychological Bulletin, 117* (1), 125-145.

Eagly, A. H., Makhijani, M. G., & Klonsky, B. G. (1992). Gender and Evaluation of Leader. *Psychological Bullettin, 111* (1), 3-22.

Eurostat (2008). *The life of women and men in Europe. A statistical portrait.* Luxemburg: Office for Official Publications of the European Communities.

Falk, E. & Kenski, K. (2006). Issue saliency and gender stereotypes: Support for women as presidents in times of war and terrorism. *Social Science Quarterly. 87*, 1-18.

Foschi, M. (1996). Double standards in the evaluation of men and women. *Social Psychology Quarterly, 59*, 237-254.

Francescato, D., & Mebane, M. E. (2011). Donne Politiche. In P. Catellani, & G. Sensales, *Psicologia della politica* (p. 253-270). Milano: Raffaello Cortina Editore.

Geis, F. L., Boston, M., & Hoffman, N. (1985). Sex of authority role models and achievement by men and women: Leade rship performance and re cognition. *Journ al of Personality and Social Psychology, 49*, 636-653.

Glick, P., & Fiske, S. T. (1999). The Ambivalence toward Men Inventory: Differentiating hostile and benevolent beliefs about men. *Psychology of Women Quarterly, 23* (3), 519-536.

Glick, P., & Fiske, S. T. (1996). The Ambivalent Sexism Inventory: Differentiating hostile and benevolent sexism. *Journal of Personality and Social Psychology, 70*, 491-512.

Glick, P., & Fiske, S. T. (2001). An ambivalent alliance. Hostile and benevolent sexism as complementary justifications for gender inequality. *American Psychologist, 56*, 109-118.

Glick, P., & Fiske, S. T. (2011). Ambivalent Sexism Revisited. *Psychology of Women Quarterly. 35*, 530-535.

Glick, P., Fiske, S.T., Masser, B., Manganelli, A.M., Huang, L., Rodriguez Castro, J., et al. (2004). Bad but bold: Ambivalent attitudes toward men predict gender inequality in 16 nations. *Journal of Personality and Social Psychology, 86*, 713-728.

Glick, P., Fiske, S., Mladinic, A., Saiz, J., Abrams, D., & Masser, B. (2000). Beyond prejudice as simple antipathy: Hostile and benevolent sexism across cultures. *Journal of Personality and Social Psychology, 79*, 763-755.

Heilman, M. E., Block, C. J., & Martell, R. F. (1995). Sex stereotypes: Do they influence perceptions of managers? *Journal of Social Behavior and Personality, 10*, 237−252.

Heilman, M. E., & Okimoto, T. G. (2007). Why are women penalized for success at male tasks? The implied communality deficit. *Journal of Applied Psychology, 92*, 81-92.

Howell, S. E., & Day, C. L. (2000). Complexities of the gendre gap. *The Journal of Politics, 62*, 858-874.

Huddy, L., & Terkildsen, N. (1993). Gender Stereotypes and the Perception of Male and Female Candidates. *American Journal of Political Science, 37* (1), 119-147.

IPU (2008). *Women in national parlaments: World classification, online database.* Tratto da www.ipu.org

Jackman, M.R. (1994). *The velvet glove: Paternalism and conflict in gender, class, and race relations.* Berkeley: University of California Press.

Jackson, D., Engstrom, E., & Emmers-Sommer, T. (2007). Think leader, think male and female: Sex vs. seating arrangement as leadership cues. *Sex Roles, 57,* 713-723.

Johanson, J.C. (2008). Perception of femininity in leadership: Modern trend or classic component? *Sex Roles, 58,* 784-789.

Johnson, S. K., Murphy, S. E., Zewdie, S., & Reichard, R. J. (2008). The strong, sensitive type: Effects of gender stereotypes and leadership prototypes on the evaluation of male and female leaders. *Organizational Behavior and Human Decision Processes, 106,* 39-60.

Koenig, A. M., Eagly, A. H., Mitchell, A. A., & Ristikari, T. (2011). Are leader stereotypes masculine? A meta-analysis of three research paradigms. *Psychological Bulletin, 137* (4), 616-642.

Lammers, J., Gordijn, E. H., & Otten, S. (2009). Iron ladies, men of steel: The effects of gender stereotyping on the perception of male and female candidates are moderated by prototypicality. *European Journal of Social Psychology, 39,* 186-195.

Lips, H. (1995). Gender-role socialization. In J: Freeman (Ed.), *Women: A feminist perspective* (pp. 128-148). Palo Alto, CA: Mayfield.

Lips, H. M. (2001). Power. Social and Interpersonal Aspects. In *Encyclopedia of Women and Gender: Sex similarities and differences and the impact of society on gender* (pp. 847-858). San Diego: Academic Press.

Manganelli Rattazzi, A.M., Volpato, C., & Canova, L. (2008). L'atteggiamento ambivalente verso donne e uomini. Un contributo alla validazione delle scale ASI e AMI. *Giornale Italiano di Psicologia. 35,* 261-287.

Masser, B.M, & Abrams, D. (2004). Reinforcing the glass ceiling: The consequences of hostile sexism for female managerial candidates. *Sex Roles, 51,* 609-615.

Matland, R., & Montgomery, K.A. (2003). *Women's access to political power in post-communist Europe.* Oxford: Oxford University Press.

Mazzoleni, G., & Sfardini, A. (2009). *Politica Pop.* Bologna: Il Mulino.

Norris, P. (2003). The gender gap: Old challenges, new approaches. In S. J. Carrol, *Women and American politics: New questions, new directions* (p. 146-172). Oxford: Oxford University Press.

Norris, P. & Lovenduski, J. (1995). *Political recruitment: Gender, race and class in the British Parliament.* Cambridge, UK: Cambridge University Press.

Powell, G. N., Butterfield, D. A., & Parent, J. D. (2002). Gender and managerial stereotypes: Have the times changed? *Journal of Management, 28,* 177-193.

Rollero, C., & Fedi, A. (2012). Ambivalent attitudes toward women and men. Recognizability of stereotypes and effects on self-perception. *Psicología Política, 44,* 69-86.

Rudman, L. A., & Glick, P. (2001). Prescriptive gender stereotypes and backlash toward agentic women. *Journal of Social Issues, 57,* 743-762.

Rudman, L. A., Moss-Racusin, C. A., Phelan, J. E., & Nauts, S. (2012). Status incongruity and backlash effects: Defending the gender hierarchy motivates prejudice against female leaders. *Journal of Experimental Social Psychology, 48* (1), 165-179.

Rule, N. O., Ambady, N., & Adams, R. B. (2010). Polling the face: Prediction and Consensus Across Cultures. *Journal of Personality and Social Psychology*, *98* (1), 1-15.

Rule, N., & Ambady, N. (2010). First Impression of the Face: Predicting Succes. *Social and Personality Psychology Compass*, *4* (8), 506-516.

Ryan, M.K., Haslam, A., Hersby S.A., & Bongiorno, R. (2011). Thing Crisis_Think Female: The Glass Cliff and Contextual Variation in the Think Manager-Think Male Stereotype. Journal of Applied Psychology, 96, 470-484.

Sakalli-Ugurlu, N. & Beydogan, B. (2002). Turkish college students' attitudes toward women managers : The effects of patriarchy, sexism, and gender differences. *The Journal of Psychology*, 136, 647-656.

Schein, V. E. (2001). A global look at psychological barriers to women's progress in management. *Journal of Social Issues, 57*, 675-688.

Scott, K. A., & Brown, D. J. (2006). Female first, leader second? Gender bias in the encoding of leadership behavior. *Organizational Behavior and Human Decision Processes, 101*, 230-242.

Sczesny, S. (2003). A closer look beneath the surface: Various facets of the think manager – think male stereotype. *Sex Roles, 49*, 353–363.

Shackelford, S., Wood, W., & Worchel, S. (1996). Behavioral styles and the influence of women in mixed-sex groups. *Social Psychology Quarterly, 59* (3), 284-293.

Sibley, C.G., & Perry, R. (2010). An opposing process model of benevolent sexism. *Sex Roles, 62*, 438-452.

Swim, J. K., Mallett, R., Russo-Devosa, Y., & Stangor, C. (2005). Judgments of sexism: A comparison of the subtlety of sexism measures and sources of variability in judgments of sexism. *Psychology of Women Quarterly, 29,* 406-411.

Thomas, S. (2002). The Personal Is the Political: Antecedents of Gendered Choices of Elected Representatives. *Sex Roles*, *47*, 445-456.

Todorov, A., Mandisodza, A. N., Goren, A., & Hall, C. C. (2005). Inferences of competence from faces predict election outcome. *Science*, *308*, 1623-1626.

In: Perspectives in Leadership
Editor: Jerry D. VanVactor

ISBN: 978-1-62417-170-3

Chapter 9

THE GENDERED IMAGE OF POWER: HOW MALE AND FEMALE LEADERS ARE PERCEIVED

Chiara Rollero * and *Norma De Piccoli*

Department of Psychology, University of Turin, Italy

ABSTRACT

Prejudice toward female leaders can arise because of the inconsistency between the communal quality associated with women and the agentic qualities stereotypically required to be a successful leader. The present study explores the perception of female and male leaders by applying free association tasks. Moreover, it investigates how demographic variables (gender and age) and leadership experience in different fields affect such perception. Three groups of Italian adults, living in the Piedmont region, were recruited ($N = 345$): political leaders, social leaders and non-leaders. Results showed that both the male and the female leader were described through agentic traits, exclusively. Political leaders and high leadership subjects showed a positive image of the male leader, whereas men expressed a negative perception of the female leader. Implications are discussed.

Keywords: Gender, leadership, language

INTRODUCTION

The present study focuses on the perception of the male and the female leader considering mainly two aspects: 1) the image people associate with the male and the female leader and 2) the differences between the respondents' characterizations (i.e. demographic variables – gender and age - and leadership experience). Concerning the first aspect, usually

* Corresponding author: Chiara Rollero (chiara.rollero@unito.it) Tel +39 011 6702055 ; Fax +39 0116702061 ;
Department of Psychology – University of Turin, Via Verdi, 10, 10124 Torino (Italy).

the research participants are presented with a list of traits that the researcher knows to be stereotypically feminine, masculine or gender neutral (e.g. Duehr & Bono, 2006; Garcia-Retamero & Lopez-Zafra, 2006; Sczesny, 2003; Sczesny et al., 2004), but this method may easily lead to misinterpretation of the data, as Willemsen pointed out (2002). If a participant rates a successful leader high on feminine traits, the researcher may suppose that this participant will think it equally probable that a woman and a man could be a leader. However, one can describe a male leader also using feminine characteristics. In other words, using feminine traits to define a successful leader should not be interpreted as describing a woman (Willemsen, 2002). Instead, our interest lies in the perceptions individuals express when they are involved in a free-association task. This method underlies more spontaneous processes and thus permits an authentic access to images people have in the mind (Abric, 2003). Moreover, we address also another question: how individual characteristics can affect such perceptions? We are interested in considering individuals with different leadership experiences in the social or in the political domain, in order to investigate how such experiences influence the perception of male and female leaders.

Several theories have been formulated to explain the sparse representation of women in leadership roles (e.g. Burgess & Borgida, 1999; Glick & Fiske, 1996; Heilman, 1983). Eagly and Karau (2002) proposed the Role Congruity Theory (RCT), an integrative approach built on social psychologists' tradition of studying prejudice and stereotyping, and organizational psychologists' tradition of studying perceptions of managerial roles. According to Eagly (1987), gender roles specify what kind of behavior is expected by an individual on the basis of his/her sexual identity. Like other forms of expectations referred to a certain role, they are consensual and exist as ideology that is socially built and shared. When judging women as actual or potential leaders, prejudice can arise in perceivers because of inconsistency between the predominantly communal qualities they associate with women and the predominantly agentic qualities they believe are required to be a successful leader (Eagly & Karau, 2002). In fact, women are expected to show relatively feminine, communal values through behaviors that are helpful, kind, and sensitive and are not expected to manifest the agentic characteristics generally associated with men and leaders. These masculine values are connected to behaviors that are assertive, ambitious, forceful, dominant, and self-confident (Eagly, 2005).

Observing an occupant of a leader role places expectations founded on gender in competition with expectations founded on leadership. In particular, when thinking about female leaders, people would combine highly divergent expectations, whereas when thinking about male leaders, people would combine largely redundant expectations (Eagly & Karau, 2002).

According to the RCT, prejudice toward female leaders and potential leaders takes on two forms. The first, which stems from the descriptive norms of gender roles, is a less favorable evaluation of women's (rather than men's) potential for leadership because leadership ability is more stereotypical of men. The second type of prejudice, connected to the injunctive norms of gender roles, is a less favorable evaluation of the actual leadership behavior of women than men because such behavior is perceived as less desirable in women (Eagly & Karau, 2002).

Thus, when individuals are requested to think of a male and a female leader in a free-association task, they should refer to agentic traits to describe both the leaders. However, as the injunctive norms of gender roles pose (Eagly & Karau, 2002), the female leader should be associated to more negative characteristics than the male leader, since agentic leadership ability is stereotypically less desirable in women.

However, the RCT argues that women would not always be targets of prejudice, since various conditions would affect these prejudices. The perceivers' gender seems to play a key role, since men often showed stronger prejudice than women (Eagly & Karau, 2002; Schein, 2001). Within the United States, young men and high school students have consistently been shown to hold more traditional views about gender roles than females (Gibbons et al., 1991; Wasserman & Weseley, 2009). Other studies have shown that this difference holds true across other nations, such as Japan, Croatia and Slovenia (Ferligoj et al., 1993). A recent study carried out in Spain with an adult sample, reported divergent data: female participants had a stronger tendency than male participants to view female leaders as less qualified than their male counterparts (Garcia-Retamero & Lopez-Zafra, 2006).

A change of attitudes about gender roles over time is also possible, although there is little evidence (i.e. Spence & Buckner, 2000). When the age of the individuals is considered, literature shows that the perception of incongruence between the leadership role and the feminine gender role is stronger and more stable in older people (Garcia-Retamero & Lopez-Zafra, 2006). Nevertheless, according to Lammers, Gordijn and Otten (2009), although expressions of sexism have become more benevolent in tone, they continue to have negative effects on how people behave towards women. Many recent studies show that not only men but also women still endorse sexist beliefs (e.g. Barreto & Ellemers, 2005; Swim et al., 2005).

As the RCT argues, stereotypes not only specify how men and women ought to be, but they also have an impact on the perception of one's competences and abilities (Eagly & Karau, 2002; Ridgeway, 2001). In general, women see themselves as less agentic and more communal than men (Bem, 1974; Spence & Buckner, 2000). They consider themselves as less suitable for respective leadership positions than men because they view themselves as possessing less of the agentic traits typically required for such positions than men do, as Bosak and Sczesny (2008) documented in their research with German management students. Results of a study conducted by Lips (2000) with a US college students sample showed that women were less optimistic than men about achieving powerful positions and also rated the roles as less positive than men did. Furthermore, women were significantly more likely than men to anticipate relationship problems in a leadership position. Similarly, Killeen, Lopés-Zafra, and Eagly (2006) found that both in Spain and in the United States young women have more difficult than young men in projecting themselves into a future as an organizational manager, although men and women regard this role as equally positive overall.

To define how individuals perceive themselves as effective leaders in sociopolitical domains, Zimmerman and Zahniser (1991) proposed the concept of leadership competence, which reflects to what extent people agree with the idea that they are leaders. Empirical research on leadership competence from a gendered perspective is controversial. Although women are generally presumed to show lower levels of leadership competence, results are not always convergent. In line with Zimmerman and Zahniser's original results (1991), Diemer and Blustein (2006) found that US urban youths do not seem to differ significantly along this dimension. Bobbio, Forchesato, Manganelli Rattazzi, and Crivellari (2005) provided contradictory evidence in an Italian sample. They suggested that among adults and university students, males tend to score higher on self-perceptions of leadership competence. Similarly, Smith and Propst (2001) showed a significant difference between men and women in a randomly selected sample of American rural residents. De Piccoli and Rollero (2010) compared three different groups of Italian adults: non-participants, social participants (i.e. individuals offering their commitment free of charge to associations in the social domain), and politicians. Their results showed no gender difference on leadership competence only for politicians, whereas men scored higher than women on this dimension both in the non-participant group and in the social participant group.

To sum up, although empirical research on leadership competence is controversial, literature seems to converge in representing the leader role mainly as a male prerogative. This perception is often shared by men and women and refers both to the organizational and to the sociopolitical domain.

**Table 1. Demographic characteristics of men
and women in the sample**

	Men	Women		
Political leaders (N = 108):	N = 52	N = 56		
Age (means and SD)	42.48 (13.84)	37.53 (12.74)	T-value = -1.60	n.s.
Low level of education (N)	10	13		
High school graduates (N)	28	27		
College graduates (N)	14	16	χ^2 (df = 2) = 2.13	n.s.
Social leaders (N = 101)	N = 50	N = 51		
Age (means and SD)	42.46 (13.18)	48.23 (15.56)	T-value = 2.01	n.s.
Low level of education (N)	10	12		
High school graduates (N)	21	27		
College graduates (N)	19	12	χ^2 (df = 2) = 2.50	n.s
Non-leaders (N = 136)	N = 59	N = 77		
Age (means and SD)	44.82 (14.38)	42.71 (15.58)	T-value = -.58	n.s.
Low level of education (N)	12	16		
High school graduates (N)	29	31		
College graduates (N)	18	30	χ^2 (df = 2) = 1.28	n.s
Total (N = 345)	N = 161	N = 184		
Age (means and SD)	43.30 (13.49)	42.66 (15.24)	T-value = -.40	n.s.
Low level of education (N)	32	41		
High school graduates (N)	78	87		
College graduates (N)	51	58	χ^2 (df = 2) = 2.90	n.s

THE CURRENT STUDY

It is well known that language plays a key role in the social construction of the reality (Billig, 1996; Gergen, 1985), as it is expression of the meanings attributed to a social object. In the present study we are interested in exploring the semantic contents people express when they think of a male leader and a female leader. Given the assumptions of the RCT (Eagly & Karau, 2002), in the case of male leader individuals should combine congruent characteristics, i.e. the agentic traits usually associated both to men and to leaders. On the contrary, in thinking of female leaders, people should combine divergent traits, i.e. the communal features associated to women and the agentic ones connected to leaders. Thus, in this case, which traits are predominant? Is the female leader perceived as agentic or as communal?

We are interested in investigating such representations in association with participants' characteristics that can affect prejudice. In particular, following the RCT (Eagly & Karau, 2002), we hypothesize that women and younger individuals will express a more positive image of female leaders than men and older individuals. Moreover, prejudices should be understood as implying not dichotomous male-female differences but general trends that emerge across situational and other individual factors (Eagly, 2009). Among situational factors, in the present study we will explore the possible role played by the kind of leadership role (being a social leader, a political leader or playing no leadership role). Among individual characteristics, we will take into account the level of leadership competence and the educational level.

In sum, the current study has two purposes: 1) exploring the representation both of male leader and female leader, and 2) investigating how such representation is affected by participants' characteristics (i.e. gender, age, educational level, leadership competence, and being or not a leader).

To reach these aims, we involved in the research both common people and individuals who are leaders in the social or in the political domain, in order to investigate if playing or not a leadership role affects the representation of the male and the female leader.

METHOD

Participants

A total of 345 Caucasian subjects living in Piedmont, a region in the north-west of Italy, were enrolled in the study. The average age of the sample was 42.96 years ($SD = 14.57$, age range: 21-65). About the education, the majority were high school graduates (48.5%), the 31.6% were college graduates, and the remaining (19.9%) had a lower level of education. No significant gender difference emerged in relation to demographic characteristics (Table 1).

The subjects were recruited in such a way as to differentiate participants according to their type of leadership. This led to the formation of three groups that were homogeneous for age ($F = 1.78$, n.s.) and education ($\chi^2 = 11.09$, df = 4, n.s.): 1) political leaders, 2) social leaders and 3) non-leaders. In detail, 108 subjects (48.1% men and 51.9% women) played a leader role in a political party: 50.5% participated in right-wing party activities and 49.5% in left-wing party activities. More specifically, they held official executive positions, with a great deal of leeway concerning the party activities and strategies. There was a total of 101 social leaders (49.5% men and 50.5% women): i.e. persons that played a leader role in associations that operate in the social assistance, social-health or cultural fields. As politicians, social leaders held official executive positions and were responsible for decisions concerning the association's activities. Twenty-four different associations, operating above all at local levels, were contacted. The 136 non-leader subjects (43.4% men and 56.6% women), were not involved in any kind of social or political activities. The kind of participation and the leadership role in the party/association were controlled through a specific section of the questionnaire.

The recruitment of politicians was done using the snowball sampling and we referred to head offices of different political parties and some institutional organizations. Politicians were approached in their offices and those who agreed to participate (response rate: 72%) were handed in a questionnaire. The social leaders were contacted through social associations operating on the territory and they were also selected by the snowball sampling. They were approached in the associations' head offices and those who agreed to participate (response rate: 84.16%) were handed in a questionnaire. Both politicians and social leaders returned the questionnaire by placing it in a marked box at the party/association office and thus anonymity was granted.

The non-participants were recruited from common persons, i.e. next-door neighbors' psychology students, according to the technique of convenience sampling. Those who agreed to participate (response rate: 68%) were handed in a questionnaire and a pen. Anonymity was granted, because the students who contacted them did not take part in the research but simply delivered the questionnaires.

Measures

Data were gathered by a self-reported questionnaire which took about 15 minutes to be completed. The questionnaire was divided into 5 sections:

4. a free-association of words in order to investigate the subjective images of a female leader. Participants were asked to answer the statement: "Think of a female leader and write the first five words that come to your mind";

5. another free-association of words referred to a male leader. Participants were asked to answer the statement: "Think of a male leader and write the first five words that come to your mind". These two free association tasks were randomized, in order to control the effect of the presentation's order. Thus, half of participants had to think of female leader first, whereas the others had to think of male leader first;

6. the *Leadership Competence Scale*. To assess the level of leadership competence, the 8-item Italian adaptation (Bobbio et al., 2005; De Piccoli & Rollero, 2010) of the Leadership Competence Scale (Zimmerman & Zahniser,1991) was used. Items were scored on a five-point scale from (1) completely untrue for me, to (5) completely true for me. Examples of items are the following statements: "I am often a leader in groups", "I can usually organize people to get things done", "Other people usually follow my ideas". Cronbach's alpha was 0.78 ($M = 3.50$, $SD = 0.67$). Globally, men showed higher levels of leadership competence. When considering the three groups of subjects separately, gender differences were no more significant for political leaders (Table 2);

7. the occupation of a leadership position in parties or association. Participants were questioned about the party/association they were member of, and about their role in the organization;

8. a socio-demographical section.

Table 2. Leadership competence: means (and standard deviations) of men and women in the sample. Scale endpoints are 1=completely untrue for me and 5= completely true for me

	Men	Women	T-value	p
Political leaders (N = 108):	N = 52	N = 56	-1.34	n.s.
	3.58 (0.66)	3.42 (0.58)		
Social leaders (N = 101)	N = 50	N = 51	-2.92	<0.01
	3.60 (0.45)	3.28 (0.63)		
Non-leaders (N = 136)	N = 59	N = 77	-2.24	<0.05
	3.69 (0.73)	3.40 (0.78)		
Total (N = 345)	N = 161	N = 184	-3.27	<0.01
	3.63 (0.63)	3.39 (0.68)		

The use of the free association of words has a long lasting tradition (see Fraisse & Piaget, 1965). From Galton (1879), pioneer in this field, until the more recent utilization in the study of social representations (Abric, 2003), its applications are numerous and in different psychological disciplines. As Abric (2003) pointed out, the free association allows gaining the access to the semantic universe of the investigated object. This method, compared to the interview, underlies more spontaneous – and thus less controlled – processes and permits an easier and faster access to the images people have in mind (Abric, 2003).

Data Analyses

The free associations of words were analyzed by software Alceste 4.6 (Reinert, 1986). The Alceste software package is a computer-based application widely used in social sciences (e.g. Brugidou, 2003; Fernandez et al., 1999; Pierre-Gerard & Perret-Catipovic, 2009; Rollero & De Piccoli, 2010; Staerklé & Clémence, 2004; Yang et al., 2009), that combines textual and statistical analyses.

It performs a descendent cluster analysis based on the lexical co-occurrences among the simple propositions of the text. The result is a hierarchy of classes, which can be represented in a tree diagram. In this case the propositions are the responses of participants to the free association of words. Alceste groups similar responses on the basis of χ^2 discriminating criteria and thereby generates a classification of the different themes present in the textual corpus. Indeed, through the χ^2 test, the software compares the within-cluster occurrence of the words with their overall occurrence on the total of responses: the highest χ^2 values correspond to the most typical words of that cluster. Thus, the researcher obtains a list of the most characteristic words for each class, along with their χ^2 statistical significance (with the minimum χ^2 value for selection set at 2.13, below which the level of statistical significance fails to reach the 10% level, using the standard χ^2 table with 1 degree of freedom). Moreover, by means of the same statistical analysis, this software makes it possible to test the association between clusters and particular characteristics of participants (considered as categorical variables). In the present study, we selected the following variables: sex, age (subgroups were based on quartiles: under 30, 30-42, 43-55, over 55), level of leadership competence (high or low, if participants were respectively higher or lower than the average), and kind of leadership role (political leaders, social leaders, non-leaders).

RESULTS

We collected 1587 words associated with the male leader. The cluster analysis enabled a good proportion of the responses (the 78.55%) to be classified into 3 classes (Figure 1).

```
Cluster 1-68responses  |-----------------------+
                                               |---------------------+
Cluster 2-73responses  |-----------------------+                     |
                                                                     |+
Cluster 3-130responses|----------------------------------------------+
```

Figure 1. Male leader. Descendent cluster analysis: the tree diagram.

Comparing the within-cluster occurrence of the words with their overall occurrence on the total of classified responses by means of a χ^2-test allowed for the identification of the words characteristic of each cluster, offering a key for its interpretation.

Table 3. Male leader: cluster 1. Characteristic words and subgroups of participants

	χ^2	occurrences in cluster	total occurrences
Elegant/elegance (*elegante/eleganza*)	56.14	19	20
Politician (*politico*)	51.89	30	44
Businessman (*imprenditore*)	45.98	16	17
Old (*vecchio*)	28.53	13	16
Cultured/culture (*colto/cultura*)	26.45	16	23
Hard-working (*lavoratore*)	24.61	8	8
Engaged (*impegnato*)	23.27	9	10
Self-confident/confidence (*sicuro di sè*)	22.46	11	14
Detached (*distaccato*)	11.07	5	6
Clever/cleverness (*astuto/astuzia*)	9.06	7	11
Intelligent (*intelligente*)	7.69	12	25
* Political leaders	18.40	37	90

Cluster 1 (25.09% of the classified responses) conveyed an image of the male leader, based on specific professions (*politician, businessmen*), *culture* and agentic traits (*self-confident, detached, clever, intelligent*). This cluster contained a significantly high number of responses given by political leaders (Table 3).

In cluster 2 (26.94% of the classified responses) the perception of the male leader was still focused on agentic characteristics, but mainly through references to *power* (*command, president, power, chief, responsibility*). In this cluster we also found benefits that can be linked to leadership (*money* and *women*), and the name of the Italian premier *Berlusconi*. Concerning participants, cluster 2 described the expressions produced by high-leadership subjects and young people (Table 4).

If the first two clusters were similar, cluster 3, the largest (47.97% of the classified responses), showed a very different perception. Indeed, in this cluster the male leader was seen as *arrogant, bully, egoist, ambitious, cold hearted*, and *presumptuous*. He was linked to *politics* and to the *abuse* of power. As expected, this negative image was expressed mainly by low-leadership participants, social leaders and older individuals (Table 5). Gender was not significantly associated to any cluster: this means that men and women express a similar perception of the male leader.

Concerning the female leader, 1557 words were used by participants. The cluster analysis classified the 77.10% of the responses. As the tree diagram shows (Figure 2), 4 classes were extracted.

Cluster 1 (16.54% of the classified responses) suggested an agentic vision of the female leader. She was perceived as *firm, enterprising, self-confident, fearless, strong,* and *determined.* This cluster contained a significantly high number of responses given by participants who played no leader role and low leadership individuals (Table 6).

Table 4. Male leader: cluster 2. Characteristic words and subgroups of participants

	χ^2	occurrences in cluster	total occurrences
Work (*lavoro*)	26.73	11	12
Money (*soldi*)	23.32	29	55
Industrialist (*industriale*)	22.36	8	8
Command (*comando*)	20.00	11	14
Charismatic/charisma (*carismatico/carisma*)19.49	7	7	
Women (*donne*)	17.55	9	11
President (*presidente*)	17.37	11	15
Berlusconi	13.72	20	39
Power (*potere*)	12.61	6	7
Chief (*capo*)	7.47	6	9
Responsible/responsibility (*responsabile*)	7.29	4	5
Strong (*forte*)	6.23	9	17
* High leadership competence	13.75	48	128
* Age: under 30	4.64	23	61

Table 5. Male leader: cluster 3. Characteristic words and subgroups of participants

	χ^2	occurrences in cluster	total occurrences
Arrogant/arrogance (*arrogante/arroganza*)	32.05	29	30
Social climber (*arrampicatore sociale*)	27.76	30	33
Bully (*prepotente*)	23.92	25	27
Egoist/egoism (*egoista/egoismo*)	20.91	18	18
Ambitious/ambition (*ambizioso/ambizione*)	17.22	15	15
Politics (*politica*)	16.01	14	14
Rich/richness (*ricco/ricchezza*)	10.99	18	22
Decision (*decisione*)	8.47	10	11
Abuse(*abuso*)	7.79	7	7
Cold hearted (*freddo*)	7.79	7	7
Presumptuous (*presuntuoso*)	6.24	8	9
* Low leadership competence	17.96	86	143
* Social leaders	10.49	50	79
* Age: over 55	9.37	43	67

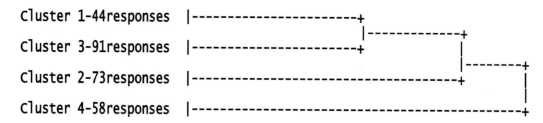

Figure 2. Female leader. Descendent cluster analysis: the tree diagram.

Table 6. Female leader: cluster 1. Characteristic words and subgroups of participants

	χ^2	occurrences in cluster	total occurrences
Firm/firmness(*decisa/decisione*)	90.63	18	19
Enterprising (*intraprendente*)	41.62	8	8
Self-confident(*sicura di sè*)	40.61	10	12
Attentive (*attenta*)	25.71	5	5
Fearless (*coraggiosa*)	15.69	5	7
Strong(*forte*)	12.06	10	24
Graduate (*laureata*)	10.05	3	4
Determined (*determinata*)	6.69	4	8
* No leader role	2.75	20	92
* Low leadership competence	2.05	27	137

Table 7. Female leader: cluster 3. Characteristic words and subgroups of participants

	χ^2	occurrences in cluster	total occurrences
Intelligent (*intelligente*)	52.18	32	37
Resolute (*risoluta*)	47.82	26	28
Beautiful (*bella*)	25.71	20	25
Work (*lavoro*)	12.92	11	14
Strong-willed (*tenace*)	10.41	7	8
Elegant/elegance (*elegante/eleganza*)	9.99	18	30
Dogged (*caparbia*)	9.68	8	10
Cultured/culture (*colta/cultura*)	9.29	9	12
Diplomatic (*diplomatica*)	9.80	5	5
* High leadership competence	7.39	40	88
* Age: 43-55	4.59	32	72

As seen in the tree diagram, cluster 3 (34.21% of the classified responses) was strongly depicted the female leader as *intelligent, resolute, strong-willed*, and *dogged*. Specific of this cluster was the reference to physical appearance, through the words *beautiful* and *elegant*. Concerning participants, the present cluster was associated with high leadership individuals and 43-55 aged (Table 7).

Cluster 2 (27.44% of the classified responses) was still focused on agentic traits, but in a negative way. Like the male leader, the female leader was perceived as *ambitious, arrogant, cold hearted, presumptuous, egoist*, and a *social climber*. The women was also considered as *lonely* and an *opportunist*. She was linked to *money* and *career*. This was the only cluster in which the respondents' gender played a significant role, given that this negative perception was mainly expressed by men. Cluster 2 was also expression of social leaders' representation (Table 8).

Table 8. Female leader: cluster 2. Characteristic words and subgroups of participants

	χ^2	occurrences in cluster	total occurrences
Ambitious/ambition (*ambiziosa/ambizione*)	33.22	12	12
Arrogant/arrogance (*arrogante/arroganza*)	27.50	14	17
Cold hearted (*fredda*)	27.47	10	10
Money (*soldi*)	25.20	12	14
(*carriera*)	18.04	15	23
Lonely (*sola*)	17.04	9	11
Social climber (*arrampicatrice sociale*)	16.98	12	17
Presumptuous (*presuntuosa*)	16.23	6	6
Opportunist (opportunista)	14.94	7	8
Egoist/egoism (*egoista/egoismo*)	10.74	4	4
* Sex: male	3.99	41	123
* Social leaders	3.72	26	72

Table 9. Female leader: cluster 4. Characteristic words and subgroups of participants

	χ^2	Occurrences in cluster	Total occurrences
Businesswoman (*imprenditrice*)	49.02	13	13
Angela Merkel	43.09	14	16
Politician (*politica*)	28.27	19	33
Chancellor (*cancelliere*)	22.01	6	6
Worker (*lavoratrice*)	17.22	6	7
Manager (*manager*)	12.90	10	18
Indira Gandhi	14.56	4	4
Condoleezza Rice	13.69	6	8
* Age: under 30	10.21	25	71
* Political leaders	7.16	31	102

Finally, cluster 4 conveyed a personification of the female leader, since it was constituted by references to famous women of power (i.e. *Angela Merkel, Indira Gandhi,* and *Condoleezza Rice*) or by references to professional positions (i.e. *businesswoman, politician, chancellor, manager, worker*). The responses of young participants and social leaders were significantly present in this cluster (Table 9).

CONCLUSION

As seen, the perception of the male leader is strongly based on agentic characteristics. In one case (Table 5) the image is exclusively negative, whereas in the other clusters the leader is described through both positive and descriptive traits. Concerning respondents, they can be distinguished mainly by their level of leadership competence and by their leader role (see the χ^2 values). This means that the image of the male leader seems not to depend on other individuals' characteristics but on what we supposed was the identification toward the leader. Indeed, on the one hand, following the assumptions of the Self Categorization Theory (Turner, 1987), we argued that when thinking of a leader, people who hold a leadership position tend to refer to a social category they belong to. On the other, since competence and stereotypes are strictly related (Eagly & Karau, 2002), who feels more leadership competent should show a less stereotypical view. In fact, low leadership subjects underline the worst traits connected to power. On the contrary, political leaders and high leadership respondents express a more complex vision (male leader is old but self-confident, detached but intelligent, he is strong but also has to face responsibilities).

In the case of the female leader, global results are different, although always focused on agentic traits. Participants seem to be less familiar with the female leader: the perception, in fact, is expressed through four different clusters (in the case of the male leader only three clusters were present) and this could indicate a less shared image, more differentiated because it less known (Reinert, 1986). The perception is similar to an expression of "ideal types", since on the one hand two clusters conveyed an exclusively positive image (Tables 6 and 7), on the other in one cluster all the characteristics are undoubtedly negative (Table 8). This distinction between a totally positive and a totally negative female leader could indicate a process of idealization, due to the less frequent presence of "real" women of power respondents can think of. It seems a perception based on two opposite poles, one completely positive and the other exclusively negative. The most concrete image of the female leader only comes by way of personification (Table 9): especially young people and political leaders try to identify a woman of power through references to famous politicians and to professional positions. Such personification might be related also to the fact that female leaders are perceived as an "exception" in respect to most women and thus they are not described with specific traits (see the contrast effects perspective, Schwarz & Bless, 1992). Regarding the respondents' characteristics, in the case of female leader, leadership competence plays no key role: both high and low leadership subjects provide a positive image. On the contrary, in this case gender has a significant influence, as men are associated with the most negative perception. Identification seems no longer to be founded on leadership competence, as for the man of power, but on gender. This is in line with recent research, arguing that men often show stronger prejudice than women (Eagly & Karau, 2002; Ferligoj et al., 1993; Garcia-Retamero & Lopez-Zafra, 2006; Gibbons et al., 1991; Jackson et al., 2007; Schein, 2001; Wasserman & Weseley, 2009).

From a theoretical perspective, these results are in line with the RCT. As this theory argues, observing an occupant of a leadership role places expectations founded on gender in competition with expectations founded on leadership (Eagly & Karau, 2002). In particular, when thinking about female leaders, people tend to combine highly divergent expectations, whereas when thinking about male leaders, people tend to combine largely redundant expectations (Eagly & Karau, 2002). The present study shows that the power is always associated with agentic traits and thus with male characteristics. In fact, even a positive perception of a female leader is exclusively founded on agentic traits. In other words, to be a good leader only agentic characteristics are required. This is in contrast with recent findings in the field of organizational psychology, where good leadership is increasingly defined in terms of the qualities of a good coach or teacher rather than a highly authoritative individual (Eagly, 2007). Most likely, individuals are more familiar with a "traditional" vision of power (Johanson, 2008; Powell et al., 2002; Schein, 2001). Particularly interesting is the vision expressed by social leaders, who shared a negative perception both of the male leader and of the female leader. Although their professional role is focused on care or social assistance and implies holding power, they criticize the agentic leadership style, but they do not propose a communal image of the leader. In other words, it seems that another way of thinking about leadership is not possible even for those who operate in the care domain. This means that it is not only a question of gender roles, but also a problem of the perception of leadership *per se*.

Indeed, given the distinctions above discussed, not only women of power are associated with negative characteristics, but also male leaders. Stereotype comes to light not through a worse evaluation of the female leader, but mainly through the association between power and agentic characteristics. Nevertheless, as above described, some individuals' characteristics affect prejudice: gender in the case of female leaders, and leadership competence and a role of power in the case of male leaders.

The free association of words is a useful methodology, since it underlies more spontaneous – and thus less controlled – processes and permits for easier access to the images people have in mind (Abric, 2003). As language reflects and preserves existing social structures (Wasserman & Weseley, 2009) this method makes it possible to avoid the misinterpretation of the data connected to the presentation of traits selected by the researcher (Willemsen, 2002). However, the present findings should be investigated in depth through other methods. Interviews, for example, could contribute to a better understanding of individuals' perceptions. Furthermore, more attention should be paid to the cultural aspects that affect the perception. Our research, in fact, provides some findings, but it is only an initial exploration.

Beall, Eagly and Sternberg (2004) pointed out that the psychology of gender should consider under what conditions gender differences are smaller or larger, and when similarity or near-similarity prevails. One of the notable developments in the psychology of gender is that researchers are posing increasingly subtle questions about the contextual patterning of difference and similarity (Beall et al., 2004). The current study aimed at following this direction, as we decided to take into account not only gender, but also leadership competence and leadership experience. As these authors underline, it is impossible to make progress on this topic without theories about how gender interacts with other variables.

REFERENCES

Abric, J. C. (2003). *Méthodes d'étude des représentations sociales.* Ramonville Saint-Agne: Editions érèes.

Barreto, M., & Ellemers, N. (2005). The burden of benevolent sexism: How it contributes to the maintenance of gender inequalities. *European Journal of Social Psychology, 35,* 633-642.

Beall, A.E., Eagly, A.H., & Sternberg, R.J. (2004). Introduction. In *The Psychology of Gender.* (pp. 1-8). New York: The Guilford Press.

Bem, S. (1974). The measurement of psychological androgyny. *Journal of Consulting and Clinical Psychology, 42*, 155-162.

Billig, M. (1996). *Arguing and thinking: A rhetorical approach to social psychology.* Cambridge: Cambridge University Press.

Bobbio, A., Forchesato, M., Manganelli Rattazzi, A. M., & Crivellari, F. (2005). La scala di controllo sociopolitico di Zimmerman e Zahniser (SPCS, 1991). Un contributo all'adattamento italiano con metodi carta e matita e web-based. *Testing, Psicometria, Metodologia, 12*, 61-82.

Bosak, J., & Sczesny, S. (2008). Am I the right candidate? Self-ascribed fit of women and men to a leadership position. *Sex Roles, 58*, 682-688.

Brugidou, M. (2003). Argumentation and values: An analysis of ordinary political competence via an open-ended question. *International Journal of Public Opinion Research, 15*, 413-430.

Burgess, D., & Borgida, E. (1999). Who women are, who women should be: Descriptive and prescriptive gender stereotyping in sex discrimination. *Psychology, Public Policy, and Law, 5*, 665-692.

Den Hartog, D.N., House, R.J., Hanges, P.J., Ruiz-Quintanilla, S.A., & Dorfman, P.W. (1999). Culture specific and cross-culturally generalizable implicit leadership theories: Are attributes of charismatic/transformational leadership universally endorsed? *Leadership Quarterly, 10*, 219-256.

De Piccoli, N., & Rollero, C. (2010). Public involvement in social and political participation processes: A gender perspective. *Journal of Community & Applied Social Psychology, 20*,167-183. Doi: 10.1002/casp.1027.

Diemer, M.A., & Blustein, D.L. (2006). Critical consciousness and career development among urban youth. *Journal of Vocational Behavior, 68*, 220-232.

Duehr, E. E., & Bono, J. E. (2006). Men, women, and managers: Are stereotypes finally changing? *Personnel Psychology, 59*, 815-846.

Eagly, A. H. (1987). *Sex differences in social behaviour: A social-role interpretation.* Hillsdale, NJ: Erlbaum.

Eagly, A. H. (2005). Achieving relational authenticity in leadership: Does gender matter? *The Leadership Quarterly, 16*, 459-474.

Eagly, A. H. (2007). Female leadership advantage and disadvantage: Resolving the contradictions. *Psychology of Women Quarterly, 31*, 1-12.

Eagly, A. H., & Karau, S. J. (2002). Role congruity theory of prejudice toward female leaders. *Psychological Review, 109*, 573-598.

Ferligoj, A., Frieze, I.H., & Marinaga, Y. (1993). Career plans and gender-role attitudes of college students in the United States, Japan, and Slovenia. *Sex Roles, 29*, 317-334.

Fernandez, L., Lafont, E., & Sztulman, H. (1999). Textual analysis of addictive behavior of cigarettes' smokers undergoing stop smoking treatment. *European Review of Applied Psychology, 49*, 199-213.

Fraisse, P., & Piaget, J. (Eds.) (1965). *Traité de Psychologie Expérimentale.* Vol. VIII. Paris : Presses Universitaires de France.

Galton, F. (1879). Psychometric experiments. *Brain, 2*, 149-162.

Garcia-Retamero, R., & Lopez-Zafra, E. (2006). Prejudice against women in male-congenial environments: Perceptions of gender role congruity in leadership. *Sex Roles, 55*, 51-61.

Gergen, K. J. (1985). The social constructionist movement in modern psychology. *American Psychologist, 40*, 266-275.

Gibbons, J.L., Shkodriani, G.M., & Stiles, D.A. (1991). Adolescents' attitudes toward family and gender roles: An international comparison. *Sex Roles, 25*, 625-643.

Glick, P., & Fiske, S. T. (1996). The Ambivalent Sexism Inventory: Differentiating hostile and benevolent sexism. *Journal of Personality and Social Psychology, 70*, 491-512.

Glick, P., Fiske, S.T., Masser, B., Manganelli, A.M., Huang, L., Rodriguez Castro, J., et al. (2004). Bad but bold: Ambivalent attitudes toward men predict gender inequality in 16 nations. *Journal of Personality and Social Psychology, 86*, 713-728.

Glick, P., Fiske, S.T., Mladinic, A., Saiz, J., Abrams, D., Masser, B., et al., (2000). Beyond prejudice as a simple antipathy: Hostile and benevolent sexism across cultures. *Journal of Personality and Social Psychology, 79*, 763-775.

Heilman, M. E. (1983). Sex bias in work setting: The lack of fit model. *Research in Organizational Behavior, 5*, 269-298.

Heilman, M. E., & Okimoto, T. G. (2007). Why are women penalized for success at male tasks? The implied communality deficit. *Journal of Applied Psychology, 92*, 81-92.

Jackson, D., Engstrom, E., & Emmers-Sommer, T. (2007). Think leader, think male and female: Sex vs. seating arrangement as leadership cues. *Sex Roles, 57*, 713-723.

Johanson, J.C. (2008). Perception of femininity in leadership: Modern trend or classic component? *Sex Roles, 58*, 784-789.

Johnson, S. K., Murphy, S. E., Zewdie, S., & Reichard, R. J. (2008). The strong, sensitive type: Effects of gender stereotypes and leadership prototypes on the evaluation of male and female leaders. *Organizational Behavior and Human Decision Processes, 106*, 39-60.

Killeen, L.A., Lopés-Zafra, E., & Eagly, A.H. (2006). Envisioning oneself as a leader: Comparisons of women and men in Spain and the United States. *Psychology of Women Quarterly, 30*, 312-322.

Lammers, J., Gordijn, E. H., & Otten, S. (2009). Iron ladies, men of steel: The effects of gender stereotyping on the perception of male and female candidates are moderated by prototypicality. *European Journal of Social Psychology, 39*, 186-195.

Lips, H.M. (2000). College students' visions of power and possibility as moderated by gender. *Psychology of Women Quarterly, 24*, 39-43.

Lips, H. M. (2001). Power. Social and Interpersonal Aspects. In *Encyclopedia of Women and Gender: Sex similarities and differences and the impact of society on gender* (pp. 847-858). San Diego: Academic Press.

Pierre-Gerard, S., & Perret-Catipovic, M. (2009). When adolescents tell us about suicide on the Internet, how do they say it to us? *Neuropsychiatrie de l'Enfance et de l'Adolescence, 57*, 128-135.

Powell, G. N., Butterfield, D. A., & Parent, J. D. (2002). Gender and managerial stereotypes: Have the times changed? *Journal of Management, 28*, 177-193.

Reinert, M. (1986). Un logiciel d'analyse lexicale: ALCESTE. *Les cahiers de l'Analyse des Données, 4*, 471–484.

Ridgeway, C.L. (2001). Gender, status and leadership. *Journal of Social Issues, 57*, 637-655.

Rollero, C., & De Piccoli, N. (2010). Place attachment, identification and environment perception: An empirical study. *Journal of Environmental Psychology, 30*, 198-205. Doi:10.1016/j.jenvp.2009.12.003.

Schein, V. E. (2001). A global look at psychological barriers to women's progress in management. *Journal of Social Issues, 57*, 675-688.

Sczesny, S. (2003). A closer look beneath the surface: Various facets of the think manager – think male stereotype. *Sex Roles, 49*, 353–363.

Sczesny, S., Bosak, J., Neff, D., & Schyns, B. (2004). Gender stereotypes and the attribution of leadership traits: A cross-cultural comparison. *Sex Roles, 51*, 631-645.

Smith, P. D., & Propst, D. B. (2001). Are topic-specific measures of socio-political control justified? Exploring the realm of citizen participation in natural resource decision making. *Journal of Community Psychology, 29*, 179-187.

Spence J. T., & Buckner, C. E. (2000). Instrumental and expressive traits, trait stereotypes, and sexist attitudes. *Psychology of Women Quarterly, 24*, 44-62.

Staerklé, C., & Clémence, A. (2004). Why people are committed to human rights and still tolerate their violation: A contextual analysis of the principle-application gap. *Social Justice Research, 17*, 389-406.

Swim, J. K., Mallett, R., Russo-Devosa, Y., & Stangor, C. (2005). Judgments of sexism: A comparison of the subtlety of sexism measures and sources of variability in judgments of sexism. *Psychology of Women Quarterly, 29*, 406-411.

Turner, J. C. (1987). A self-categorization theory. In J.C. Turner, M. A. Hogg, P., J. Oakes, S.D. Reicher, & M.S. Wetherell. (Eds.), *Rediscovering the social group: A self-categorization theory* (pp. 42-67). Oxford and New York: Blackwell.

Wasserman, B.D., & Weseley, A.J. (2009). ¿Qué? Quoi? Do languages with grammatical gender promote sexist attitudes? *Sex Roles, 61*, 634-643.

Willemsen, T.M. (2002). Gender typing of the successful manager – A stereotype reconsidered. *Sex Roles, 46,* 385-391.

Williams, J.E., & Best, D.L. (1990). *Measuring sex stereotypes. A multination study.* Newbury Park, CA: Sage.

Yang, S., Kadouri, A., Révah-Lévy, A., Mulvey, E. P., & Falissard, B. (2009). Doing time: A qualitative study of long-term incarceration and the impact of mental illness. *International Journal of Law and Psychiatry, 5*, 294-303.

Zimmerman, M. A., & Zahniser, J. H. (1991). Refinements of sphere-specific measures of perceived control: Development of a socio-political control scale. *Journal of Community Psychology, 19*, 189-204.

In: Perspectives in Leadership
Editor: Jerry D. VanVactor

ISBN: 978-1-62417-170-3
© 2013 Nova Science Publishers, Inc.

Chapter 10

THE CURT FLOOD EFFECT AND ITS IMPACT ON WORKPLACE LEADERSHIP

*Tony J. Gill**
Gill Advisors Inc.
The Corporate Real Estate, Department at Canadian
Tire Corporation, Toronto, Ontario, Canada

ABSTRACT

In 1969, Curt Flood, an outfielder with the St. Louis Cardinals, steadfastly refused a trade to the Philadelphia Phillies, violating the terms of baseball's Reserve Clause. Flood ended up sitting out the entire 1970 season, and he filed suit in court. Although he eventually lost in the U.S. Supreme Court, he set the wheels in motion for free agency in professional sports. The impact of Flood's stand reverberated into other realms as well, including the corporate world. As sports teams had to adjust to the newfound power of players, it also had to transform the manner in which they were effectively managed to maximize the productivity of the player, and the success of the organization. This paper argues that the effective coach or manager of a new-age athlete possesses leadership skills similar to those required managing workers in a knowledge economy.

Keywords: Knowledge economy, staff free agents, workplace free agency, leadership

INTRODUCTION

On an early May evening in the spring of 1967, George Armstrong, captain of the Toronto Maple Leafs, gingerly guided a loose puck into an empty net to seal the deal. The Leafs, an original charter team of the National Hockey League, had not only clinched the Stanley Cup for that season, but had just won their fourth league championship in that decade.

---

* Correspondence concerning this article should be directed to tony@gillinc.com. Tony Gill currently manages strategic projects for the Corporate Real Estate.

The victory firmly stamped the 'dynasty' label on the team for the success they achieved over that decade. Much of the credit for their victory went to their coach and general manager George "Punch" Imlach, who built the team from scratch. Despite Imlach's popularity with the press and the city of Toronto, he was anything but a kind and benevolent soul to his players.

Behind the veneer of a polished, media-savvy hockey executive was a relentlessly tough and unforgiving task master. Though players on those storied teams were embraced as heroes and media darlings by adoring fans, Imlach tended to treat them more like chattels that belonged to the hockey club. He demanded complete obedience from his players, letting them know that the mighty Maple Leaf was bigger than any one of them, and none of them were to dare fall out of line. If they did, there would be hell to pay. For instance, if a player believed he was entitled to more money at contact renewal time, Imlach would respond by using the media as an instrument to demean them until they bowed to his will [1]. If a star player sustained a career-threatening injury, the team felt no obligation to provide any type of compensation. The insurance policy for such a player was provided not in the form of a financial instrument, but often by moonlighting (the most famous example of this involved Maple Leaf defenseman Tim Horton, who partnered with an ex-police officer in starting a local doughnut shop, which today is the biggest fast-food chain in Canada) [2]. In short, players were assets owned by the team until such time they were deemed expendable. In retrospect, it seems that what Imlach controlled in those dynasty years of the Maple Leafs were a collection of abundantly talented, yet often demoralized, assets. The iron fist ways of the Toronto Maple Leafs would have long-term repercussions that still impact the team today.

While the Leafs were building their dynasty in Toronto, a swift centerfielder was making his mark with the St. Louis Cardinals. In fact in the same year the Leafs won their last cup, Curt Flood was putting together a career season. He had been a key cog in the Cardinals' success of the 1960's and by the '67 campaign had been named one of the team's co-captains, while leading the team in batting. The good times in St. Louis wouldn't last. Two years later, Flood's numbers were down, and he began squabbling with team management. By the end of the year, the Cardinals had had enough and decided to package Flood off in a trade to the Philadelphia Phillies.

Up until that moment, such a move would go unquestioned, as baseball's reserve clause effectively gave teams the right to own a player's rights until they were deemed expendable. Perhaps emboldened by the civil rights movement of the 60's (Flood was an African American from Texas), he rationalized that the reserve clause created an environment where players, regardless of compensation, were treated by owners no differently than slaves were treated by their masters. Curt Flood wanted no part of it, and balked at the trade. He sat out the entire 1970 season and filed a lawsuit against Major League Baseball, which would eventually find its way all the way to the Supreme Court. Although he eventually lost that battle, the genie had been released from the bottle.

It was just a few years later in 1974 when Jim "Catfish" Hunter, coming off championship years with the Oakland A's, decided to use his newfound power and sign a five-year $3.75 million dollar contract with the New York Yankees, which at the time was the richest contract ever offered to a baseball player. A tide of high profile free agent signings would follow in the 70's, including the Yankees' signing of slugger Reggie Jackson. It was only a matter of time before players associations in the NFL, NBA and NHL followed suit.

Curt Flood's dream of player emancipation, fuelled by the experiences of his past, was now complete.

What Flood had inadvertently done was not only set in motion a transformational change that would permanently impact the relationship between players and owners in baseball, but throughout professional sports. Gone was the unwritten rule that a player was considered the permanent property of a team – they now became partners with the organizations to whom they provided their services. The Flood impact was significant as it also set a precedent extending well beyond the boundaries of professional sports, and into a multitude of environments defined by an employer/employee relationship. This, in turn, imposed new challenges on the way in which managers would have to lead players (or in the case of the work world, their staff) who now had the freedom of mobility, not to mention a significant amount of power.

In fact there are startling parallels between what happened in professional sports and to large organizations within developed countries in the post-industrial world, as the notion of lifetime loyalty to one organization gave way to the concept of the free agent, regardless of whether that free agent took the form of a big league ballplayer, or a contemporary knowledge worker with a skill-set coveted by companies across a number of industries. Thus, valuable lessons in leading people who have the freedom to move if their work environment is sub-optimal can be gained by examining how successful professional sports teams maintained their edge even though players were bound to the teams for whom they plied their trade, only for the duration of their contracts. More significantly however, it might be argued that Curt Flood's one symbolic gesture of refusing a trade to the Phillies was the catalyst in redefining the qualifications required to lead in a contemporary workplace environment.

POWER DYNAMICS IN SPORTS REVERSED

When it became clear there was no going back and owners would never wield the same power over players they previously did, new realities began to dawn. Players who previously had to ply their skills to the whims of task masters like Maple Leaf coach Punch Imlach and others of his ilk no longer had to buy in. If they didn't feel comfortable in a particular situation, they now had the power to move (when their contracts expired) - often for a significantly more money. Thus, the only way in which a team had any realistic chance of keeping a prized player on a team was to not only treat them well, but to create an atmosphere where their players could be successful. What was once an environment where players were effectively told to only speak when spoken to, was now flipped on its head into one where player needs were placed at the forefront. The change was dramatic in its swiftness, however, it didn't occur without growing pains and miscalculations about how management should effectively engage with high-priced players.

For instance consider the New York Yankees approach to trying to maintain the upper hand on a new generation of rich ball players. Billy Martin played second base with the Yankees in the 50's and was always regarded as a tough, fiery competitor who would never back away from a good fight, including an incident that occurred in 1969 while managing the Minnesota Twins where he engaged in a bar fight with pitcher Dave Boswell that resulted in the latter needing twenty stitches [3]. When Yankees owner George Steinbrenner went on a spending spree to restore the team's glory in the 1970's, he knew he had to bring in a tough manager to cut through the egos that were flying high in the Yankees dressing room. Martin was his man, and for the most part, it was a successful choice, but one not completely devoid of a few bumps along the way.

On a nationally-televised game between the Yankees and the Red Sox, Martin was reaching his boiling point with the play of his high-priced outfielder Reggie Jackson. Jackson, he believed, was loafing in the outfield, so Martin pulled him from the game. When Jackson confronted Martin between innings in full view of the national TV audience, the two nearly came to blows. Incidents like this demonstrated that a new approach may have been required to better manage the egos of a cadre of new millionaires whose loyalty to a team was limited to the length of a contract.

As the landscape changed, it forced sports owners to re-evaluate the types of leaders required to skillfully manage players and in turn get the biggest return for their investment. The Yankees, now competing with the highest payroll in baseball including mega-stars like Reggie Jackson, initially thought the way to manage these newly minted millionaires was through intimidation. Over time, however, it became abundantly clear that the prerequisite to manage players demanded more than being a master tactician in the mould of Sparky Anderson, whose approach to managing was likened to a gruff, yet brilliant professor who had zero tolerance for deviance from a system he put into place. Anderson-like leaders didn't need to bother dealing with issues other than game strategy and ensuring all players fell into line. The new leader needed to be an individual with the ability to tame the egos, get buy-in from everyone and create an underlying sense of cohesion – a formula, if executed properly would result in winning.

In the bold new world of free agency, the power dynamic between player and coach is turned upside down. In the pre-Flood baseball era, it was relatively certain that a manager was earning more than his player, so purely from an ego standpoint, the manager held all the cards. In the bold new post-free agency world, a manager might now only be making a small fraction of what his star players are earning. Could an Imlach-like manager still be successful in such a power dynamic? Probably not. The prerequisite for success in such a situation was not intimidation but gently massaging egos and leading through example without completely bowing to the whims of the player. So in a very tangible way, the key success driver in such a situation is the ability to skillfully manage egos when the player now holds the psychological cards and be strong enough to gain buy-in to a team system from a player.

A NEW KIND OF LEADER ASSUMES CONTROL IN THE LOCKER ROOM

But the successful manager in this situation is not only responsible for the individual needs of a player, but needs to somehow create a formula for success that ultimately benefits the entire organization. Create a good locker room atmosphere where players feel a sense of cohesion and joint purpose, regardless of the wide disparity that exists in player salaries, and the first step to on-field success is achieved. If executed properly, this translates to higher revenues to owners. Skilled coaches and managers don't go unrecognized; in fact they attract skilled players into their fold. Consider the process associated with a free agent signing with a new team. That player's agent is very aware that the team his client signs with should have the type of coach or manager that will bring out the best in that player to assure that when it comes to contract renewal time, their market value is maximized. Successful players who command large salaries want to attach themselves to the types of leaders known not only for being a player's coach, but has a track record of winning. Welcome to the world of the new-age coach who brings an entirely different approach to the locker room. Consider the following examples.

As a former basketball player with the Lakers, Pat Riley entered the coaching ranks and led the Lakers and Heat to NBA championships. One of the Riley's biggest influences was Sun Tzu's *The Art of War*, an ancient treatise on military engagement that he applied to the approach he took to coaching. In addition to the respect he commanded from his players from his strategic approach to the game, he also won their respect by being perhaps the nattiest-dressed coach in all of professional sports. With his trade-marked coiffe of slicked-back hair, and his tailored Armani suits, he gained a tangible visible advantage over his competitors and literally seduced his players through his very appearance [4].

Terry Francona, the son of a former Major League ball player, was a utility player with the Montreal Expos, who supplemented the knowledge he first gained from his father, by becoming a student of the game while riding the bench for the Expos. It is significant to note that in addition to studying the game from his perch (usually next to his managers in Montreal), he also was a teammate of the first generation of millionaires including speedster Tim Raines, and future Hall of Famers Andre Dawson and Gary Carter. Playing and living with ballplayers who had reached stratospheric heights in terms of earning ability, Francona was able to learn what made these players tick and how to maintain their levels of motivation. Terry Francona would eventually become a manager himself, rising through the minor league ranks until he was appointed manager of the Boston Red Sox, where he would guide his team to two World Series Championships, the first since 1917, thus breaking the dreaded "Curse of the Bambino".

Bill Belichick perhaps most benefitted from being the son of a football coach at the U.S. Naval Academy. By carefully watching the disciplinary aspects of coaching football players who also serve in the military gave Belichick a unique perspective from which he could ply his trade. Needless to say, Belichick's Patriots are regarded as one of the most successful franchises in NFL history.

Ken Hitchcock never played professional hockey, but instead anonymously toiled for years as a junior hockey coach in Western Canada. He is said to have always been a master strategist, and surrounded himself with exceptional coaching staffs. He was also an avid Civil War buff, knowing the particulars of most battles and how they were won and lost [5]. When he got his big break and landed a head-coaching job in the NHL with the Dallas Stars, the heavy-set leader with a shock of white hair and a neatly-groomed moustache immediately connected with his players as a level-headed, avuncular tactician. Under Hitchcock's guidance, the Stars captured their first Stanley Cup in 1999.

In the brave new landscape of professional sports, the hard-liners of the past such as Anderson and Imlach gave way to a new generation of masterful (and indeed, sometimes quirky) tacticians such Riley, Francona, Belichick and Hitchcock, who combined a certain degree of "street cred" with an uncanny ability to connect to players. Leaders like this generally share certain characteristics that when combined have optimized a particular recipe for success. All seem to have developed the ability to draw something from deep inside to get the rich athletes they manage to buy into a system and remain committed to the collective; in this case, the team. Many of these managers seem to also share characteristics of somehow not being overbearing, immersing themselves into the work ethos expected from the players (In 2010, HBO's critically acclaimed show *24/7 Penguins/Capitals: Road to the NHL Winter Classic* poignantly depicted Penguins head coach Dan Bylsma participating with his players in exhausting skating drills, and giving enough room for his superstar players to share some of the leadership duties in the locker room, while still being able to make tough coaching decisions such as scratching players from the line-up, having them sent down to the minors or even traded).

The dynamics associated with leadership requirements stemming from the Flood effect are not unique to just professional sports. College sports has also had to adapt, as more and more student athletes who compete at large Division I schools are effectively playing in a quasi-professional environment. If a supremely gifted athlete can perform at a high level, even after a year or two, he can forsake the remaining years in college and declare himself eligible for the draft. This provides a challenge for the colleges who invest so much in recruiting. If that student has a positive experience at the school and puts off the decision to go to the pros, it can lead to a high degree of on-field success, which in turn drives alumni contributions and successful recruiting drives in the future (the key component required to build a successful, top-tier program). The system used to be set up in such a way that the student had to remain before being draft eligible, but the system is now structured in a very similar manner to free agency. Thus, the student athlete needs to have a very positive environment in which to succeed. The new-age coach has become the standard at large Division I schools, the one who is a players' guy and bonds with the team to get buy-in. Gone are the days where coaches like Joe Paterno, Bear Bryant, Bobby Knight and Woody Hayes ruled the roost, and at least as far as the latter two are concerned thought nothing about assaulting players (regardless of what side they played for) to assert their power.

CONNECTING SPORTS HISTORY TO THE CONTEMPORARY WORKPLACE: THE END OF THE COVENANT

Having analyzed some of the change dynamics associated with the impact of free agency on professional sports, the question now becomes to what degree are they applicable to changes that have occurred within other spheres of work? The variables are in fact remarkably similar in terms of timeline and the rules governing the relationship between employer and employee. Consider first the world that existed until changes started to take hold. America entered an era of unprecedented prosperity beginning at the end of the Second World War. Economic growth and industrial expansion fuelled a phenomenon that came to be known as consumerism. The goods sold to consumers were produced by large companies who hired industrial workers. Given the optimism that took hold in the 40's and 50's and the underlying belief that prosperity had no boundaries, an unwritten covenant was struck between employers and their employees which was simply that once an employee was hired, they were hired for life.

For the most part, this unwritten bond remained unchallenged until the winds of change began to blow. America's manufacturing engine began to stall, as it gradually lost its competitive advantage to foreign markets in what was becoming an increasingly global marketplace, the dynamics of which are apty described by Thomas Friedman in his 2005 book, *The World is Flat* [6]. Industrial towns such as Newark, Toledo and Buffalo began to experience the closure of large manufacturing plants which served as key economic drivers for their respective communities [7]. At the same time, the entire labor movement seemed to be losing ground in its bargaining power, a phenomenon best illustrated by President Reagan's decision to fire all federal air traffic controllers who went on strike to secure higher wages shortly after Reagan was inaugurated in 1981. Events such as this signalled the symbolic end of that unwritten code that was once assumed to be unassailable existed between employers and employees. As employers symbolically fired the first shot over the bow, breaking the jobs for life code, employees soon followed suit. Lifelong loyalty to a particular company became a vestige of a bye-gone era, as employees became increasingly motivated by employers who would operate the best employment package. This new approach was particularly characteristic of a new type of worker who instead of using his/her hands to manufacture products, used their mind to conduct what increasingly came to be known as knowledge work. This transforms working environments into not a white collar or blue collar workplace, but one noted urbanist Richard Florida refers to as the "no-collar" workplace [8].

As loyalty eroded on both sides, so too did the rules of engagement characterizing the relationship between employer and employee. If we continue our discussion concentrating on the work patterns associated with knowledge-based work (assuming manufacturing has reached a point of maturity), many of the dynamics we observed in an era of sports free agency find direct parallels in the contemporary workplace. Workers who perhaps detect their employers sense of loyalty towards them is based less on tenure and past performance as opposed to an approach constantly begging the question "what have you done for me lately?" become expedient, enter survival mode, and actually begin adopting the same attitude of emancipated ball players. This is the point where management needs to question whether the best approach to managing is taking a more authoritarian stance reminiscent of Punch Imlach or one requiring more of a delicate touch such as the one taken by Dan Bylsma.

WORKING PATTERNS AND ASSUMPTIONS FROM ANOTHER ERA AND THE NEED TO ADAPT

When an employee had little opportunity to move between companies (in fact, workers used to move to where the jobs were), management had a much greater ability to impose more of a rigid command and control structure within the organization. The personal attributes of a particular worker were not generally considered to be a huge consideration, given the fact that manufacturing work tended to be rote. If for any reason an employee could no longer continue with his duties, that position could be easily replaced. In such an environment, an employee has little leverage, and management practices become standardized.

This, in turn has a direct impact on the way in which management hierarchies are structured, and staff are managed. Consider, for instance an organization that utilizes a vertical management structure. Vertically-integrated organizations function in such a manner that large, macro ideas are articulated from the top, ownership or sponsorship of one of these ideas is then granted to a level below (perhaps at a VP level), who then delegate management of the components of that ideas to a level below that (and AVP or a Director), who then will leave the execution of these tasks to the two or more layers that fall below. The question becomes, how strategic does such an approach remain if the nature of the work is one where staff, particularly at lower levels, have exceptional skill sets, but are not given an opportunity to flourish given the restrictive nature of the tight hierarchy that has been imposed upon them? Remember, this is an era where bright workers have the ability to move between jobs, if they feel their full potential isn't being realized in environments restricting their opportunities to showcase their talents to those who have the ability to allow them to rise. In a sense, skilled knowledge workers such as those characterized above are essentially the corporate equivalents of free agents.

I first made the connection between knowledge workers and professional athletes through a personal experience in the early years of the internet era. Having completed an MBA in 1994, just about the time platforms like Netscape and AOL were first gaining traction, I knew I was ready to dive head-long into the corporate world, with a relatively high level of assurance that my newly-minted credentials would take me to a place where I could quickly rise through the corporate ranks. Only at this time, I still operated under the assumption that my career rise would occur in *one* place, going through the necessary machinations associated with a hierarchical organization. The thought of vertical movement energized by moving between companies was not even considered.

I landed that first job, but within a short time, maybe a year, I realized that the people charged with managing me, weren't fully tapping into my potential and putting me in situations that allowed me to put my best foot forward. In the institutional real estate world, there's an expression referred to as *highest and best use*, and this about assuring that a particular piece of real estate is developed in such a way that it yields the maximum amount of return. So erecting a small hardware store, for instance, at the busiest intersection in a large metropolitan area would not yield the same amount of financial return as say building a 50-storey luxury condominium, and would not constitute its highest and best use. I bring up this well-worn piece of real estate terminology, because it can directly be applied to how well-trained knowledge workers are put to use in the workplace. If they are given menial tasks that don't challenge them, their potential is not being put to its highest and best use. Thus, a worker in this situation can end up feeling bored and professionally unfulfilled.

This diversion ties back to the story of Curt Flood and the dawn of the internet era. After feeling as though my capabilities were not being maximized, a friend alerted me to a new website that seemed to be tailored just to me. It was called MBA Free Agents (since renamed MBA GlobalNet), and its value proposition was predicated upon the fact that given the value an MBA brought to the table, they could actually position themselves in the working world, the way pro ball players could in MLB, i.e. they could sign contracts with companies for set periods of time (literally, high paying contract work), work through the contract and then move to the next assignment.

MIDDLE MANAGEMENT ANGST

This single realization had a profound impact on the way in which I viewed workplaces. Especially in a time where the primary GDP drivers of the economy had shifted from a production-based orientation to one much more skewed toward knowledge work, I was sure that profound change would follow. For the most part, the events that have unfolded over the last 30 years (i.e. the decline of manufacturing and the subsequent rise of the knowledge economy) have been just about as significant as societal changes that occurred at the onset of the Industrial Revolution.

Despite the widespread changes that have occurred as a result of the rise of the knowledge economy, there are still companies who doggedly maintain the management structures that have remained in place for decades, and such an approach may lead to the erosion of competitive position in an increasingly competitive global environment. A large organization that relies upon an overly structured hierarchy in an environment where knowledge work is undertaken runs a risk of losing talented employees, if insecure middle managers stand in the way of their personal growth. I have found myself in the middle of large-scale change management initiatives within the organizations where I have worked involving the adoption of enterprise-wide mobility programs. Programs such as these transform the very way in which work is carried out by leveraging technology and innovative space design. It is done so by first identifying staff capable of carrying out their duties remotely. Such workers may adopt a 'hotelling' work arrangement, where they check into the office perhaps once or twice per week, and work from alternate locations (including home) on the other days. There are many advantages associated with adopting such a work culture, however there are those who despite whatever advantages may exist, will resist at every turn. More times than not, the resistance comes from middle managers insistent on taking more of a command and control approach to the way in which work.

This anecdote not only is presented to demonstrate where pockets of resistance may originate from, but to also provide a glimpse of where the future of work may reside and how managers in the future will be required to oversee teams. By its very nature, remote work requires a superior to manage staff remotely, thus the manner in which employees are evaluated will change. It will not be through intangible measures including the time spent at desk and charisma, but through a more quantitative strategy measuring the degree to which a set amount of deliverables have been accomplished. In this environment, the manager still needs to be able to create a platform that allows the contributions of remote workers to be recognized, so they, in turn will have their chance to rise within the ranks.

Perhaps the perceived complexity of this task is one that creates an understandable degree of uncertainty in the manager's mind, but an employee in a position of leadership should be motivated by the fact that if they are successful in adapting to this environment, they could very well find themselves in a pioneering position of management, as the concept of mobility is only now gaining traction. A manager who agrees to take on this challenge *and is successful* could in fact be likened to a pitcher who is a 20-game winner in the final year of a current contract. In other words, their free-agent potential is limitless.

Returning to the example of middle managers in rigidly-structured organizations resistant to change, we find that a majority of them insist that their staff need to be within their line of sight in order to be effective. As far as sight is concerned, in a knowledge economy, such insistence and adherence to an archaic way of managing might be considered myopic. Managers who cling to such beliefs often assume such a stance only because they might lack the confidence to give their staff more autonomy. As a group, middle managers could be characterized as the most anxious cogs within an organization, because they are the ones who have been chosen from the staff ranks to rise and depending on how they perform their duties, future promotions could come as well. The promise of future upward movement can at times create uncertainty and insecurity.

For instance, if they allow a bright and talented staff member to see the light of day (i.e. get an audience with managers at higher levels), they might get skittish about the possibility of that staff member rising more quickly. In a bygone era where employee mobility was unheard of, middle managers such as these held all the cards, and could easily afford to speak to staff in patronizing tones, and assert that because of their position they could assume they knew more than the workers lower in the organization's hierarchy. In the era of staff free-agency, such assumptions can have a detrimental effect due to the underlying cost of talent. The parallels to the plight of athletes in the era just before free agency is striking.

THE COST OF TALENT

In 1993, Derek Bok, the former President of Harvard wrote a book entitled *The Cost of Talent* which discussed how high excessively high compensation packages for executives was not in society's best interest, especially as highly-trained, and educated workers were required to drive a knowledge economy. He also pointed out that within professions where knowledge work was being applied, those people working in those environments considered the non-pecuniary aspects of professional work several times more valuable than compensation [9]. This is significant, as it suggests that a sub-optimal working environment could lead to a talented employee leaving, regardless of their compensation level. I applied what I read in the book to knowledge workers in today's economy. Large organizations often discount the value of a skilled employee, and may be paying little heed to the costs associated with talented employees. Organizations who hired skilled staff assume the cost not only of hiring, training and acclimatizing the new employee to the subtleties of an organization (a period of perhaps 6-12 months), where salary is considered a sunk cost, but also the cost gap associated with the high skill level of a departed employee and a somewhat less skilled replacement, resulting in a productivity gap. Indeed, to many contemporary knowledge-based organizations, it is the employees who often drive the creative soul of the companies they represent.

In an era where cost management is of tantamount concern (bear in mind organizations can sustain growth either by increasing revenues or managing costs), the subtleties associated with the cost of talent always need to be kept top of mind. The cost of talent, especially when that talent is free to leave the organization where he/she is not able to maximize their potential becomes a direct and tangible threat to an organization's bottom line. It is thus incumbent upon them to preserve and effectively manage what is perhaps an organization's greatest asset: its people. In order to fully understand the impact of the cost of talent, management needs to first remove itself from the assumptions from a previous time when the skill sets of staff could be easily replaced because the underlying nature of work was rote, and realize that in a world of knowledge work, employees bring a wide range of unique talents to the job that once lost are often difficult to replace.

WORKPLACE FREE AGENTS

Given the magnitude of changes that have unfolded as a result of a decline in collective bargaining and manufacturing and a rise in knowledge work, an entirely new set of demands are placed on those who are put in the position of managing people who now have the ability to move on a moment's notice.

In order to be successful, a contemporary manager first needs to understand how workgroups operate. In a hierarchical organization that was previously described, a middle manager needs to understand that it is their primary responsibility to delegate tasks to a team where ideas are packaged and delivered to the manager, who in turn makes final modifications to the information and presents it to others. Thus, the middle manager in this dynamic will naturally lose some control of the end-deliverable, as others are often putting those pieces together. A skittish manager tries to maintain control through micro-management, often creating information silos between team members, and storing all information bits in their vest pocket until it is presented as something they created in isolation. A staff member who gets wind of such an approach will be demoralized, thereby becoming a prime candidate to seek greener pastures elsewhere. A confident, forward-looking manager, on the other hand, embraces the skills of all the components involved in the process, doing whatever is required to ensure their staff remain as productive as possible and the deliverable is met. They also are sure to acknowledge the contribution of employees whose efforts were particularly noteworthy, without going so far as to be excessive in the amount of praise that is doled out. If this requires partaking in a tough skating drill with the players to keep them motivated and collectively bought into a system, then so be it.

This also requires the leader to step outside of themselves and look beyond the short term and think to themselves "If I am going to rise, I need to ensure that my best assets (brightest staff) remain motivated and happy enough to stick around to ensure I make my next move up the ladder". In short, this is the essence of contemporary leadership, and bears a striking similarity to the approach that must be taken by successful coaches in the free agent world of pro sports.

ANECDOTES FOR SUCCESS AND LESSONS LEARNED

Given the main points stressed in this chapter, perhaps the best way to conclude is to anecdotally describe some of the situations I have seen that separate great managers from all the rest, as well as other factors to consider as workplaces further evolve to a place where staff free-agency may perhaps rule the day.

I begin with an example of a former boss of mine named Stefan who ran the office real estate portfolio of a large Canadian bank. By their very nature, Canadian banks are very large, hierarchical and structured. It is an environment where employees are hand-picked to rise by those immediately above them. Thus, in most cases the recipe for success requires continuous face time, jockeying for visibility by continuously presenting minute accomplishments (often in ways similar to a toddler who seeks validation from a teacher for scoring well in a spelling test), and by developing an often superficial personal bond between superior and subordinate. Under such a dynamic, the actual quality of end-deliverables is often secondary. This was not the way Stefan managed his staff. It was all about empowering each member of the team by articulating a broad mandate that the entire group had to buy into. He encouraged collaboration (as opposed to creating information silos between his people), and during bi-weekly meetings demanded the team share their thoughts ensuring large deliverables were met. Collaboration thus significantly enhanced the end-deliverable.

He took input from others, synthesized the information and made decisions based on input from everyone. It should come as little surprise that perhaps Stefan's greatest attribute was that he was a highly-skilled listener, and possessed an exceedingly large amount of self-confidence (though in those bi-weekly meetings, it often escaped those who were in attendance that he ran the show, given his velvety approach to leadership). Like Ken Hitchcock, Stefan surrounded himself with good people who he regularly solicited input from. The example of Stefan shows that a skilled leader in a contemporary environment needs to arm his/her people with the skills, confidence and resources required for his people to advance. He never thought twice about showcasing his best and brightest people to executives many levels above, because at the end of the day, their attributes and skills were ultimately a reflection of himself. Stefan's approach and belief in the importance of collaboration is noted in Don Tapscott's *Grown Up Digital*, where Tapscott suggests that today's best and brightest seek innovative companies as employers and are constantly looking for innovative ways to collaborate. [10]

After moving to a large player in Canada's retailing space, I worked under the guidance of a forward-looking real estate strategist names Peter. Actually, when I joined, it was within another group, where I quickly found there was a significant gap between the requirements of the job and my particular skill set. During a two-hour meeting I attended in the place of my boss (from the group I was affiliated with when hired), I spoke exactly twice briefly commenting on some of the challenges associated with mobility. Peter, a Vice President attended that meeting, and solely based on my brief contributions to that forum, took my then boss aside and asked if I could switch to his team. After a brief period of negotiation, I made the move. Arriving in my new position, I found an environment characterized by personal empowerment, where all team members bought into a collective sense of purpose, while Peter along the sidelines gently moved us forward, encouraging us along the way to always put our best foot forward.

Like Stefan, Peter relished the opportunity of showcasing his people in front of those at higher levels, as this approach demonstrated to those above how skilled he was in sourcing talent, and getting the most from their contributions. Peter did something else too which turned out to be significant. He created a seamless succession plan that would kick in if any personnel changes took place. Because he had a tremendous amount of self-confidence, he sought those who either possessed a similar sense of confidence, or those who with a few tweaks could become their best under his leadership. When Peter ultimately left the organization to pursue another opportunity, his successor Kim assumed the reigns without missing a beat. As a leader Kim put her best employees in the spotlight and continually sought input from a staff she encouraged to be open as possible. All the while, Kim maintained a steadiness and level-headed approach that has moved the team along the same trajectory of success Peter had plotted out from the beginning. Together, Stefan, Peter and Kim are the best leaders I have ever worked for and possess all the characteristics of the types of coaches and managers who successfully lead teams in an era of free agency.

FORTY PLUS YEARS LATER …

In their 2011 ranking of the value of sports franchises, *Forbes* ranked the Toronto Maple Leafs as the most valuable team in the National Hockey League with a value of $521 million [11]. From the standpoint of pure history, the Leafs are a storied franchise with a multitude of fans across the country and beyond. The team has sold out each of their home games since the end of the Second World War. In addition to standard gate receipts, they command huge revenues through the sale of private boxes and licensing agreements tagged to their most expensive seats. The sale of merchandise for the team is a cash cow that keeps delivering huge revenues, so much so, the team has entered a phase where every few years, they will make subtle tweaks to their uniform to satisfy the insatiable appetite their fans have for new team jerseys (which can sell in the hundreds of dollars each). The Leafs even have their own cable channel that operates in continuous programming loops on a 7/24 basis to provide an easy fix for Leaf fans in the wee hours of the night as a more action-packed alternative to late night infomercials.

The Toronto Maple Leaf brand, it seems, is all powerful. Perhaps due to all the financial success the team has achieved, it has little incentive to change the way their core hockey operations are run. When interviewed on Leafs TV or any other outlet, the players seem to always refer to the honour associated with playing for such a storied franchise. Perhaps this provides a glimpse of the fact that the team still thrives on the glory of the past, and with it, management practices from a by-gone era. Coaches over the past forty plus years, have for the most part maintained a distance from players, and authoritarian approach to managing players. As the old saying goes, if it ain't broke, why fix it. Thus, it seems that the mighty Maple Leaf still rules the day.

It is notable then to take stock about how the team has fared since Curt Flood's career season in 1967. They have not won a Stanley Cup since. In fact, they currently have the league's longest futility streak, having gone the longest without winning the cup. All of the charter teams from the league – called The Original Six – have won at least one Stanley Cup since '67 except for the Maple Leafs. The Leafs also currently have another dubious distinction; in the spring of 2012, due to one of the worst slumps in franchise history that began in February they will miss the playoffs for the seventh consecutive year. It is a sad state of affairs in Leaf Nation, but somehow the revenues keep coming in. Given these facts, one might suggest the ghost of Punch Imlach has not quite left the building.

REFERENCES

The Big M: *The Life and Times of Frank Mahovlich* (2006). Retrieved from http://www.cbc.ca/lifeandtimes/mahovlich.html.

Melanie, S. (2000). Krispy Kreme vs. Tim Horton: Let us compare mythologies. *Saturday Night Magazine,* Issue Number 3953, p. 68-91.

Fighting Teamates (no date). *Sports Illustrated Vault.* Retrieved from http:// sportsillustrated. cnn.com/vault/gallery/featured/GAL1143695/18/18/index.htm.

Ashburner, S. (2008). *With his unique style and attitude, Pat Riley changed the game.* Retrieved from http://sportsillustrated.cnn.com/ 2008/writers/steve_aschburner/09/ 05/riley.hall.fame/index.html

Whyte, K. (2006). *Interview with Ken Hitchcock, The NHL Coach talks about dynamics in the dressing room, leadership, and making sacrifices.* Retrieved from http://www.macleans.ca/culture/sports/article.jsp? content=20061225_138474_138474

Friedman, T.L. (2005). *The world is flat: a brief history of the twenty-first century.* New York, NY: Farrar, Straus and Giroux

Kunstler, J.H. (1993). *The geography of nowhere: the rise and decline of America's man-made landscape.* New York, NY: Touchstone (division of Simon & Shuster Inc.)

Florida, R. (2002). *The Rise of the Creative Class.* New York, NY: Basic Books, A member of the Perseus Books Group

Bok, D. (1993). *The cost of talent: how executives and professionals are paid and how it affects America.* New York, NY: The Free Press, A Division of Simon & Shuster

Tapscott, D. (2009). *Grown up digital: how the net generation is changing the world.* New York, NY: McGraw Hill.

Ozanian, M. (2011). *The Business of Hockey: Team values hit all-time high.* Retrieved from http://www.forbes.com/sites/mikeozanian/2011/ 11/30/the-business-of-hockey/

In: Perspectives in Leadership
Editor: Jerry D. VanVactor

Chapter 11

ENTREPRENEURIAL LEADERSHIP: THE DARK SIDE REVISITED

William L. Tullar[*] and Dianne H. B. Welsh[†]

Department of Management, Bryan School of Business and Economics,
University of North Carolina at Greensboro, Greensboro, NC, US

ABSTRACT

As entrepreneurship has gained curriculum entries in schools of business, many have noted the contribution that entrepreneurs make to society in general and the economy in particular. Many view the entrepreneur as an economic hero, raising up new ventures against a growing tide of regulation, monopolistic big business, and foreign competition. Entrepreneurs come in all shapes and sizes and with considerable variation in personality traits. However, they are, as a class of people, susceptible to certain common problems. This is what we are calling the dark side of entrepreneurial leadership: characteristics that make the entrepreneur a leader, but that also have a significant downside both for the entrepreneur him/herself and for the other stakeholders in his/her business. This article examines these dark side characteristics and suggests how university curricula might mitigate them.

INTRODUCTION

Entrepreneurship in universities has gained popularity in the last twenty years from relatively few courses and programs to a great variety. Solomon now estimates there are 1,600 courses up from 1,200 courses in 2001 that were offered just in business schools (Katz, 2008; Weaver, Dickson, & Solomon, 2007). The first entrepreneurship course was offered in 1947 (Katz, 2008). The Global Consortium of Entrepreneurship Centers now has over two-

[*] # 366 Department of Business Administration, 516 Stirling Street, P.O. Box 26170, Bryan School of Business and Economics, University of North Carolina at Greensboro, Greensboro, NC 27402-1760; wltullar@uncg.edu; (336) 334-4526.
[†] dhwelsh@uncg.edu; (336) 256-8507; (336) 334-5580 Fax.

hundred universities as members (www.globalconsortiumentrepreneurshipcenters.org) and academic and professional organizations have grown in numbers and popularity. Clearly, academe has discovered entrepreneurship as a fertile area for teaching and research.

Economists, public policy experts, and the popular press have noted the contribution that entrepreneurs make to society in general and the economy in particular. Many view the entrepreneur as an economic hero, launching and growing new ventures against a growing plethora of regulations, monopolistic big businesses, and increasing foreign competition, while worldwide currency valuation has continued to affect import and export costs. Entrepreneurship has long been recognized as a driver of economic development (e.g., Acs, Desai, & Hessels 2008; Kuratko & Hodgetts, 1989). Meanwhile, economic and management literature also suggests that the leader's task is to "mobilize" the firm's resources and its creditors (Brazeal & Herbert, 1999; Howell & Higgins, 1990; Morris &Jones, 1999; Jelinek & Litterer, 1995). This view has led many of the business schools both in the U. S. and around the world to develop curriculum to further the skill sets of students to start businesses through internships, experiential learning, practicums, and real stores on campus. For example, The University of North Carolina at Greensboro (Welsh & Dragusin, 2011), Millikin University, and The University of Vermont all have student-run retail stores, ranging from printing businesses to art and first-hand products made by faculty, staff, and students. We hold that this is a laudable goal, and that business schools are helping their communities by producing a cadre of more successful entrepreneurs with real experience before they leave the college campus. However, the focus of this effort has been on cognitive, declarative functional knowledge: marketing, finance, legal issues, strategy, and management. While these functional areas of study are integral for entrepreneurs to know, we argue that self-knowledge is as important as cognitive declarative knowledge (Kickul, Maxfield, & Krueger 2005; Krueger, 2000; Krueger, 2007; Shepard, Maxfield, & Krueger, 2005)

The merging of the concepts of leadership and entrepreneurship begins with the Austrian Economist, Joseph Schumpeter. Schumpeter asserted that entrepreneurship was "a special case of the social phenomenon of leadership" (Schumpeter, 1928: 379). He also pointed out that the relationship between entrepreneurship and general leadership is a complex one, and that entrepreneurship is essentially a subcategory of leadership. It is not surprising then, that entrepreneurial leadership is a major topic in business schools. If entrepreneurs are generally considered to be leaders, then it is primarily the leadership characteristics of entrepreneurs that we focus on here.

Entrepreneurs are not more maladjusted than any other categorizations of people, although there are many a tale of entrepreneurs and their peculiarities. It is these stories that create legends around entrepreneurs. Despite cultural differences, entrepreneurs share many of the same motives and personality characteristics (Tullar, 2001). Welsh, Luthans, and Sommer (1993a, 1993b) found that managers and employees responded to positive psychology and management techniques despite major cultural differences between the U.S. and Russia. Entrepreneurs come in all shapes and sizes and with variation in personality traits. On the other hand, they are, as a class of people, susceptible to certain common problems. This is what we are calling the "dark side" of entrepreneurial leadership: characteristics that make the entrepreneur a leader, but that also have a significant downside both for the entrepreneur him/herself and for the other stakeholders in his/her business. These characteristics may have negative consequences.

Vision, self-assurance, desire for success, and optimism are all characteristics of good leaders and good entrepreneurs. However, consider the dark side of these characteristics: the vision may only be seen with rose colored glasses, the self-assurance may lead to an overestimate of personal ability, the desire for success may blind the entrepreneur to employee and personal problems, and even optimism can be unrealistic. We argue here that entrepreneurial leaders need to be aware of these possibilities so that they can pursue their strategies knowing these personal potential pitfalls. It is our purpose to explore these dark side characteristics with an eye to providing entrepreneurs with feedback during their formal education which will point them to the personal problems they are likely to encounter and by increasing their awareness of these pitfalls, hopefully to avoid falling prey to them.

We have divided these traits/characteristics into two classes: characteristics that are harmful to the entrepreneur him/herself and characteristics that are harmful to others. Let us examine the two classes briefly here, and then we will examine them in more detail later. Those characteristics that are harmful to the entrepreneur him/herself we include risk taking behavior, psychic risk, over-commitment, overwork, and stress. Those characteristics that are harmful to others include a great need for control, a sense of mistrust, an overriding desire for success, a need for applause, unrealistic optimism, splitting, acting out internal discomfort and chaos into the business, impulse control problems and generalized anxiety and depression. These characteristics are likely contributors to the very high failure rate of new businesses that start each year.

It is our intent to discuss each of these characteristics in detail showing how it negatively affects the entrepreneur, his/her personal relationships, and the stakeholders of his/her business. While we will employ the scientific literature as much as possible, for some characteristics we will speculate. This is necessary because some dark side characteristics have not had much research attention. We then propose some additions to collegiate business school curriculum to help students who are going to become entrepreneurs deal with their own dark side characteristics. In order for students to gain knowledge of these dark side characteristics, a complete entrepreneurial assessment should be done at the beginning of their program to measure the dark side characteristics of the individual. From this information, feedback can be given to the budding entrepreneur on what his/her dark side liabilities are. This could then be followed by personalized online training to assist the entrepreneur in overcoming these problems before they occur.

At the outset of our discussion, let us be clear that we are not proposing any sort of psychotherapy for business school curriculums. Some of the aspiring student entrepreneurs will probably need psychotherapy, but probably not any more than most other adult populations. What we propose is to help students gain self-insight so that they can see indications of the dark side problems coming before they actually have to deal with them on a personal basis in a crisis situation.

ENTREPRENEURIAL LEADERSHIP TRAITS HARMFUL TO SELF

Risk Taking Behavior

Financial Risk

Recent studies of risk taking behavior in Poland (Tyszka, Cieślik, Domurat, & Macko, 2011) and India (Mani, 2011) show that risk taking behavior is central to entrepreneurship, even entrepreneurship outside a first world context. The Tyszka, et al. (2011) study concluded that entrepreneur's reported more everyday risky investment activities than wage earners did. They interpreted this observation in terms of the necessity of entrepreneurs for risk-taking, rather than personal preference and liking shows that risk taking is the variable most related to entrepreneurial success. Since McClelland's *The Achieving Society* (1959) was published, it has been an axiom of entrepreneurial theory that entrepreneurs take *moderate* risks. Singh (1989) found that enterprises run by high risk takers generally showed either static or declining growth. But in sum, entrepreneurs are risk takers, and as such, some of the risks they take aren't successful. Most entrepreneurs experience failure before experiencing success. Gompers, Kovner, Lerner, and Scharfstein (2008) found that all else being equal, a successful entrepreneur who is venture-backed and takes her company public has a 30% greater chance of succeeding in her next venture. Comparably, first-time entrepreneurs would have an 18% chance of success and entrepreneurs who had previously failed would have a 20% chance of success. The reasons new ventures fail include product or market problems, financial difficulties, and managerial issues. Examples of product/market problems are poor timing, product design issues, inappropriate distribution strategies, unclear business definitions, overreliance on one customer, undercapitalization, assuming too much debt too early, and venture capital relationship problems. Managerial issues include misunderstanding of the team approach, including hiring not based on qualifications and poor relationships with the parent company and venture capitalists, and human resource issues, such as ego, employee-related concerns, and control issues (Bruno, Leidecker, & Harder, 1987; Karakaya & Kobu, 1994). Dominant problems in start-up ventures include sales/marketing (38 percent), obtaining external financing (17 percent), internal financial management (16 percent), general management (11 percent). In the growth stage, sales/marketing was the most dominant again (22 percent), internal financial management (21 percent), human resource management (17 percent), and general management (14 percent) (Terpstra & Olson, 1993).

Consider the case of Steve Jobs chronicled in the new book by Isaacson (2011). He took great risks when he launched innovative new products, relying solely on his own instincts rather than the usual crutches of focus groups and market research, which he shunned. Jobs had a number of humiliating failures but always rebounded: he sold few Apple I's, but the Apple II was a blockbuster. The Lisa failed, but the Macintosh eventually succeeded after a slow start (Deutschman, 2011). Here is the archetypal risk taker, but he was probably willing to assume higher levels of risk (both financial and personal) than most entrepreneurs. Hope played a great part in his success as well as other entrepreneurs (Welsh & Raven, 2011). His turbulent personal and professional relationships were also well chronicled and represent a good example of the dark side of an entrepreneur.

One of the problems of the risk propensity of entrepreneurs is that most studies consider risk propensity as a stable personality trait, thereby covering only one of the research streams on risk taking behavior. Hack & Lammers (2011) consider the situational factors of risk propensity as described by prospect theory. They showed that entrepreneurs set significantly higher reference points than do non-entrepreneurs. For a given distribution of outcomes, this behavior can explain a subsequent willingness to take on more risks.

Another of the issues of entrepreneur risk taking may be that entrepreneurs think about risks differently than non-entrepreneurs. That is, entrepreneurs see risks as an opportunity to be measured rather than the impossible. This shows how entrepreneurs think differently about risk in that their perception of what is risky is different than non-entrepreneurs. Their frame of understanding the problem is simply different.

In any case, depending on the environment and the venture that the entrepreneur proposes to engage in, risks may involve the loss of one's life savings, one's residence, and many other personal possessions as well as debt for an extended period of time. Indeed, studies have shown repeatedly that entrepreneurs often fail three or four times before they succeed. Yamakawa, Peng, & Deeds (2010, p. 284) observe that "under certain conditions, previous failures indeed stimulate entrepreneurs to learn, which, in turn, can foster new entrepreneurial growth." Even so, failure can be personally devastating, leading to depression for the entrepreneur and the stakeholders who believed in his/her venture. Risk taking leads to loss at least some of the time. A significant number of failures may undermine the entrepreneur's feelings of self-efficacy and thus delay or totally prevent any attempts to begin another venture.

Career Risk

This is a relatively under-researched aspect of entrepreneurial experience. However, it is clear that many entrepreneurs quit jobs at which they are performing satisfactorily to pursue their own business. Such a move produces a resume gap that is hard to explain away. If a person was intent on pursuing a career in B to B marketing, why did she drop out of corporate life for five years to pursue a business opportunity that ultimately failed? A resume gap and the ability to explain the failure of a business may make it very difficult for an entrepreneur to re-enter corporate life and get a coherent career started again (Will, 2009; Ireland, 2002).

A recent study of nurses who start their own business/practice was conducted in Finland. It provides a good example of how entrepreneurs view managers and management in general. The nurse entrepreneurs had a positive attitude towards management in general, but they had difficulties in adopting the manager's role. They also showed a lack of managerial assertiveness. Half of the respondents in the survey indicated that they had development needs and one-third indicated training needs in relation to necessary management skills. The authors concluded that nurses who are planning to start up their own practice or business need to have prior leadership experience and also need some form of management training (Sankelo & Åkerblad, 2008). It was clear from the study that nurse entrepreneurs have difficulty with management skills. When entrepreneurs take time out to run their own businesses, they are not developing skills that would give them a better career trajectory in a larger organizational setting. Indeed, authors have found that leadership traits do differ from managerial traits (DiPietro, Severt, Welsh, & Raven, 2008).

If we look at a person's potential career as having a certain monetary value, gaps in that career can be costly. That is, taking time out for a business that fails can be costly not just in losing one's life savings but also in creating a lower career trajectory since re-entry into the corporate world may have to be at a lower level than qualifications warrant.

Family Risk

Entrepreneurs are typically self-exploiters who throw themselves into their work with the idea that their success is going to be determined by the total number of hours per week they invest in their businesses. Since there are a fixed number of hours in a week, the hours spent at work cannot be spent attending to personal or family matters. However, in many cases married couples take on a business venture together. There is some research that shows some real advantages to this (Fielden & Davidson, 2005; Moore & Buttner, 1997). For instance, a study in Slovenia showed that the entrepreneur's spouse can significantly influence the family firm's network performance. The partner is part of all cliques formed in the entrepreneur's network. This allows the spouse to obtain information from different sources, and to influence the decision making process in the network. The spouse is also well connected with other network members, and is a major player in the information acquisition process for the enterprise. Since the spouse has a central position in the network's structure, this gives the power to reach other network members quicker. The spouse can reach other persons at shorter path distances than the entrepreneur. Therefore, the entrepreneur's spouse can be an important information provider for the entrepreneur's network. The most interesting contribution of this study is that the spouse can be as important as or even more important than the entrepreneur in the resource and information provision for the firm (Bratkovič, Antončič, & Ruzzier, 2009). This study raises another issue. While husband and wife are both throwing all their energies into making the family enterprise go, these energies cannot be directed to their children or their personal relationships.

A qualitative study done in Russia by Finnish academics expose some of the family problems woman entrepreneurs commonly encounter. The authors outline some of the strains on the family by having the wife and mother own and run her own business. Interestingly, they found that while four times as many Russian men as women claim to be entrepreneurs, when actual ownership statistics are checked, there are about as many women as men who own their own business. However, given Russian societal norms, women are supposed to be successful wives and mothers first and this can create role conflict (Salmenniemi, Karhunen, &Kosonen, 2011).

Social Risk

In this context, social risk can be defined as the risk of falling out of a given economic class into a lower economic class because of a business failure. When entrepreneurs invest all or a substantial portion of their life savings in a business, failure may temporarily or permanently cause the entrepreneur and his/her family to fall into a state of financial destitution. The family may lose the house, the cars, and financial assets. While this may seem less of a risk for single people, married individuals carry others with them down the Socioeconomic Status Scale. Bankruptcy often greatly strains marriage and family relationships may leave the family in difficult financial straits for some period of time. This may result in divorce and/or alienation from the children as well as financial embarrassment. Likewise, there are personal repercussions, such as loss of friends and social status. Homes, cars, and lifestyles may be casualties if the business goes Chapter 11.

Stress

Type A Behavior

Type A behavior is a known concomitant of stress. The theory of Type A and Type B behavior identifies the Type A individual as "ambitious, aggressive, business-like, controlling, highly competitive, preoccupied with his or her status, time-conscious, arrogant and tightly-wound" (Williams, 2001; p. 236). People with Type A personalities are often high-achieving "workaholics" who multi-task, push themselves with deadlines, and hate both delays and ambivalence. In *Type A Behavior: Its Diagnosis and Treatment* Friedman (1996) argues that Type A behavior demonstrates three major symptoms: free-floating hostility, which can be set off by even minor incidents; a strong sense of time urgency and thus impatience, and a competitive drive, which naturally causes stress. Of course, the free-floating hostility is more of a covert indicator while the time urgency and the competitive drive are much more overt. Criticism of the theory has arisen from researchers and statistical results have varied dramatically. It appears that only hostility is statistically significant as it relates to coronary problems. The other components of the Type A personality do not appear to be predictable (Williams, 2001).

While there are legitimate questions surrounding whether Type A behavior is a contributor to coronary disease, there is little doubt that time urgency and the competitive drive are associated with stress. Korotkov, et al. (2011) found that Type A individuals would engage in less preventive and more risk-related behaviors under high stress than Type B's. Six out of seven regression analyses results showed that Type A's engaged in less preventive, and more risk-related behaviors under high stress, than those who self-reported as Type B.

Félix Raya, Antonio Moriana, and Herruzo (2010) found that Type A behavior was strongly predictive of burnout. While their study involved teachers, not entrepreneurs, but they found high correlations between overload, hostility, and impatience with measures of stress. While more conclusive studies of entrepreneurs and Type A behavior remain to be done, it is clear that there is a relationship between the description of the Type A person and the description of the entrepreneur. The effects of high stress levels have well-known costs. One of those costs is burnout and its attendant career effects. Physical effects of stress on entrepreneurs have been reported to include back problems, indigestion, insomnia, or headaches (Akande, 1992; Buttner, 1992; Rabin, 1996).

Multi-Tasking

A well-known theory called the Single Channel of Attention explains why multi-tasking often doesn't work. Welford (1967) argued that the brain's central decision mechanism can deal with data from only one signal, or a group of signals, at one time. Data from a signal arriving during the reaction time to a previous signal must wait until the decision mechanism becomes free. It is possible that the decision mechanism can become occupied by feedback from responding movements so that delays may occur when a signal arrives during or shortly after the response to a previous signal. Restak (1994) concluded that multi-tasking is actually a myth - what is actually happening is sequential processing, or attending to stimuli in a round robin. Focus is probably really lost with multi-tasking.

A recent study examined the impact of multi-tasking with digital technologies while attempting to learn from real-time classroom lectures in a university setting. Four digitally-based multi-tasking activities (texting using a cell-phone, emailing, MSN messaging, and Facebook™) were compared to three control groups (paper-and-pencil note-taking, word-processing note-taking, and an electronic notepad usage) over three consecutive lectures. The study showed that participants using Facebook and MSN conditions performed worse than those in the paper-and-pencil use control group. Those participants who did not use any technologies in the lectures outperformed students who used some form of technology. Consistent with the Cognitive Bottleneck Theory of Attention (Welford, 1967), and contrary to popular beliefs, attempting to attend to lectures and engage digital technologies for off-task activities can have a detrimental impact on learning (Wood, et al., 2012). So multi-tasking may be a tactic used by many entrepreneurs, but it probably doesn't help them acquire or integrate information as fast as focused attention would.

On the other hand, given the ubiquitous nature of technology, decision making tasks typically involve using information technology in order to bring additional knowledge to bear on a given decision. Multi-tasking appears to have a detrimental effect on decision-making, but this has seemingly not had an effect on overall organizational productivity. There were steady increases in overall productivity for the first decade of the twenty-first century (Appelbaum, Marchionni, & Fernandez, 2008). What this points to is that there are strategies that can be used by decision makers to incorporate technology to make more information available for a given decision, and thus diminish (but not eliminate) the negative effects of multi-tasking on decision making. While multi-tasking is a characteristic of entrepreneurs, it is clear from the evidence from a variety of sources that multi-tasking produces inferior decisions and inferior attention and recall. Thus, this is a handicap that must entrepreneurs must be cognizant of and cope with.

Neglect of Everything but Work

Another frequently observed characteristic of entrepreneurs is that they throw themselves into their work with abandon and often do it to the exclusion of everything else. This typically leads to role conflict for the entrepreneur. Conflict can occur between family demands and family responsibilities, and between demands of work and need for recreation. Brady, Rodanovitch, & Rotunda (2008) collected data from university employees and Society for Human Resource Management (SHRM) members in a study on the relationship of workaholism on work-family conflict, job satisfaction, and perceptions of leisure time. They used two different measures of workaholism. The results indicated that greater scores on the Workaholic Risk Test were significantly related to higher levels of work-family conflict and lower levels of satisfaction with their time away from work. Clearly, neglect of everything but work tends to make other features of life less successful.

Indeed, there is a Nigerian study that showed that loneliness was one of the stressors encountered by entrepreneurs. Akande (1992) found that entrepreneurs often feel isolated, although an outside observer might believe they could not suffer from loneliness due to the many people who usually surround them. However, entrepreneurs are isolated from people they can confide in. Many of them said that it is difficult approaching anybody who can be a confident because the person who is most likely to understand your situation is probably competing with you. The entrepreneurs in this sample said that loneliness was their greatest problem (Akande, 1992).

Problems Dealing with People

Entrepreneurs commonly have problems relating to others. In a study of Turkish entrepreneurs, Benzing, Chu, & Kara (2009) found that entrepreneurs consider problems with employees as one of the greatest problems that they face. Entrepreneurial obsession with control over the work often strains relationships with employees. Micromanagement, common among the entrepreneur ranks, is often an alienating force with employees. Such alienation makes for a toxic atmosphere in the workplace and adds to stress and frustration for all parties.

ENTREPRENEURSHIP TRAITS POTENTIALLY HARMFUL TO OTHERS

The Overpowering Need for Control

Control is an interesting factor in the life of entrepreneurs. Many of them are drawn to entrepreneurial activity because it allows more control over life activities. Indeed, the European Commission advertises the various benefits of entrepreneurship, claiming that the entrepreneur's job allows one to be one's own boss. This means, according to the Commission almost unlimited decision autonomy, freedom of choice in the tasks to do, time schedule flexibility, utilization, and development of skills (European Commission, 2004b). Additionally, entrepreneurs themselves often mention the same aspects of their jobs when asked why they choose an entrepreneurial career (Birley & Westhead, 1994). The control appears to benefit entrepreneurs' health: Compared with other professions, entrepreneurs showed significantly lower overall somatic and mental morbidity, lower blood pressure, lower prevalence rates of hypertension, and somatoform disorders, as well as higher well-being and more favorable behavioral health indicators (Stephan & Roesler, 2010).

While control may be positive for the entrepreneur him/herself, it is less salutary for employees. In the original article pointing out the dark side of entrepreneurism, Kets de Vries (1986) presents an interesting clinical study that illustrates the point. He examined clinical data from 38 entrepreneurs. One of the overriding characteristics he found was an obsession with control. There are certainly adequate anecdotal tales from employees of entrepreneurial organizations of the nit picking and detail focus of their owner/boss. Ironically, what may produce health in the entrepreneur may produce illness in the employee. Kets de Vries (1985) notes excessive concern with details, which often makes them poor collaborators. The job characteristics model lists autonomy as the first of the five characteristics that determine the motivating potential of jobs (e.g. Hackman & Lawler, 1971). Employee autonomy and entrepreneur control are diametrically opposed. Thus, the entrepreneurial obsession with control may reduce the motivating potential of all the jobs that s/he supervises.

Sense of Mistrust

Entrepreneurs have a natural fear of competitors. They see themselves as being the lone sentinel looking out for the business. This, coupled with a natural tendency for splitting, makes entrepreneurs untrusting of employees, vendors, and even customers. As evidence for this, we find first that entrepreneurs are lower on the Big Five Dimension of Agreeableness (Zhao & Seibert, 2006) - - that is they don't necessarily go along to get along. However, we must also note that studies which examine Neuroticism of entrepreneurs have generally found that levels of Neuroticism are generally lower in entrepreneurial populations than they are in managerial ones.

Entrepreneurs are typically focusing on peotential competitors. The idea that an employee might leave them and join a competitor is always a tempting thought. We argue that the extreme environmental scanning and general mistrust make for sycophantic employees. The only ones who last understand that to survive you have to keep on the boss's good side.

Desire for Success

While entrepreneurs may have their own definition of what success is (see Kananui, Thomas, Sherman, Waters, & Gilea, 2010), since McClelland (1959) a desire for success is one of the distinguishing characteristics. Singh (1970; p. 121) argues that "An entrepreneur is driven by a desire to achieve success and not to fail in business. He is motivated with a 'three stage motivational intensity: wish fulfillment, push toward reality, and defense.'" Brandstätter (2010) observes that entrepreneurs are driven more by a vision of success than by a fear of failure. But success for whom? The entrepreneur is free to define success for him/herself, but how does that success fit with the aspirations of employees. For instance, in the work of Kananui, et. al (2010) the authors hold that spirituality plays a role in how entrepreneurs define success. Our view of that is that an entrepreneur's focus on his/her vision of success may or may not include employees' aspirations.

Need for Applause

Kets de Vries (1996) explains from a clinician's point of view the inner workings of the entrepreneurial mind. In the clinical case of a 44 year old entrepreneur, he observes that this case provides 'unique insight into the complex "inner theater" of the *entrepreneur*. A desire for *applause* ... appears to be (one of the) common themes in this man's thought. For this particular entrepreneur, running a business doesn't seem to be a rational process, but more 'a retrospective rationalizing of decisions.' In his earlier clinical studies, Kets de Vries (1986) mentions the need for applause as a common theme in the entrepreneur patients he discusses. He argues that entrepreneurs have a need to be seen as heroic and that the Genesis of this need is the reaction against the feeling of being insignificant.

Again the need for applause and approval may impel the entrepreneur to hire and keep those employees who will feed his/her ego. Rather than having a staff that reflects the brutal reality of the marketplace, an entrepreneur may greatly prefer staff that flatters and praises.

Unrealistic Optimism

A recent study (Casar, 2010) tests the hypothesis that entrepreneurs tend to be overly optimistic. Consistent with conjectures regarding entry into self-employment, he finds substantial overoptimism in nascent entrepreneurs' expectations. Entrepreneurs clearly overestimate the probability that their nascent activity will result in an ongoing business. Just as Kahneman & Tversky (1973) showed the irrationality people exercise in making decisions, Casar (2010) shows the irrational optimism entrepreneurs show as they view a potential venture.

Still worse, for those ventures that do manage to achieve operation, individuals overestimate the expected future sales and employment. Casar concludes: "the findings demonstrate a general forecasting bias in those entering venturing. An awareness of the biased forecasting tendencies of those in similar decision-making settings *may allow individuals considering future entrepreneurial activity to incorporate knowledge of overoptimism* into future expectations (Casar, 2010; p. 837, italics ours)."

Splitting

Splitting is a psychoanalytic defense mechanism. Kets de Vries (1985) suggests that splitting is a way of coping with the environment. Splitting is a tendency to see everything as either all good or all bad. The way splitters see themselves and others is dramatically oversimplified. Entrepreneurs may fail to appreciate or simply refuse to recognize the complexity and ambiguity inherent in human relationships. They tend to see things in extremes when dealing with other people, especially with their employees.

Projection

Projection is a psychological defense mechanism in which a person subconsciously denies his or her own attributes, thoughts, and emotions, which are then attributed to other people. Thus, projection entails imagining the belief that others originate those feelings. According to psychoanalytic theory, projection relieves anxiety by allowing the expression of unwanted unconscious impulses without letting the conscious mind admit them.

We all have a tendency to externalize internal problems: we "project" our discomforts and fears onto others. When we attribute a threat we feel to someone else or to an event, it becomes more manageable. However, if a person uses this as their dominant way to relieve stress, it can be problematic. One of the harmful effects of projection may include scapegoating. The entrepreneur may see him/herself as blameless for enterprise failures. Failures in this system of thought are always caused by incompetence or malign intention of others. The problem in entrepreneurial organizations where the entrepreneur projects in this manner is that the employees are the reason for the chaos and failure. Getting rid of one or more of them is then an attractive answer for current problems and chaos.

WHAT CAN BE DONE?

We have outlined a somewhat discouraging look at entrepreneurship in our narrative, but we want to assure our readers that we are enthusiastic proponents of entrepreneurial activity.

Clearly, for some subset of the population, running one's own business is the only satisfying career. Although we have just recounted a litany of problems entrepreneurs and their employees face, we believe that education is Aremedy for many of these ills. If entrepreneurs are cautioned ahead of time of the problems they are likely to encounter, they can avoid at least some of them.

We propose that entrepreneurial education should include individual assessment based on the categories we have advanced in this paper. Based on a foreknowledge of what their problems are likely to be, faculty can counsel entrepreneurs how they can best handle some of these problems. While we are not recommending therapy, we are recommending that the programs which teach entrepreneurship should do more than give cognitive declarative knowledge: they should help students to see their own prospective personal problems and weaknesses as potential impediments to their own success. This can be accomplished by a thorough assessment of these dark side factors not only in business schools, but across the curriculum. Research should identify valid and reliable measures of dark side factors that include motivational and personality constructs as well as content and knowledge skills. These must be developed to aid future entrepreneurs to be more successful and to allow entrepreneurship programs to add more value to the students they educate.

In addition, investigators have not generally sought to examine the "dark side" of entrepreneurship. We argue that research can shed light on the "dark side" of entrepreneurship and how these characteristics affect entrepreneurial firms. In so doing, it can facilitate better outcomes for new startups and fragile small businesses. If we are successful in adding this component in enough of the university and college entrepreneurship programs perhaps we can help lower the failure rate of new business start-ups. In any case, recognizing that there is a 'dark side' to entrepreneurship and helping future entrepreneurs to understand it is a worthy goal for both research and teaching.

REFERENCES

Acs, Z. J., Desai, S., & Hessels, J. (2008). Entrepreneurship, economic development and institutions. *Small Business Economics, 31*(3), 219-234.

Akande, A., & Obafemi, A. U. (1992). Coping with entrepreneurial stress: A Nigerian case study. *Leadership & Organization Development Journal, 13*(2), 27-32.

Appelbaum, S. H., Marchionni, & A., Fernandez, A. (2008).*The multi-tasking paradox: perceptions, problems and strategies. Management Decision, 46*(9), 1313-1325.

Benzing, C., Chu, H. M., & Kara, O. (2009).Entrepreneurs in Turkey: A factor analysis of motivations, success factors, and problems. *Journal of Small Business Management, 47*(1), 58-91.

Brady, B. R., Vodanovich, S. J., & Rotunda, R. (2008, July). The impact of workaholism on work-family conflict, job satisfaction, and perception of leisure activities. *Psychologist-Manager Journal, 11*(2), 241-263.

Bratkovič, T., Antončič, B., & Ruzzier, M.(2009). Managing global transitions. *International Research Journal, 7*(2), 171-190.

Brazeal, D.V. & Herbert, T.T. (1999). The genesis of entrepreneurship'. *Entrepreneurship Theory and Practice, 23*(3), 29-45.

Bruno, A.V., Leidecker, J.K., & Harder, J.W. (1987, March/April). Why firms fail. *Business Horizons*, 50-58.

Buttner, E.H. (1992, summer). Entrepreneurial stress: Is it hazardous to your health? *Journal of Managerial, 4*(2), 223-240.

Casar, G. (2010). Are individuals entering self-employment overly optimistic? An empirical test of plans and projections on nascent entrepreneur expectations. *Strategic Management Journal, 31*, 822-840.

DiPietro, R.B., Severt, D., Welsh, D.H.B., & Raven, P.V. (2008). Franchisee leadership traits v manager leadership traits: An exploratory study comparing hope, leadership, commitment, and service quality delivery. *International Entrepreneurship and Management Journal, 4*(1), 63-78.

Deutschman, A. (2011, September 5). Exit the king. *Newsweek, 158*(10), 30-34.

Felix, R., Moriana, A., Javier, J. H. (2010, June). *Ansiedad y Estres, 16*(1), 61-70.

Fielden, S. L., & Davidson, M. J. (Eds.) (2005). *International handbook of women and small business entrepreneurship.* London, UK: Edward Elgar.

Friedman, M. (Eds.) (1996). *Type A Behavior: Its diagnosis and treatment.* New York, NY: Plenum Press.

Gompers, P., Kovner, A., Lerner, J., & Scharfstein, D. (2008, July). *Performance persistence in entrepreneurship.* Unpublished manuscript, Harvard University.

Hack, A., & Lammers, F. (2011). Why are entrepreneurs more risk loving? On the reference dependencies of entrepreneurial decision making [Abstract]. *Proceedings of the NeuroPsychoEconomics Conference*, Munich, Germany, p. 35.

Hackman, J. R. & Lawler, E.E. (1971). Employee reactions to job characteristics. *Journal of Applied Psychology*, 55(3), 259-286.

Howell, J. M., & Higgins, C. A. (1990). Champions of technological innovation. *Administrative Science Quarterly*, 35(2), 317-341.

Ireland, S. (2002, July/August). *Searcher, 10*(7), 98-110.

Isaacson, W. (Ed.) (2011). *Steve Jobs.* New York, NY: Simon & Schuster.

Jelinek M., & Litterer, J. A. (1995). Toward entrepreneurial organizations: Meeting ambiguity with engagement. *Entrepreneurship Theory Practice, 19*(3), 137-56.

Karakaya, F. & Kobu, B. (1994, January). New product development process: An investigation of success and failure in high technology and non-high technology firms. *Journal of Business Venturing, 9*(1), 49-66.

Katz, J.A. (2008). Fully mature but not fully legitimate: A different perspective on the state of entrepreneurship education. *Journal of Small Business Management, 46*(4), 550-566.

Kickul, J., Maxfield, S., & Krueger, N.F. (2005). Measurement issues in entrepreneurship studies (editors' introduction), *New England Journal of Entrepreneurship, 8*(2), 5-7.

Korotkov, D., Perunovic, M., Claybourn, M., Fraser, I., Houlihan, M., Macdonald, & Korotkov, K. A. (2011, April). The Type B behavior pattern as a moderating variable of the relationship between stressor chronicity and health behavior. *Journal of Health Psychology, 16*(3), 397-409.

Krueger, N.F. (2000). The cognitive infrastructure of opportunity emergence. *Entrepreneurship Theory & Practice, 24*(3), 5-23.

Krueger, N.F. (2007). What Lies Beneath? The experiential essence of entrepreneurial thinking. *Entrepreneurship Theory & Practice, 31*(1), 123-138.

Kuratko, D. F., & Hodgetts, R. M. (Eds.) (1989). *Entrepreneurship: a contemporary approach.* Chicago, IL: Dryden Press.

Mani, C. (2011, September). Forces behind entrepreneurship of women- an economic study. *International Journal of Bio-Resource & Stress Management, 2*(3), 355-358.

Moore, D. P., & Buttner, E. H. (Eds.) (1997). *Women entrepreneurs: Moving beyond the glass ceiling.* New Delhi, India: Sage Publications.

Morris, Michael H., & Foard F. Jones. (1999). Entrepreneurship in established organizations: The case of the public sector. *Entrepreneurship Theory and Practice 24*(1), 71–91.

McClelland, D. C. (Eds.) (1961). *The achieving society.* Princeton, NJ: Van Nostrand.

Rabin, M.A. (1996, January). Stress, strain, and their moderators: An empirical comparison of entrepreneurs and managers. *Journal of Small Business Management, 34*(1), 46-58.

Restak, R. M. (Ed.) (1994). *Receptors.* New York, NY: Bantam Books.

Salmenniemi, S., Karhunen, P., & Kosonen, R. (2011, January). Between business and Byt: Experiences of women entrepreneurs in contemporary Russia. *Europe-Asia Studies, 63*(1), 77-98.

Sankelo, M., & Akerblad, L. (2008, October). Nurse entrepreneurs' attitudes to management, their adoption of the manager's role and managerial assertiveness. *Journal of Nursing Management, 16*(7), 829-836.

Schumpeter, J.A., (1928). The instability of capitalism. *Economic Journal,38*(151), 361-386.

Singh, N. (1970). Risk taking, achievement imagery, and personnel functions in entrepreneurship: A psychological analysis. *Indian Journal of Psychology, 45*(2), Jun, 1970. pp. 121-139.

Singh, S. (1989, December). Personality characteristics, work values, and life styles of fast- and slow-progressing small-scale industrial entrepreners. *Journal of Social Psychology, 129*(6), 801-806.

Shepherd, D.A. & Krueger, N.F. (2002). Entrepreneurial teams and social cognition: An intentions-based perspective. *Entrepreneurship Theory & Practice, special issue on cognition, 27*(2), 167-185.

Stephan, U. & Roesler, U. (2010). Health of entrepreneurs versus employees in a national representative sample. *Journal of Occupational and Organizational Psychology, 83,* 717–738.

Terpstra, D.E. & Olson, P.D. (1993, spring). Entrepreneurial start-up and growth: A classification of problems. *Entrepreneurship Theory &Practice, 17*(3), 5-20.

Tullar, W. L. (2001). Russian entrepreneurial motive patterns: A validation of the Miner Sentence Completion Scale in Russia. *International Journal of Applied Psychology, 21*(2), 422-435.

Tyszka, T., Cieślik, J., Domurat, A., & Macko, A. (2011, April). Motivation, self-efficacy, and risk attitudes among entrepreneurs during transition to a market economy. *Journal of Socio-Economics, 40* (2), 124-131.

Will, K.H. (2009, July 10). The mind gap. *Chronicle of Higher Education, 55*(41), A36.

Weaver, M., Dickson, P., & Solomon, G. (2007). Entrepreneurship and Education: What is known and not known about the links between education and entrepreneurial activity. *The Small Business Economy for Data Year 2005: A Report to the President.*

Welford, A.T. (1967). Single channel operation in the brain. *Acta Psychologica, 27,* 5-21.

Welsh, D.H.B. & Dragusin, M. (2011). Entrepreneurship education in higher education institutions as a requirement in building excellence in business: The case of The

University of North Carolina at Greensboro. *Forum Ware International Journal*, http://forumware.wu-wien.ac.at/, (in press).

Welsh, D.H.B., Luthans, F., & Sommer, S.M. (1993a, February). Managing Russian factory workers: The impact of U.S.-based behavioral and participative techniques. *Academy of Management Journal*, *36*(1), 58-79.

Welsh, D.H.B., Luthans, F., & Sommer, S.M. (1993b). Organizational behavior modification goes to Russia: Replicating an experimental analysis across cultures and tasks. *Journal of Organizational Behavior Management*, *13*(2), 15-35.

Welsh, D.H.B., & Raven, P.V. (2011). Hope among franchise leaders: Why hope has practical relevance to franchising-An exploratory study. *Canadian Journal of Administrative Sciences*, *28*(2), 134-142.

Washington, DC: U.S. Small Business Administration.

Williams, R. B. (2001). Hostility: Effects on health and the potential for successful behavioral approaches to prevention and treatment. In A. Baum, T. A. Revenson & J. E. Singer (Eds.), *Handbook of health psychology*. Mahwah, NJ: Erlbaum

Wood, E., Zivcakova, L., Gentile, P., Archer, K., De Pasquale, D., & Nosko, A. (2012, January). Examining the impact of off-task multi-tasking with technology on real-time classroom learning. *Computers & Education*, *58*(1), 365-374.

Yamakawa, Y., Peng, M.W., & Deeds, D.L. (2010, August). How does experience of previous entrepreneurial failure impact future entrepreneurship? *Proceedings of the Academy of Management Annual Meeting, Montréal, Canada*.

In: Perspectives in Leadership
Editor: Jerry D. VanVactor

Chapter 12

WISDOM FOR THE COMMON GOOD: TALES OF THREE LEADERS

Shih-ying Yang*

Department of Educational Policy and Administration,
National Chi Nan University, Puli, Nantou, Taiwan

ABSTRACT

The ultimate goal of wisdom is to promote a meaningful and satisfying life for everyone. When wisdom is manifested through leadership, it generates positive effects not only for the leader, but also for others at the individual, organizational, and societal level. Thus, if achieving a group goal fails to produce positive results that enhance a good life for both the leader and the members of the larger community, one has achieved something less than wisdom. This paper, which adopts a process view of wisdom and leadership, suggests that multiple levels of positive influence should be emphasized when we discuss wisdom in leadership. Specifically, this paper describes how three leaders manifested wisdom: Solomon, Confucius, and Mother Teresa, with an emphasis on the different levels of positive influence their leadership achieved. Suggestions about how to foster wisdom in leadership are provided at the end.

INTRODUCTION: RECONNECTING WISDOM TO LEADERSHIP

The connection between wisdom and leadership was made early in human civilization. In the hunting period, people followed those who were not only strong and mighty, but who also enabled many to live a good life, a satisfying and meaningful life (King and Napa, 1998). Leaders who fulfilled this requirement were deemed wise. Plato (1957) asserted that there is no leadership without wisdom. For Plato, the critical difference between leaders and followers is the ability and vision to move people toward wisdom. The ultimate criterion for outstanding leadership is not a specific competency, but rather wisdom, which guides and

* Emai: shihying@ncnu.edu.tw, Tel: +886-49-2910960#2761, 2856, Fax: +886-49-2917191

helps the human community to the Good. Similarly, ancient Confucian scholars believed that wisdom enables a sage to rule, influence, and gain respect from all people (*The Doctrine of The Mean*, 31, cited in Chan, 1963). Disciples followed Confucius because they believed he and his way could bring harmony to the world (*Confusius: The Analects*; *Great Learning*). Other traditions have held similar views. In the classical Hindu text *Vedanta*, for example, a person can be a true leader only after he or she understands cosmic truths and hence attains wisdom (Chakraborty, 1995).

Thus, leaders throughout history have attracted followers to their visions of a good life and to their ability to embody such a vision. People willingly follow those who have a clear vision of what a good life is, whose behavior embodies the way to live a good life, who have great compassion for their fellows, and who demonstrate great enthusiasm for the kind of world they believe people can create (Assmann, 1994). It is therefore not surprising that throughout human history, individuals who have been perceived as wise, such as Socrates, Confucius, the Buddha, and Jesus, have also been considered great leaders.

Since the industrial revolution, which initiated the formation of complex organizations and globalized institutions, leadership has often been linked to effectiveness and efficiency in promoting organizational performance and profits (Collins, 2001; Nahavandi, 2000). People often enter organizations first and foremost for paychecks and are introduced to leaders without knowing their personal vision. Even mission statements often emerge only after organizations have been established, rather than being the cause of their establishment. Leadership, therefore, tends to emphasize leaders' personalities, behaviors, styles of interaction with followers, and actions or decisions that move people to accomplish group goals, which are often for-profit and decided by others through top-down processes. Leadership is thus rarely considered in relation to wisdom (Srivastva and Cooperrider, 1998), which has as its aim the promotion of a good life for everyone (Baltes and Staudinger, 1993; Kekes, 1983; Sternberg, 1998; Yang, 2001, 2008a, 2008b).

As a result of this emphasis on organizational efficiency and profit, researchers generally disregard wisdom as an important factor in outstanding leadership (Beyer and Niño, 1998; Khandwalla, 1998). Until recently, wisdom has not been mentioned in scholarly discussions of leadership, nor has it been a predominant research topic (Kessler and Bailey, 2007). Professors of Business, as compared to professors in other fields, tend to consider wisdom as negatively related to creativity (Sternberg, 1985), which is more often perceived as the driving force of organizational performance (Yang, 2011a).

However, neglecting the value of wisdom in leadership can have very negative consequences (Bennis, 2007). As evidenced by recent events (e.g., global environmental and financial crises), the harmful effects of leaders' lack of wisdom often spill outside their organizations (Andrews, 2008 October 24; Chapman and Smith, 2011, November 3; Cooperrider and Srivastva, 1998). Many scholars predict that wisdom will succeed knowledge as the next key construct for leadership and management (Bierly, Kessler, and Christensen, 2000; Iredale, 2007; Small, 2004). If the past overemphasis on profit and efficiency has led to a lack of wisdom, then we need to work together to transform the present knowledge-based economy and society toward one that emphasizes wisdom.

As wisdom is now recognized as a research topic in social science fields, the time is ripe to reconsider the connection between leadership and wisdom. To begin, we must first understand what wisdom is, and then return to fundamentals by asking ourselves why wisdom is important for leadership in the first place.

UNDERSTANDING WISDOM

Terms for "wisdom" exist in many languages (Assmann, 1994, Birren and Fisher, 1990; Holliday and Chandler, 1986; Levitt, 1999; Takaharshi, 2000; Yang, 2001); it is therefore a concept important to members of different cultures. Wisdom can be seen as real-life phenomena that lead to success in handling human affairs or in the effort to live a good life (Ardelt, 1997; Baltes and Staudinger, 2000). People seek wisdom because it can promote a good life for everyone (Sternberg, 1998; Yang, 2008a).

Three views of wisdom have been widely discussed in the literature over the last 30 years. According to the first view, wisdom is defined as a personal quality or competency (Ardelt, 2003; Arlin, 1990; Erikson, 1982; Kramer, 2000; Labouvie-Vief, 1990; Malan and Kriger, 1998). From this perspective, such a quality or competency can help people understand paradoxical human nature and resolve developmental crises, and hence foster good living. According to the second view, wisdom is defined as a collective system of knowledge concerning the meaning and conduct of life (Baltes et al., 1995; Smith, Staudinger, and Baltes, 1994; Staudinger, et al., 1992). For scholars in this group, this collective system of knowledge can contribute to success in life planning, life management, and life review, and hence equips a person to live the best life possible. According to the third view, wisdom is defined as a real-life process that both requires and produces actions that generate positive influence (Küpers, 2007; McKenna, Rooney, and Boal, 2009; Sternberg, 2007; Walter, 1993; Yang, 2001, 2008a, 2008b, 2011a). For scholars who propose such a view, wisdom is manifested only if one's decision or action generates positive effects for oneself and others. Such manifestations of wisdom thus help many people to live a good life. This paper adopts this view of wisdom and the process model forms the basis for the discussion below.

A PROCESS VIEW OF WISDOM

A process view of wisdom is necessarily a broad view, since it treats wisdom as a real-life process encompassing many elements (Küpers, 2007; McKenna, Rooney, and Boal, 2009; Sternberg, 2007; Walter, 1993). Yang (2001, 2008a, 2008b, 2011a) defines wisdom as a process, and asserts that at least three core components work together to produce the phenomenon of wisdom: (1) the *cognitive integration* of what are ordinarily considered separate or conflicting systems to form a vision promoting a good life, (2) the actions that *embody* integrated thought or vision, and (3) the *positive effects* of these actions on the actor and others. Thus, wisdom is manifested when a person integrates ideas that are usually deemed disparate, puts the integrated thought into action, and embodies the thought in actions that generate positive effects for oneself as well as others (Yang, 2001, 2008a, 2008b, 2011a).

In real life, wisdom is rare, since it involves these three components, which seldom occur together. Moreover, it is by virtue of the positive effects generated by embodiment that wisdom is ultimately related to achieving the common good in the long run (Baltes et al., 1995; Sternberg, 2007; Yang, 2008a). Empirical results support this view of wisdom (Yang, 2008a, 2008b, 2011a).

Because thought and actions, and their influence on others are essential parts of leadership, the present study adopts Yang's process view of wisdom to explore the relationship between the manifestation of wisdom and leadership.

WHY WISDOM IS IMPORTANT TO LEADERSHIP

Leadership is "a process whereby an individual influences a group of individuals to achieve a common goal" (Northouse, 2004, p. 3). Leaders are those who often represent organizations and face unforeseen challenges. Leadership experience thus differs from managerial or administrative experience, in which one applies proven solutions to known problems (Day, 2000). When wisdom is manifested through leadership, it often generates pervasive positive effects (Küpers, 2007) and helps people to live a good life. Greater positive influence at multiple levels and on a larger scale can be expected if wisdom is manifested through leadership. It is precisely this potential for multi-level and widespread positive influences that makes wisdom important to leadership. Previous research on wisdom manifested through leadership has found that leaders nominated as wise persons tend to manifest wisdom by responding to societal needs. They often pursue self-defined missions, and tend to found new organizations when existing organizations are inadequate to solve social problems. They value the common good as much as organizational benefit (Yang, 2011a). Empirical results show that wisdom manifested through leadership often produces positive effects for members of an organization and for society in general.

WISDOM FOR THE COMMON GOOD: TALES OF THREE LEADERS

Manifestations of wisdom by three leaders throughout human history -- Solomon, Confucius, and Mother Teresa -- illustrate this point that wisdom contributes to the common good and promotes a good life for everyone.

Taking a process view of wisdom, manifestations of wisdom can occur over three different lengths of time. The first form of wisdom occurs on a relatively short timeline; it involves successfully resolving individual challenges and problems encountered in daily life. Solomon's judgment is one example of the first form of wisdom.

As the story goes, two prostitutes came to King Solomon quarreling over a young boy, each insisting she was the child's mother. Solomon offered to cut the living child in half and give each woman half of the child. One of the women begged Solomon not to kill the child, but instead to give him to the other woman. The second woman agreed to take half of the child. Solomon then gave his verdict: "Give the living baby to the first woman. Do not kill him; she is his mother. When all Israel heard the verdict the king had gave, they held the king in awe, because they saw that he had wisdom from God to administer justice" (I Kings 3: 16-28, New International Version). In this story, the baby boy's fate, its mother's well-being, Solomon's power, the morale of Israel, the relationship between the young king and the people, and even the spiritual relationship between the people and God, were all positively transformed by Solomon's verdict. King Solomon thus manifested wisdom by integrating the conflict between love and killing, embodying this insight in his action, and generating positive effects for himself and others.

The second form of wisdom can occur over a longer period of an individual's life; it involves successfully managing life challenges, so that the nature and content of subsequent life experiences is set in a positive direction, and leads to further self-actualization. This helps to progress toward living a good life, and facilitates future manifestations of wisdom.

Confucius' life management in his earlier years is one possible example of the second form of wisdom. Growing up fatherless in a poor family (Szuma Chien, 97 BC/1974), Confucius set his heart on learning at the age of fifteen; as a result, "at thirty I took my stand; at forty I came to be free from doubts; at fifty I understood the Decree of Heaven; at sixty my ears were attuned; at seventy I followed my heart's desire without violating the moral principles" (*Confucius: The Analects,* II: 4). As a result of such a personal example, people throughout generations have been moved to cultivate themselves to be better ethical beings.

Wisdom can also be manifested through the act of contributing to the common good over the long term, generating widespread positive influences not only for one's contemporaries, but also for future generations. This is a third form of wisdom and takes the longest time to manifest. The work of Mother Teresa exemplifies the third form of wisdom.

By integrating two seemingly conflict ideas -- serving God and serving the poor -- Mother Teresa embodied her idea by working and living in the slums to serve the poorest of the poor. As a result, her work generated widespread positive influence at multiple levels. First, her work generated positive effects for herself. Mother Teresa experienced a sense of accomplishment and enjoyment through her success in achieving what she set out to do: loving God through serving the poor. She stated, "[the] people of Calcutta have come to know and love the poor. No one is left to die on the road... People of all faiths come to share in the work. They say, 'Mother Teresa, we want to help.' They are willing to touch the poor" (Chawla, 1992, p. 195). Second, many people in Calcutta were helped and saved by Mother Teresa's work on a personal level. Third, Mother Teresa's actions generated social change. Tens of thousands people were helped by the new homes the Missionaries of Charity opened around the world: in Albania, Bangladesh, Brazil, Burundi, England, Ethiopia, the Gaza Strip, Japan, Jordan, Northern Ireland, Papua New Guinea, the Philippines, Panama, Portugal, Rome, Sicily, South Africa, USA, the USSR, Venezuela, Yemen, and many parts of Eastern Europe -- altogether 120 nations (Chawla, 1992). Finally, because of the efforts of Mother Teresa, many people's conceptions of a good life have been transformed. Bharati Mukherjee, a former student of the school run by the Sisters of Loreto, who grew up seeing Mother Teresa on the campus, noted such a transformation: "Lepers were a common sight all over India and in every part of Calcutta, but extending help beyond dropping a coin or two into their rag-wrapped stumps was not... Her care of lepers changed the mind of many Calcuttans. Young physician began to sign up as volunteers" (1999, June 14, p. 90). Chawla also notes that in 1992, when dwindling attendance was a matter of concern to the church, Mother Teresa's Missionaries of Charity numbered almost 4,000. Several hundred girls, often well-educated and from good families, anxiously awaited acceptance into a life of almost absurd hardship. Thus, Mother Teresa's actions generated positive effects for her contemporaries, as well as for future generations.

All the above examples illustrate that wisdom manifested by leaders can contribute to the common good. What these three leaders had in common is that they had visions of a good life. Solomon sought a right ruling over his people: "So give your servant a discerning heart to govern your people and to distinguish between right and wrong" (1 Kings 3:5, 7, 9-12). Confucius pursued peace and harmony in the world (*The Doctrine of the Mean; The Great Learning*). Mother Teresa wrote in her journal:

> I believe some are saying what use of working among this lowest of the low that [as] the great, the learned and the rich are ready to come, it is better to give full force to them. Yes, let them all do it. If the rich people can have the full service and devotion of so many nuns and priests, surely the poorest of the poor and the lowest of the low can have the love and devotion of us few – "the Slum Sister" they call me, and I am glad to be just that for His love and glory. (Chawla, 1992, p. 44)

These examples make clear that in real life, leadership in wisdom involves integrating disconnected or conflicting ideas to attain a vision of the good life, actions that embody this vision, and the positive effects of these actions for both oneself and others.

HOW CAN WE FOSTER WISDOM IN LEADERSHIP

Seen as a process, wisdom is not a quality that can be developed intrapersonally. However, leadership learning fosters opportunities and the ability to manifest wisdom. Different manifestations of wisdom require different abilities, and these abilities can be developed through real-life experiences. Here "real-life" refers to events in one's own life. Wisdom is manifested in real-life contexts (Baltes, Staudinger, Maercker, and Smith, 1995; Kramer, 2000; Sternberg, 2007; Yang, 2008b), and requires tacit knowledge, which can only be acquired through active participation in real-life events (Polanyi, 1958). Thus, abilities to manifest wisdom must also be developed in real-life situations.

Real-life challenges and problems are complex, long-term, dynamic, ambiguous, uncertain, and contradictory (Bigelow, 1992). They are often ill-structured, poorly defined, emotion- and value-laden, and may have contrasting timeframes that either take a long time to resolve (Jaques, 1979), or come as emergencies and crises allowing little time for response (Yang, 2008b). These challenges and problems are often tied to a person's personal goals, purpose in life, and may have significant consequences (Van Velsor and McCauley, 2004; Yang, 2008b). Real-life challenges and problems thus differ qualitatively from hypothetical cases presented in classrooms or examination settings, even if these are derived from actual events (Gragg, 1954).

Results of a previous study (Yang, 2011b) showed that leaders acquired multi-dimensional learning from their on-the-job experience over a two-year period. This finding corresponds to predictions made by many scholars (Bennis, 2007; Bigelow, 1992; Waters, 1980; Zaccaro, Kemp, and Bader, 2004). On-the- job leadership learning was found to include learning related to oneself, learning related to multiple perspectives and knowledge of contexts, learning related to leadership knowledge and skills, and learning related to long-term perspective and overall vision. Moreover, learning acquired through real-life leadership experience helped leaders develop a more inclusive and holistic perspective.

However, the results showed that even for higher educational leaders, for whom creating knowledge to promote the common good of mankind and improve the human condition is an important aim, the long-term perspective and vision they developed as a result of their leadership experience tend to relate more to themselves rather than to their organizations or the society as a whole. Although those leaders served extra-organizational communities, the study found little evidence they had developed inspiring and forward-moving visions of better institutions, customs, social relations, or better ways of living for others through their leadership experience.

When we compare this finding with the visions of Solomon, Confucius, Mother Teresa, and leaders who were nominated as wise persons (Yang, 2011a), it is reasonable to conclude that sensitivity to societal needs and visions of a good life may pre-date this process of leadership learning. Leadership learning simply enables leaders who already have strong motivation to fulfill their visions to refine or gain knowledge, skills, reasoning, viewpoints, and practices that are necessary to embody their visions.

A contrast between two leaders recorded in *The Records of the Grand Historian* (97 B.C./1974), one of the best known historical texts in ancient China, written by the famous historian Szuma Chien, shows the importance of such a vision:

> Chao Sheh was a very capable general in the State of Chao [the weakest state] in the Warring States Period of ancient China (403 B.C. - 221 B.C.), and he won battles in the most desperate situations. In 260 B.C. the mighty State of Chin [the state that unified China in 221 B.C.] attacked the State of Chao. At that time Chao Sheh had already died. The young king of Chao wanted to appoint Sheh's son Chao Kuo to be the commander....
>
> Chao Kuo [the son] had studied military science and discussed strategy since boyhood. He was confident that no one in the world was a match for him. Once he even bettered his father Chao Sheh in a discussion on strategy, yet he could not win his father's approval. When Chao Kuo's mother asked why, Chao Sheh [the father] said, "War is a matter of life and death, but he makes light of it. I can only hope he never becomes our state's commander. If he does, he will destroy our army."
>
> .... So when Chao Kuo [the son] was about to set out with his troops, his mother wrote to beg the king not to send him. Asked for her reasons, she replied, "When I was first married to his father [Sheh], who was then a commander, he offered food and wine to dozens of men at his meals and treated hundreds as his friends, distributing his gifts from Your Majesty and others of the royal house among his officers and friends. From the day he took the command he gave no further thought to family affairs. But as soon as Chao Kuo [her son] became a commander he put on such airs that none of his officers or men dare look him in the eye. When you give him gold and silk he takes it home, and he looks every day for cheap property to buy. How does he compare with his father, would you say? Since father and son are so different, I hope you will not send him."
>
> "Leave it to me," said the king. "I have made the decision." ... After Chao Kuo [the son] took over, he rescinded all previous orders and appointments. When General Pai Chi of the State of Chin learned of this, he made a surprise attack, feigned a retreat, cut Chao's supply route and split the army into two so that both officers and men lost heart. When his army was starving some forty days later, Chao Kuo led picked troops out to fight and the men of Chin shot and killed him. The State of Chao was defeated and hundreds of thousands of its men surrendered, only to be buried alive by the State of Chin. In all, the State of Chao lost four hundred and fifty thousand men [450,000]. (Chapter 81, trans. 1974)

This disastrous battle, which is known as the Battle of Changping (長平之戰), was considered a decisive battle that ultimately allowed the State of Chin to conquer and unify China decades later (http://en.wikipedia.org/wiki/Battle_of_Changping).

Chao Sheh [the father] is by no means a prominent figure in ancient Chinese history. His name was recorded in history probably because of his son's horrible failure. However, it is only by comparing his actions with the son's failure that we realize how many lives were saved by the father's efforts. What distinguishes the father from the son, or a good leader from a bad leader, was not knowledge, but their differing visions of the common good -- how much they cared about others' lives and deaths relatively to their own. The difference in their visions led to the subsequent difference in their approach to serving as generals, which in turn led to difference in the results of their leadership, particularly in times of emergency.

However, given that leadership experience aids in understanding the broader context of complex issues (Bierly et al., 2000) and allows leaders to see the connectedness of things (Bigelow, 1992), leadership learning should play a role in fostering grand and inspiring visions. Thus, we may also speculate that more than the two years used in the study are needed to develop visions for the common good. Gardner's (1993) study on creativity claims that it takes roughly ten years to develop a groundbreaking thought. An integrated and inspiring vision that promotes the common good may also need many years to develop.

Thus, many would argue that just as Rome wasn't built in a day, it probably took Chao Sheh many experiences in combat and long involvement in the military to understand that life and death are no light matters. So he developed a goal to be a good general, and his daily practice gained him further respect from his followers, and allowed him to give commands efficiently in times of emergency.

However, taking Chao Kuo as an example, how many chances would a bad leader be given to revise his vision? If self-interested leaders are indeed given chances to change their visions, the aforementioned finding suggests that more than two years are probably necessary to do so. Hence, a good leader, who has the potential to manifest wisdom, should have a vision of the common good to begin with. Only then could his or her vision be refined through his or her leadership experience.

Thus, two conclusions can be drawn from the above discussion. First, we should select leaders with visions of the common good. Best of all, we should recruit those who have a history of manifestations of wisdom to be leaders. Aspiring leaders should show their visions of the common good and demonstrate past manifestations of wisdom. Moreover, during the recruiting interview, potential organizational leaders should be asked to predict the effects their leadership may generate for themselves, for other individuals, and for the continuing development and prosperity of surrounding communities. These descriptions should be evaluated and used as a supplemental criterion.

Second, we should cultivate sensitivity to societal needs and visions of a good life in students, because many of them will become future leaders. Students should be encouraged to participate in activities that would increase their sensitivity to societal needs, examine their conceptions of a good life, reflect and make further cognitive integration to form visions that can promote a good life for many, take actions to realize these visions, and explore their success in generating positive influences through their actions.

To conclude, the world is in need of leaders who manifest wisdom that not only benefits organizations, but also serves the well-being of the society. All of us should participate in fostering wisdom in leadership that can transform leaders and organizations, and move the present knowledge-based economy and society toward a wisdom-based economy and society. Through our efforts to pursue wisdom, together we can live better lives and transform the world into a better place for us all to live.

REFERENCES

Andrews, E. L. (2008, October 24). Greenspan concedes error on regulation. *New York Times*. p. B1.

Ardelt, M. (1997). Wisdom and life satisfaction in old age. *Journal of Gerontology: Psychological Sciences, 52B*, 15-27.

Ardelt, M. (2003).Empirical assessment of a three-dimensional wisdom scale. *Research on Aging, 25*, 275-324.

Arlin, P. K. (1990). Wisdom: The art of problem finding. In R. J. Sternberg (Ed.), *Wisdom: Its nature, origins, and development* (pp. 230-243). New York: Cambridge University Press.

Assmann, A. (1994). Wholesome knowledge: Concepts of wisdom in a historical and cross-cultural perspective. In D. L. Featherman, R. M. Lerner, and M. Perlmutter (Eds.), *Life-span development and behavior* (Vol. 12, pp. 187–224). Hillsdale, NJ: Lawrence Erlbaum.

Baltes, P. B., and Staudinger, U. M. (1993). The search for a psychology of wisdom. *Current Directions in Psychological Science, 2*, 75-80.

Baltes, P. B., and Staudinger, U. M. (2000). Wisdom: A metaheuristic (pragmatic) to orchestrate mind and virtue toward excellence. *American Psychologist, 55*, 122-136.

Baltes, P. B., Staudinger, U. M., Maercker, A., and Smith, J. (1995). People nominated as wise: A comparative study of wisdom-related knowledge. *Psychology and Aging, 10*, 155-166.

Bennis, W. (2007). The challenges of leadership in the modern world: Introduction to the special issue. *American Psychologist, 62 (1)*, 2-5.

Beyer, J. M., and Niño, D. (1998).Facing the future: Backing courage with wisdom. In S. Srivastva and D. L. Cooperrider (Eds.), *Organizational wisdom and executive courage* (pp. 65-100). San Francisco: Jossey-Bass.

Bierly, P., Kessler, E., and Christensen, E. (2000). Organizational learning knowledge and wisdom. *Journal of Organization Change, 13 (6)*, 595-618.

Bigekow, J. (1992). Developing managerial wisdom. *Journal of Management Inquiry, 1(2)*, 143-153.

Birren, J. E., and Fisher, L. M. (1990). The elements of wisdom: Overview and integration. In R. J. Sternberg (Ed.), *Wisdom: Its nature, origins, and development* (pp. 317-332). New York: Cambridge University Press.

Chakraborty, S. K. (1995). Wisdom leadership: Leading self by the self. *Journal of Human Values, 1(2)*, 205-220.

Chan, W.-T. (1963). *A source book in Chinese philosophy (translated and compiled)*. Princeton, New Jersey: Princeton University Press.

Chan, W.-T. (1963). *Instructions for practical living and other Neo-Confucian writings by Wang Yang-ming (translated, with notes)*. New York: Columbia University Press.

Chapman, J., and Smith, G. (2011, November, 3). *Greek farce! PM calls off referendum and refuses to quit in eurozone fiasco*. Retrieved from http://www.dailymail.co.uk/news /article-2055872/Greece-bailout-crisis-George-Papandreou-calls-referendum-refuses-quit.html#ixzz1eKKPgRCJ.

Chawla, N. (1992). *Mother Teresa: The authorized biography*. Boston: Element Books Inc.

Collins, J. (2001). *Good to great.* New York: HarperBusiness.

Cooperrider, D., and Srivastva, S. (1998). An invitation to organizational wisdom and executive courage. In S. Srivastva and D. L. Cooperrider (Eds.), *Organizational wisdom and executive courage* (pp. 1-24). San Francisco: The New Lexington Press.

Day, D. (2000). Leadership development: A review in context. *Leadership Quarterly, 11,* 581-613.

Erikson, E. (1982). *The life cycle completed.* New York: W. W. Norton and Company.

Gardner, H. (1993). *Creating minds.* New York: Basic Books.

Gragg, C. I. (1954). Because wisdom can't be told. In M. P. McNair (Ed.), *The case method at the Harvard Business School.* New York: McGraw-Hill.

Holliday, S. G., and Chandler, M. J. (1986). Wisdom: explorations in adult competence. *Contributions to Human Development, 17,* 1-96.

Jaques, E. (1979). Taking time seriously in evaluating job. *Harvard Business Review, 57,* 124-132.

Kekes, J. (1983). Wisdom. *American Philosophical Quarterly, 20,* 277-286.

Kessler, E. H. and Bailey, J. R. (2007). Introduction: Understanding, applying, and developing organizational and managerial wisdom. In E. H. Kessler and J. R. Bailey (Eds.), *Handbook of organizational and managerial wisdom* (pp. xv-lxxiv). Los Angeles: Sage.

Khandwalla, P. N. (1998). Thorny glory: Toward organizational greatness. In S. Srivastva and D. L. Cooperrider (Eds.), *Organizational wisdom and executive courage* (pp. 157-204). San Francisco: The New Lexington Press.

King, L. A., & Napa, C. K. (1998). What makes life good? *Journal of Personality and Social Psychology, 75,* 156–165.

Kramer, D. A. (2000). Wisdom as a classical source of human strength: Conceptualization and empirical inquiry. *Journal of Social and Clinical Psychology, 19,* 83-101.

Küpers, W. M. (2007). Phenomenology and integral phenol-practice of wisdom in leadership and organization. *Social Epistemology, 21 (2),* 169-193.

Labouvie-Vief, G. (1990). Wisdom as integrated thought: historical and developmental perspectives. In R. J. Sternberg (Ed.), *Wisdom: Its nature, origins, and development* (pp. 52-86). New York: Cambridge University Press.

Levitt, B., and Lave, C. A. (1988). Organizational learning. *Annual Review of Sociology, 14,* 319-340.

Malan, L. C., and Kriger, M. P. (1998). Making sense of managerial wisdom. *Journal of Management Inquiry, 7 (3),* 242-251.

McKenna, B., Rooney, D., and Boal, K. (2009). Wisdom principles as a meta-theoretical basis for evaluating leadership. *Leadership Quarterly, 20,* 177-190.

Mukherjee, B. (1999, June 14). Mother Teresa. *Time 100: Heros and icons of the 20th century, 153 (23),* 88-90.

Nahavandi, A. (2000). *The art and science of leadership.* Upper Saddle River, NJ: Prentice Hall.

Northous, P. G. (2004). *Leadership: Theory and practice.* London: Sage.

Plato (1957). Theaetetus. In *Plato's theory of knowledge: The Theatetus and the Sophist of Plato* (F. M. Conford, Trans.) (pp. 445-470). New York: Bobbs-Merrill.

Polanyi, M. (1958). *Personal knowledge: towards a post-critical philosophy.* Chicago: The University of Chicago Press.

Smith, J., Staudinger, U. M, and Baltes, P. B. (1994). Occupational settings facilitating wisdom-related knowledge: The sample case of clinical psychologists. *Journal of Consulting and Clinical Psychology, 62(5),* 989-999.

Srivastva, S., and Cooperrider, D. L. (Eds.), (1998). *Organizational wisdom and executive courage.* San Francisco: The New Lexington Press.

Staudinger, U. M., Smith, J., and Baltes, P. B. (1992). Wisdom-related knowledge in a life review task: Age differences and the role of professional specialization. *Psychology and Aging, 7(2),* 271-281.

Sternberg, R. J. (1985). Implicit theories of intelligence, creativity, and wisdom. *Journal of Personality and Social Psychology, 49,* 607-627.

Sternberg, R. J. (1998). A balance theory of wisdom. *Review of General Psychology, 2,* 347-365.

Sternberg, R. J. (2007). A system model of leadership. *American Psychologist, 62 (1),* 34-42.

Szuma Chien (97 B.C./1974). *Records of the Historian.* (H. -Y. Yang and Y. Gladys, Trans.). Hong Kong: The Commercial Press.

Takahashi, M. (2000). Toward a culturally inclusive understanding of wisdom: Historical roots in the East and West. *International Journal of Aging and Human Development, 51,* 217-230.

Van Velsor, E. and McCauley, C. D. (2004). Our View of Leadership Development. In C. D. McCauley and E. Van Velsor (eds.), *The Center for Creative Leadership Handbook of Leadership Development (2nd ed.).* San Francisco: Jossey-Bass, 1-22.

Walter, G. A. (1993). Wisdom's critical requirement for scientific objectivity in organizational behavior research: Explicit reporting of research values. In R. T. Golembiewski (Ed.), *Handbook of organizational behavior* (pp. 491-524). New York: M. Dekker.

Waters, J. A. (1980). Managerial skill development. *Academy of Management Review, 5 (3),* 449-453.

Yang, S.-Y. (2001). Conceptions of wisdom among Taiwanese Chinese. *Journal of Cross-Cultural Psychology, 32,* 662-680.

Yang, S.-Y. (2008a). A process view of wisdom. *Journal of Adult Development, 15(2),* 62-75

Yang, S.-Y. (2008b). Real-life contextual manifestations of wisdom. *International Journal of Aging and Human Development, 67(4),* 273-303.

Yang, S.-Y. (2011a). Wisdom displayed through leadership: Exploring leadership-related wisdom. *The Leadership Quarterly, 22,* 616–632.

Yang, S.-Y. (2011b). Leadership learning and the manifestation of wisdom. Unpublished manuscript, National Chi Nan University. Puli: Taiwan.

Zaccaro, S. J., Kemp, C., and Bader, P. (2004). Leader traits and attributes. In J. Antonakis, A. T. Cianciolo, and R. J. Sternberg (Eds.), *The nature of leadership* (pp. 101-124). Thousand Oaks, CA: Sage.

In: Perspectives in Leadership
Editor: Jerry D. VanVactor

ISBN: 978-1-62417-170-3
© 2013 Nova Science Publishers, Inc.

Chapter 13

LEADERSHIP IS DEAD, LONG LIVE LEADERSHIP: A SHIFTING PARADIGM

Billy Brocato[1] and Gene L. Theodori[2]
[1]Sam Houston State University, Department
of Sociology, Huntsville, Texas, US
[2] Sam Houston State University, Huntsville, Texas, US

ABSTRACT

Twenty-first century management principles require a new theoretical paradigm that expands previous attempts to describe the efficacy of a more democratic, cooperative work environment. In this chapter, we advance a new theoretical orientation of leadership. We begin our discussion by highlighting the results of a content analysis of leadership studies from a 10-year period. The content analysis revealed that operational definitions tied to leadership traits have remained ambiguous and too rigid to adequately capture the changing dynamics of leader-worker behaviors. Following the content analysis, we develop a parsimonious measure constructed from the social, personal, and organizational heuristics used by subjects in group settings. We conclude our findings with a discussion for the need to use more robust operational constructs to meet leadership needs in the postmodern era.

INTRODUCTION

In this postmodern era, leadership has remained a significant topic of research interest (Erickson, Shaw, & Agabe, 2007; Guzman, 2007). In fact, a simple Google inquiry of "leaders" produced more than one billion hits. Similarly, a Google inquiry into "leadership" resulted in the return of 115 million hits. Most significant for our research, we found that common leadership symbols found in the arts and sciences have continued to describe leaders as powerful, knowledgeable, transactional, transformative, and charismatic persons who were

---

[1] 1901 Avenue I, Suite 270, Huntsville, Texas 77341; Phone: 936-294-4537;Email: BRB029@SHSU.EDU
[2] Email: GL002@SHSU.EDU

responsible for the social, moral, and economic progress of modern and pre-modern societies (Branden, 1969; Lundberg, 1988; Handy, 1991; Ackoff, 1999; Pillai, Schriesheim, & Williams, 1999; Cantor, 2001; Hoyt & Blascovich, 2003; Becker, 2007; Kouzes & Posner, 2009). Although there was a brief period following the end of the Cold War where management researchers began downplaying hierarchical work relations and stressed the democratization of the shop floor (Kilduff & Krackhardt, 2008), more recently, researchers have returned to traditional command-control scenarios.

Hoopes (2003) has argued that much of the social science research of the past several decades that focused on management developing social conscious or egalitarian political relationships on the shop floor has undermined management's legitimate power to maintain control and profitability. Other researchers have simply described such leadership models as pseudo-transformational (Barling & Turner, 2008). However, we argue that this narrative of the personal leader – the mythic hero that has grown over the centuries, culminating in the new modernist leader found in early twentieth century organizational research (Wren, 2005) – has become an outdated paradigm in a postmodern world (Harvey, 1990). As noted by Bolman and Deal (2008), modernist management research has focused on legitimating a hierarchical, authoritarian standard: managers as leaders and workers as simply followers. In our paper, we offer an alternative to Hoopes' thesis that marketplace success was dependent on management retaining authoritarian control of the work setting. We believe that twenty-first century management principles require a new theoretical paradigm that expands previous attempts to describe the efficacy of a more democratic, cooperative work environment. To that end, we will provide a meta-analysis of the management literature and propose a more robust measurement instrument.

A NEW LEADERSHIP PARADIGM

The popular television and film success of the science fiction novel, *Star Trek*, by the late Gene Roddenberry, resonates with inherited organizational and leadership symbols stemming from early Greek civilization to post-World War II American heroes (Cantor, 2001). Similarly, leadership studies have been little different in their sweep-of-history tales, illustrating modernist narratives that have reinforced classical models of rational, directed action in work settings instead of recognizing the nexus of social cooperation required in a postmodern world (Baudrillard, 1994; Travica, 1999; Gherardi, 2000; Gilovich & Griffin, 2002; Sillince, 2007; Albritton & Anderson, 2008; Herold, Fedor, Caldwell, & Liu, 2008; Hamel, 2009). These meta-narratives have demonstrated management perspectives tied to neoliberal ideologies, but they have not adequately considered workers' social frames or their cooperative roles in changing leadership settings (Berger & Luckman, 1966; Blumer, 1969; Kotlyar & Karakowsky, 2007). For example, the latest *Star Trek: The Next Generation* television series and movies, stands in sharp contrast with prior *Star Trek* themes.

Earlier *Star Trek* plots illustrated a single-edged requirement of the successful leader and his team. Captain Kirk, an emotional but strong hero-leader and his compliment, the logical, all-too-rational Mr. Spock, were able to solve any puzzle and escape any predicament because Kirk was best at exploiting his crew's capabilities through charismatic appeals. Spock remained Kirk's underling but offered tactical options with evidentiary probabilities. The modernist symmetry was unavoidably clear. Fast-forward several decades and *Star Trek: The Next Generation* symbolic gestures (Collins, 2010) harken to significant shifts in leadership behaviors. Capt. Picard represented the transformational and transactional leader – relying on his crew to make their decisions as he ensured their career path development. Additionally, the introduction of an android, Mr. Data, sets in motion an expanded social role in comparison to Kirk's Mr. Spock. Data continued Spock's evidentiary logic and close relationship to Capt. Kirk as demonstrated in the earlier *Star Trek* series, but extended Spock's failure to fully appreciate the Enlightenment project. Spock relied on pure reason, logic as reflected in the early history of the Enlightenment period. But Data demonstrated an adaptation to the Enlightenment promise by insisting on the superiority of human will over instrumental reason by insisting on his moral right to pursue his existential quest for authenticity.

In the case of the latest *Star Trek* galactic encounters, leadership and subordinate relationships no longer reflected or mirrored rigid modernist chains of command. Instead, leadership decision-making emerged through the crew's interactions and situational contexts. This is an important distinction because *Star Trek: The Next Generation* remained grounded in the modernist paradigm, but conversely demonstrated that leadership and group roles had expanded to include mutual trust (Covey, 2006). Capt. Picard was not a mythic hero; instead, he represented a shift in the behavior of leadership: decision making as an emergent, cooperative endeavor among the crew and its executive officers. Our comparison of the different leadership models as illustrated by the two very different *Star Trek* television series highlights a significant shift in leadership models. In the following sections, we will pursue the schemas linked to socio-cultural emergent behaviors in group settings.

Borrowing liberally from decision-making and social realist theorists, we propose that group behavioral responses grow more complex as actors require increased information when faced with increased uncertainty (Kahneman & Tversky, 1982; 2000; Kahneman & Frederick, 2002; Gilovich, Griffin, & Kahneman, 2002; Archer, 2007). This is a critical critique of the traditional leader-worker dyad paradigm often used given the complexities associated with organizational cooperation in global markets and in expanded computer-mediated, virtual work places. To that end, in the next sections we will propose a shift in the theoretical orientation of leadership. Additionally, we will demonstrate from a content analysis of leadership studies over a 10-year period that operational definitions tied to leadership traits have remained ambiguous and too rigid to adequately capture the changing dynamics of leader-worker behaviors (Brocato & Theodori, 2011). Following the content analysis, we develop a parsimonious measure constructed from the social, personal, and organizational heuristics used by subjects in group settings. We conclude our findings with a discussion for the need to use more robust operational constructs to meet leadership needs in the postmodern era. This is a significant departure from traditional behavioral models because as Margaret Archer (2007) has written, "Through such a *modus vivendi*, a subject's personal identity is aligned with her social identity. Arriving at that alignment is a dialectical process, generally requiring adjustment and accommodation between the personal and the social." (p. 88).

THEORY

Our expanded leadership model proposes a synthesis of organizational power constructs, interpersonal, and intrapersonal belief structures that contextualize the heuristic biases people use in their daily social settings (Herman, 2010). Similar to Foucault's (1986) *epistrophē eis heauton*, where actors' intentions were inferred from cooperative or uncooperative contexts (Brocato & Gold, 2010) and Archer's (2007) work on the social consequences linked to reflexivity, we have triangulated the social-cultural, the psychological, and the organizational structures to better reflect the emergent conditions that give rise to successful or unsuccessful group behaviors. Returning to the pioneering work of Kaheman and Tversky on decision-making heuristics, we accept their premise that individual cognitive schemas that give rise to successful and fallible judgments were grounded in personal and group experiences similar to the construct of *habitus* (Bourdieu, 1998). Moreover, relying on Margaret Archer's description of reflexivity to ensure actors remained at-once autonomous and socially constructed, we believe the subjective powers of self-dialogue, of reflexivity in contemporary settings have surpassed earlier social understandings tied to the beginning of the modernity project (Gadamer, 1976). Just as Archer's theoretical orientation has bridged intersubjectivity, social context, and emergent behaviors with the added structure of meaningful agency, we concur that people in an organizational setting are active, not passive agents. Leaders and workers are "'active agents', people who can exercise some governance in their own lives, as opposed to 'passive agents' to who things simply happen" (2007: 6). Archer has proposed that "The subjective powers of reflexivity mediate the role that objective structural or cultural powers play in influencing social action and are thus indispensable to explaining social outcomes" (2007: 5). We are not concerned with the mediating influence as much as the significance this plays in the emergence of behaviors that lead to cooperative or uncooperative behaviors.

Archer's thesis, unique as it may appear, resembles the work of George Herbert Mead's social psychology and Jürgen Habermas' theory of communicative action. Mead (1934) and Habermas (1987) have located the self through its relations with the *other*, but that relationship is not a simple causal stimulus-response scheme or simply perceptual recognition of an object that exists separate from us. Mead demonstrated that the exchange, use, and understanding implicit in the act of human communication provided the foundation of social cooperation. As noted by Mead (1934:225), "The individual enters as such into his own experience only as an object, not as subject; and he can enter as an object only on the basis of social relations and interaction, only by means of his experiential transactions with other individuals in an organized social environment." We conclude that consciousness is an emergent condition and has more to say about social situations than mapping individual behavioral traits. Similarly, Habermas detailed human communicative rationales within an individual's life worlds, explicating the cooperative through intentionality structured "between an external world, which has consolidated into an institutional reality, and an inner world of spontaneous experiences, which come out not through norm-conforming actions but only through communicative self-preservation" (Habermas, 1987: 42).

As a simple explanation of the heuristics adopted for this paper, Table 1 provides an illustration of the complexity of decision making for any task *T* (Frith, 2007). In this scenario,

Table 1. Decision Frame - Hypothetical Leadership Perception Model

Description	A. Minimal Account: General Perception	B. Tropical Account: Personal Perception/Bias	C. Comprehensive Account: Perceptions Constructed/Context-Oriented
Perceptual Referents and conginitive framing	1. Refers to basic associative differences; minimal is simply what the brain registers what the eye beholds	1. Refers to differences perceived as in learned biases; topical is the brain computing similar/dissimilar images the eye has beheld	1. Refers to differences perceived as in learned biases modified in terms of context; comprehensive is the mind providing a probalistic but contextual inference that what the eye is behold is comparable to past circumstances and outcomes
Framing	2. Example: A recent published leadership study lists the following traits as important to company success. How confident are you with this finding?	2. Example: Please rank leadership traits you believe are essential at your company. How confident are you that your rankings on this scale approximate what others in your work group would choose?	2. Example: Please rank the following leadership traits as you believe are displayed at your company. How close do you think your rankings match your company's leadership?
Responses in %	25%, 40%, 60%, 75%, 100%	25%, 40%, 60%, 75%, 100%	25%, 40%, 60%, 75%, 100%
Hypotheses	$A_1 < B_1$; $A_1 < C_1$	$B_1 < A_1$; $B_1 <$ or $= C_1$	$C_1 < A_1$; $C_1 >$ or $= B_1$

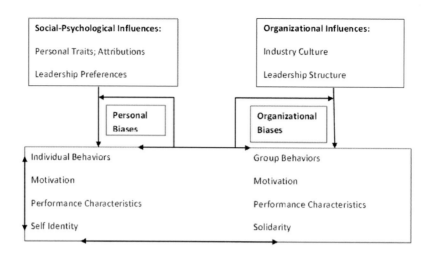

Figure 1. Casual Diagram of Personality and Organizational Theory of Group Performance.

employees hypothetically are presented with three different contexts linked to an organizational setting. In each case, employees rely on different cognitive states to frame their general perception of leadership and their consequent behavior. In the simplest frame (T^1), employees would simply make a judgment based on their personal knowledge (agree or disagree). The second frame (T^2) requires employees to make a judgment and compare their decision in light of another group's likely judgment (how similar do *we* match up). The third frame (T^3) asks employees to judge external organizational leadership symbols with their leaders' behaviors (comparative judgment predicated on *external perceptions linked to context and personal bias*). Simply, Table 1 demonstrates the triangulated context linked to decision making that results in an emergent, interactive, and evolving structure of beliefs and intentional actions (Law, 2004; Konorti, 2008). We further illustrate our theory of the dynamic quality of socio-cultural heuristics and decision making for actors in Figure 1. To test our theory, we proceeded to complete a content analysis of a sample of leadership research findings published in refereed journals.

METHODOLOGY & FINDINGS

To categorize the empirical reliability of leadership traits research found in management studies, we relied on a content analysis of transformational and charismatic concepts found in a convenience sample of leadership research from a search of the EBSCO library database (Table 2). The terms leadership, transformational, and charismatic were selected for the database search. To minimize research time, published management articles were selected from refereed journals from 1998 to 2008. The content analysis examined articles for specific descriptions and definitions related to transformational and charismatic leadership traits (see Tichy & Devanna, 1986, for expanded descriptions of the transformational leader). Secondly, we examined the researchers' *stated* studies' intentions. For example, we reviewed researchers' survey questions to determine whether the survey was asking workers to rate their satisfaction with organizational goals or with their manager. This is an important distinction because the researchers' intention *framed* the subjects' responses.

Table 2. Transformational and Charismatic Traits: A Literature Review Summary

Transformational	Charismatic	Context	Studies
	Interpersonal strength; magnetism; forceful; fair	Group perceptions, behaviors; exchange relationship	Scott, Colquitt, & Zapata-Phelan, 2007
	Symbolic, meaningful behavior; idealist; visionary; emotionally influential	Organizational fit of subordinates; organizational behaviors internalized	Huang, Cheng, & Chou, 2005
Idealized influence moral values; communication; role clarity; mission clarity	Ethical, moral consequences;	Affect subordinate behaviors; organizational effectiveness	Hinkin & Tracey, 1999
	Affects followers perceptions; emotional intelligence, social intelligence, social control; emotional displays	Organizational change management	Grover, 2005
	Affect attitudes; visionary; emotionally-charged; emotional contagion	Job satisfaction; group performance	Erez, Misangyi, Johnson, LePine, & Halverson, 2008
	Manipulative; ethical; visionary; empowerment	Organizational outcomes; change management	Tuomo, 2006
Idealized influence; inspirational; intellectual; vision, trust; respect; risk-taker; integrity; role model	(considered a component of transformational)	Organization-directed; group performance	Stone, Russell, & Patterson, 2004
Motivational; trust; charismatic; inspirational; intellectual, individualized communication	(Charisma as a central concept)	Exchange-oriented; organizational behaviors; group commitment	Pillai, Schriesheim, & Williams, 1999
Affective; motivational; empowering, role model, visionary; change agent; moral	Self-confident; visionary; unconventional; self-interested	Group performance needs; affect worker attitudes	McLaurin & Al Amri, 2008
Affect beliefs; values, visionary; moral; empowering	(Charismatic used synonymously)	Follower change commitment; change management	Herold, Fedor, Caldwell, & Liu, 2008
Role model; inspirational; intellectual; individualized consideration		Affect group performance; organizational commitment	Felfe & Schyns, 2004

Table 2. (Continued)

Transformational	Charismatic	Context	Studies
Empowering, intellectual; vision-sharing; role model; mediator; emotionally intelligent	(Considered a component of transformational)	Relationship management; group performance in multicultural settings	Manning, 2003
Motivational; moral; social contagion; goal-directed; communicative	(Mainly a component of transformational, but case sensitive)	Organizational change process; inducing change in followers	Pawar, 2003
Authority; visionary; role model; problem solving; inspirational; idealism; risk taker; networking	(Considered a component of transformational)	Organizational power; legitimate authority; affect changes in followers; environment sensitive	Pearce, et al., 2003
Visionary, role model; inspirational; individualized consideration		Motivate change in others; aware of subordinates emotional/perceptions	Hautala, 2005
Stimulates; motivates; selfless; individualized consideration; inspirational; visionary; intellectual; fairness	(Idealized influences)	Organizational change; subordinate perceptions; group performance	Wu, Neubert, & Xiang 2007
Trustworthy; inspirational; communicative; intellectual; individual consideration; trust; moral; empowering, respect	(Considered a component of transformational, but can be different based on context)	Group satisfaction; group performance as a subjective assessment by followers; subordinates identify with group	Hoyt & Blascovich, 2003

Charismatic and Transformational Constructs

Table 2 provides a description of the categories charismatic, transformational, and the context of the research question posed in the selected studies. Additionally, the operational definitions provided in the published articles relied on traditional descriptors of charismatic leaders. In this case, charismatic leaders possessed an interpersonal force that exerted considerable influence on subjects' willingness to act (Den Hartog, De Hoogh, & Keegan, 2007). Other authors associated charismatic with emotional states that provoked uplifting and inspirational states in workers – something akin to fostering spiritual experiences in followers (Katz & Kahn, 1978). Researchers also described charismatic leaders as those who possess artful styles, promoting group cohesion and commitment to leadership goals, and at times exerting influences that were contradictory to social norms (Huang, et. al., 2005; Choi, 2006; Tuomo, 2006; Miller, 2007; Gehrke, 2008; Walumbwa, Avolio, & Zhu, 2008). There was also the work of Grover (2005), Hinkin and Tracey (1999), and Huang, et al, (2005) where charismatic qualities or traits portend some improvement in an organization through the willingness of followers to act on the wishes of their leader(s). Cranti and Bateman (2000) described charismatic traits as those that "include prosocial assertiveness, creativity and innovation, risk-seeking propensity, self-confidence, social sensitivity, and sensitivity to follower needs" (p. 64).

The content analysis revealed that researchers used a continuum of adjectives to illustrate transformational leadership traits and behaviors. Manning described transformational leaders with a psychological strength that could empower group members and display "intellectual openness, vision-sharing, and role modeling" (2003: 21). Correlatively, Pillai, Schriesheim, and Williams ascribed leaders with a power to foster "organizational citizenship behaviors", including "conscientiousness, sportsmanship, civic virtue, courtesy, and altruism" (1999: 898). Other researchers described transformational leadership traits on a continuum that included a servant leader dimension. Stone, Russell, and Patterson (2003) explained the difference between transformational and a servant leader as one of leadership "focus", where transformational leaders were more concerned with "organizational objectives" and servant leaders focused more on "the people who are followers" (p. 349).

Hoyt and Blascovich (2003) investigated transformational and transactional leadership traits in face-to-face and virtual experimental settings. Their findings also demonstrated transactional leaders were more organizationally focused, whereas transformational leaders were charismatic, inspirational, intellectually stimulating, innovative, and "demonstrated a high degree of personal concern for the followers' needs" (p. 680). Hautala (2005) examined the effects transformational leaders would have on employee ratings of superiors, employing the same operationalization of transactional versus transformational leadership continuum as previously mentioned. Subjects were asked to rate an exchange-oriented leader or a leader who raised "subordinates' motivation" (p.85). The researcher operationalized transformational in this case as a leader's ability to motivate subordinates "to see deeper purposes behind their work, thus making them achieve high levels of (self) motivation" (p. 85).

The content analysis showed that researchers' operational definitions of charismatic, transformational, or transactional were guided by the stated research purpose. This was considered a logical fallacy. In a majority of cases reviewed, researchers were looking for organizational alignment based on leaders and workers relationships in a given organizational setting. In a second stage to the content analysis, we looked at *how* the researchers' intent helped to contextualize the meaning they had ascribed to leadership traits. For example, leaders and subordinates with similar extraversion and introversion traits resulted in positive correlations with organizational goals, group alignment, and reports of satisfaction with a group's managers. We believe this finding was spurious because there was not a discussion that would explain extraneous conditions affecting the hypothesized independent and dependent variables.

Wu, Neubert, and Yi (2007) examined the effect transformational leaders' actions had on employee perceptions regarding justice or fairness in a large Chinese company. Similar to prior researchers' efforts, they operationalized transformational leadership on four dimensions: "individualized consideration, inspirational motivation, idealized influence (trait and behavior), and intellectual stimulation" (p. 331). These four dimensions helped them explain transformational behavior, but they also found that subordinates perceptions were mediated based on "informational justice and interpersonal justice" (p. 338). This implied that where employees perceived their work group as cohesive, they were more in line with change management strategies. Of particular importance, however, is their conclusion: "A significant contribution of this study is that it uncovers the followers' psychological processes by which transformational leadership yields its influence on employees" (p. 345). However, this study did not control for the extraneous conditions that would have led workers to perceive their mangers as just individuals.

We in no way want to downplay the significance of the employee profiles, correlations, or related alignment strategies discussed in the literature we reviewed, but we do question the effectiveness attributed to a leader who possesses a continuously expanded behavioral trait in each of these representative studies. Although researchers have associated transformational or charismatic traits with historical figures, their findings failed to demonstrate which came first. Is it a leader's charismatic persona, workers' psychological susceptibility or malleability, or the interactive consequences that lead to successful goal attainment in a historically structured context? For example, Figure 2 demonstrates the use of particular leadership traits from the current management literature linked to a specified group effect. However, in reality, the traits remain a simple projection of a researcher's conceptual ideation of a leadership trait and do not provide explanatory power in regards to group performance or outcome.

Essentially, a researcher could replace each conceptualized trait with another concept and replicate the associational links demonstrated in Figure 2. For example, replace transactional with flex work schedule; replace transformational with group-led actions; and replace charismatic with company-sponsored weekly outings. In these cases, have researchers discovered or uncovered what relationship between management and workers best fits group performance? We think not. Mechanistic or simple associational properties were not explanatory simply because a researcher attributes properties in an ambiguous context – a decidedly *ad hoc* approach to hypothesis generation and testing. Instead, the responsibility of researchers was to consider those phenomena that signify behaviors and locate the referents in an objective space that would uncover emergent conditions such as group performance, willingness, or cooperation. In either case, the answer should result in an investigation into past researchers' underlying biases that guided their leader-follower research and how they operationalized behavioral traits when describing group communication, interaction, acceptance, and performance (Green, 2007; Kearney, 2008).

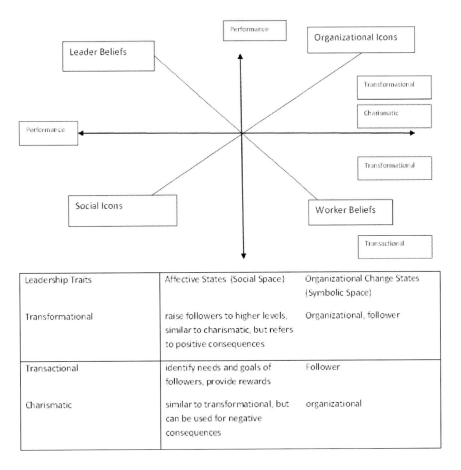

Figure 2. Leader-Worker Habitus.

Assembling the Social

Following the initial content analysis, the second stage revealed a substantial list of adjectives used to describe transformational and charismatic traits as presented in Table 3. As shown in Table 3, two additional categories were added to synthesize the adjectives attached to the two leadership traits under study. The categories fell upon a continuum of interpersonal or internalized meanings and organizational, external meanings that we constructed using a grounded theory approach (Glaser & Strauss, 1967). What we identified was an organizational habitus of stakeholders' leadership perceptions that informed a socio-cultural structure made up of five distinctive intrapersonal and five interpersonal referents linked to an organizational manger's conduct (Table 3). For example, from the 13 adjectives that were used in studies to determine the effectiveness of managers to align workers with organizational purposes, we developed five general characteristics of an organizational leader: a leader's expert knowledge, ownership in the company, prestige in the industry, professional networking capability, and ability to garner trust. Additionally, there were 10 adjectives used in the literature consistently to describe charismatic traits. These definitions in turn were reduced to five intrapersonal icons that represented implied social and organizational biases subjects used in their decision-making (as shown in Table 4).

Table 3. Organizational & Social Beliefs Linkage to Transformational and Charismatic Traits

	Organizational/Power Icons	Self/Group Icons
Transformational/Transactional	1. Interpersonal skills aimed at organizational effectiveness 2. Multicultural competencies 3. Transcend role through internal drive to succeed 4. Powerful, 5. Knowledgeable 6. Respected 7. Change agents 8. Courageous 9. Empower others 10. Ethical 11. Life-long learners 12. Emotional Intelligence 13. Visionaries	1. Expert 2. Ownership 3. Prestige 4. Networking 5. Trust
Charismatic	1. Manipulative 2. Culture-specific 3. Trustworthy 4. Multiple Intelligences 5. Unconventional behavior 6. Visionaries/Idealists 7. Self-confident 8. High self esteem 9. Motivated by power 10. High Performers	1. Leads by example 2. Team focused 3. Fair, just, ethical 4. Emotional intelligence 5. Innovative

Table 4. Organizational Power and Individual Leadership Traits Matrix

Subject Ranks: Organizational/Intrapersonal Power Icons	1. Expert 2. Ownership 3. Prestige 4. Networking 5. Trust	Subject Ranks:
= Weighted Values	= Overall Score	= Weighted Values
Subject Ranks Interpersonal Power Icons	1. Leads by example 2. Team focused 3. Fair, just, ethical 4. Emotional intelligence 5. Innovative	Subject Ranks:

Having developed a social-organizational continuum proved an important theoretical model because it highlighted the underlying heuristics that informed leaders and followers emergent behaviors in a work setting (Gherardi, 2000). Essentially, the five organizational icons and five individual icons we identified mirrored organizational and cultural structures of conduct and normative behavior that led to expectations among group members (Gibbard, 1990; Merton, 1996). From this habitus of conduct and decision-making, we developed a weighted evaluation matrix as given in Table 5 to further illustrate the interconnectedness of the structural and cultural factors informing stakeholders' perceptions and interactions. We believe the weighted score evaluation matrix would prove parsimonious and empirically feasible instead of using correlational studies that appeared to reify a leader's ephemeral traits or simply workers' self-reports about management effectiveness.

Table 5. Weighted Evaluation Matrix: Organizational Power and Individual Leadership Traits

Leadership Solution Evaluation Matrix		Power Traits (perceived)					
		Expert Knowledge	Ownership Power	Prestige power	Network Power	Trustworthy Power	Final Rating
Relative Importance (Weight)==>		3	1	5	4	2	
Primary CANDIDATE TRAITS							
Psychometric Self-Report	A) Leads by Example	5	1	5	1	5	**3.67**
	B) Team-focused	1	2	2	5	3	**2.73**
	C) Fair & Just; ethical	3	3	4	3	2	**3.20**
	D) Emotional Intelligence	4	5	3	4	4	**3.73**
	E) Innovative	2	4	1	2	1	**1.67**
AVATAR TRAITS							
							-
							-
							-

Using our postmodern behavioral matrix (as illustrated in Table 5) in place of contemporary modernist models would eliminate ambivalent leadership traits as causal paths of analysis and provide researchers a more robust analytical tool to examine socially and culturally structured biases that result in successful or unsuccessful group performances. Table 5 would provide researchers with a reliable and valid measurement of each subject's heuristic biases that result in their alignment with other stakeholders. For example, a manger could rank order each socio-cultural item with a specific organizational icon. This would result in a weighted score that demonstrates their alignment along the organizational habitus structure. A worker or a board of directors could fill out the evaluation matrix questionnaire and compare their scores with their other stakeholders. Thus, the scores would allow for direct comparison on structural or organizational characteristics and their personal, socio-cultural beliefs. This would allow for stakeholders to examine where their differences lay and inform their alignment strategies going forward.

CONCLUSION

New Problems in a New World

Why a new theory of management? As more companies employ advanced information and communications technologies to organize work in virtual environments, human resources managers need parsimonious metrics to evaluate the compatibility of strategic initiatives, implementation costs, communication, and media requirements. Especially difficult will be the development of management models that can mitigate organization/stakeholders' cross-cultural, cross-gender, and cross-generational communication biases that lead to individual and group conflicts (Hine, 2000; Thompson, 2010). As Collins (2001) has argued, successful companies were not the product of a miracle moment of recognition, but instead represent a culmination of many efforts over time that came to represent a gestalt of business activities. Other researchers have described that some of the most successful companies may have reached their pinnacle simply as a consequence of luck, and that behavioral approaches to strategic management should be wary of case studies that used simple comparative models (Bromiley, 2005).

As mentioned earlier in this paper, Hoopes (2003) went so far as to criticize psychological notions of leadership, instead preferring to remain fixed on the core requirements of market capitalism, the reasonable exercise of power, and the fiduciary responsibility of the firm. Additionally, Mintzberg et al. (2003) have provided a comprehensive review of organizational case studies that continued to demonstrate successful and unsuccessful management strategies linked to effective or ineffective top managers. However, as our research has shown, management studies have not penetrated the organizational habitus where the interaction of leaders and workers actually takes place. Essentially, we have demonstrated that modern management claims of organizational and behavioral uniformity appeared far less appropriate in the global and virtual work setting. As touched on previously, the literature often overlooked gender differences and workers' social contexts, choosing instead to focus on scientific management philosophies or the emotional/multiple intelligences managers have learned and brought to the workplace (Gardner, 1983; 2006; 2007; Handy, 1991; Engen, Leeden, & Willemsen, 2001; LePelley, 2001; Rahim & Psenicka, 2002; Fiedeldey-Van Dijk, & Freedman, 2007; Anderson, Spataro, & Flynn, 2008). Consequently, a postmodern model would re-examine organizations' systems designs, structures, and strategies without limiting analytical findings to bounded rationality assumptions found in management research (Travica, 1999; Bromiley, 2005; Barney & Clark, 2007; Davenport & Harris, 2007).

Just as neuroscientists have suggested that the mind pragmatically anchors objects and space through relational actions, our expanded paradigm posits that work behaviors were anchored in biased codes, schemas, networks, and frames of conduct (Katz & Kahn, 1978; Lundberg, 1988; Huber, 1990; Drucker, 1997; Chisnall, 2001; Doolin, 2003; Rizzolatti & Sinigaglia, 2006; Soulsby & Clark, 2007; Wu, Neubert, & Xiang, 2007; Ehin, 2008; Hesselbein & Goldsmith, 2009; Kallinikos, 2009). Our postmodern model posits that "in a complex world there are no simple binaries" (Law & Mol, 2002, p. 20) and that current leadership models have remained too linear, failing to recognize the heterogeneous micro-cultures within and without an organization's "strategic action fields" (Fligstein & McAdam, 2011: 6). We have demonstrated that the published conclusions drawn from defining transformational and charismatic traits of leaders appeared ambiguous at best (Brocato & Theodori, 2011; Brocato, Jelen, Schmidt, & Gold, 2011; Brocato & Gold, 2010). In particular, past operational definitions where researchers developed simple causal connections between either the manager-worker or worker-manager dyad did not allow for the emergent, dynamic behaviors grounded in each stakeholder group's perceptions, their consequent assessment of each group's effectiveness, and their overall alignment with their organization's goals (Ling, Chia, & Fang, 2000; Tekleab, Sims, Yun, Tesluk, & Cox, 2008; Kotlyar & Karakowsky, 2007). We found that this was an important research error because cognitive psychologists (judgment and decision making research), neuroscience, social psychology, sociology, organizational, and management studies have well demonstrated that social behaviors have remained heterogeneous (Goffman, 1959, 1974; Thaler, 2000; DeLanda, 2006).

In a technologically advanced communication environment, leaders and followers' interactions are qualitatively different, more complex and stretch beyond modernist definitions of space and time (Appadurai, 1996; Hancock & Tyler, 2001). The guiding principles of Taylorism (Taylor, 1911) and Fordism (Esser & Hirsch, 1994) are not adequate in a new multi-media, virtual world as Marcuse's (1964) insights about alienation and technological totalitarianism have demonstrated. We believe that the hamartia of modernist research literature has missed the mark by not focusing on the intrapersonal and group complexities that occur based on biased decision-making patterns and emergent behaviors or practices. Thus, we proposed a postmodern approach that would investigate emergent group interaction as a nexus of socio-cultural biases, intuition, and organizational influences located in a global milieu (Goldman, 1999; Morris, 2006; Choi, 2006; Neuhauser, 2007; Taylor, 2007; Goleman & Boyatzis, 2008; Todorovic & Schlosser, 2007; Jacoby, 2008).

To that end, this paper re-conceptualized leadership in a dynamic, emergent postmodern frame (Latour, 2005). We believe that re-conceptualizing leadership as contingent on the personal, socio-cultural biases of leaders and followers alike, instead of traditional personality traits, would provide insight into productive (or unproductive) decision making in uncertain situations (Varner & Beamer, 2005). To better describe the causal connections and pathways of complex social relations in organizational settings, we developed an evaluation matrix[1] to address leader and worker organizational and intrapersonal belief structures. We offered this multidimensional scale as a first step toward a parsimonious metric of the complex heuristics actors would likely use in organizational settings.

---

[1] The hypothetical evaluation matrix was presented in earlier published studies (see Brocato & Theodori, 2011).

REFERENCES

Ackoff, R. L. (1999, Jan-Feb). Transformational leadership. Strategy & Leadership, 2(1), 20(6).

Albritton, M., Oswald, S., & Anderson, J. (2008). Leadership quality and follower affect: A study of U.S. presidential candidates. Journal of Leadership Studies, 1 (4), 6-22. Retrieved October 25, 2008 from http://dx.doi.org/10.1002/jls.20035

Anderson, C., Spataro, S., & Flynn, F. (2008, May). Personality and organizational culture as determinants of influence. Journal of Applied Psychology, 93(3), 702-710. Retrieved February 19, 2009, doi:10.1037/0021-9010.93.3.702

Appadurai, A. (1996). Modernity at large: Cultural dimensions of globalization (public works, vol. 1). Minneapolis: University of Minnesota Press.

Archer, Margaret. (2007). *Making Our Way Through the World: Human Reflexivity and Social Mobility*. Cambridge: Cambridge University Press.

Barling, J., Christie, A., & Turner, N. (2008). Pseudo-transformational leadership: towards the development and test of a model. Journal of Business Ethics, 81(4), 851-861. Retrieved February 16, 2009, from ABI/INFORM Global database. (Document ID: 1518109831).

Barney, J.B. & Clark, D.N. (2007). Resource-based theory: Creating and sustaining competitive advantage. Oxford: Oxford University Press.

Baudrillard, J. (1994). Simulacra and simulation (Sheila Faria Glaser, Trans.). Ann Arbor: The University of Michigan Press.

Becker, G. F. (2007, November). Organizational climate and culture: Competing dynamics for transformational leadership. *Review of Business Research*, 7, 6. p.116(8). Retrieved April 27, 2008, from Academic OneFile via Gale: http://find.galegroup.com/ips/start.do?prodId=IPS

Berger, P.L. & Luckman, T. (1966). The social construction of reality: A treatise in the sociology of knowledge. New York: Random House Inc.

Blumer, H. (1969). Symbolic interactionism: Perspective and method. Berkeley: University of California Press.

Bolman, L.G. & Deal, T.E. (2008). Reframing organizations: Artistry, choice, and leadership (4rd ed.). San Francisco: Jossey-Bass.

Bourdieu, P. (1998). Practical reason: On the theory of action. Stanford: Stanford University Press.

Branden, N. (1969). The psychology of self-esteem. San Francisco: Jossey-Bass.

Bromiley, P. (2005). The behavioral foundations of strategic management. Malden, MA: Blackwell Publishing.

Brocato, Billy R. & Stuart S. Gold. (2010). Leadership Ambiguity and Ambivalence: A Critical Solution. *Global Management Journal*, 2(2): 5-15.

Brocato, Billy R. , Jonatan Jelen, Thomas Schmidt, and Stuart Gold. (2011). Leadership Conceptual Ambiguities: A Post-Positivistic Critique. *Journal of Leadership Studies*, 5(1): 35-50.

Brocato, Billy R. & Gene L. Theodori. 2011. "Resolving Leadership Conceptual Ambiguities: A postmodern Sociological Resolution." *International Journal of Business and Social Sciences [Special Issue], 2*(19): 23-34.

Callon, M. (2002). Writing and re(writing) devices as tools for managing complexity. In Law, J. & Mol, A. (Eds.), Complexities: Social studies of knowledge practices (pp. 191-217). Durham: Duke University Press.

Cantor, P.A. (2001). Gilligan unbound: Pop culture in the age of globalization. London: Rowman & Littlefield Publishers, Inc.

Chia, R. (1996). The problem of reflexivity in organizational research: Towards a postmodern science of organization. Organization, 3(1), 31-59. Retrieved February 26, 2009 from http://org.sagepub.com/cgi/content/abstract/3/1/31. DOI: 10.1177/135050849631003

Chisnall, P.S. (2001). Virtual ethnography [Review of the book Virtual ethnography]. International Journal of Market Research, 43(3), 354-356. Retrieved July 17, 2009, from ProQuest Psychology Journals.

Choi, J. (2006, Summer). A motivational theory of charismatic leadership: envisioning, empathy, and empowerment. *Journal of Leadership & Organizational Studies (Baker College), 13(1),* 24-43. Retrieved April 25, 2008, from Business Source Complete database.

Collins, J. (2001). Good to great: Why some companies make the leap and others don't. New York: HarperCollins Publishers, Inc.

Collins, R. (2010). The contentious social interactionism of Charles Tilly. Social Psychology Quarterly, 73(1): 5-10. DOI: 10. 1177/01902725093359616.

Covey, S.M.R. (2006). The speed of trust: The one thing that changes everything. New York: Free Press.

Cranti, J., & Bateman, T. (2000). Charismatic leadership viewed from above: The impact of proactive personality. Journal of Organizational Behavior, 21(1), 63-75. Retrieved from Business Source Complete database.

DeLanda, M. (2006). A new philosophy of society: Assemblage theory and social complexity. London: Continuum.

Davenport, T.H. & Harris, J.G. (2007. Competing on analytics: The new science of winning. Boston: The Harvard Business School Press.

Den Hartog, D., De Hoogh, A., & Keegan, A. (2007, July). The interactive effects of belongingness and charisma on helping and compliance. *Journal of Applied Psychology, 92(4),* 1131-1139. Retrieved April 25, 2008, from Business Source Complete database.

Doolin, B. (2003). Narratives of change: Discourse, technology and organization. Organization, 10 (4), 751-770.

Drucker, P.F. (1997). Toward the new organization. In Hesselbein, F., Goldsmith, M. & Beckhard, R. (Eds.), The organization of the future (pp. 1-5). New York: The Peter F. Drucker Foundation for Nonprofit Management.

Ehin, C. (2008). Un-managing knowledge workers. Journal of Intellectual Capital, 9(3), 337-350.

Engen, M.L., Leeden, R., & Willemsen, T.M. (2001). Gender, context and leadership styles: A field study. *Journal of Occupational and Organizational Psychology*, 5(74), 581-598.

Erez, A., Misangyi, V., Johnson, D., LePine, M., & Halverson, K. (2008, May). Stirring the hearts of followers: Charismatic leadership as the transferal of affect. *Journal of Applied Psychology*, 93(3), 602-616.

Erickson, A., Shaw, J., & Agabe, Z. (2007, Fall). An empirical investigation of the antecedents, behaviors, and outcomes of bad leadership. Journal of Leadership Studies, 1(3), 26-43.

Esser, J. & Hirsch, J. (1994). The crisis of fordism and the dimensions of a 'post-fordiat' regional and urban structure. In A. Amin (Ed.): Post-Fordism: A reader (pp. 71-97). Oxford: Blackwell Publishers Ltd.

Felfe, J. & Schyns, B. (2004). Is similarity in leadership related to organizational outcomes? The case of transformational leadership. Journal of Leadership and Organizational Studies, 10 (4), 92-102. Retrieved November 4, 2008 from http://swtuopproxy.museglobal.com/MuseSessionID=81a1993273f952d303484dcaf8c74 6e/MuseHost=jlo.sagepub.com/MusePath/cgi/reprint/10/4/92.

Fiedeldey-Van Dijk, C., & Freedman, J. (2007). Differentiating emotional intelligence in leadership. Journal of Leadership Studies, 1 (2), 8-20. Retrieved October 25, 2008 from http://dx.doi.org/10.1002/jls.20012

Fligstein, Neil & Diug McAdams. (2011). Toward a General Theory of Strategic Action Fields. *Sociological Theory, 29*(1): 1-26.

Foucault, M.(1986). The care of self: Volume 3 of the history of sexuality (R. Hurley, trans.). New York: Vintage Books

Frith, C. (2007). Making up the mind: How the brain creates our mental world. Malden: Blackwell Publishing

Gadamer, H. (1976). Philosophical hermeneutics. (D.E. Linge, Trans). Berkeley: University of California Press.

Gardner, H. (1983). Frames of mind: The theory of multiple intelligences. New York: Basic Books, a member of the Perseus Books Group.

Gardner, H. (2006). Multiple intelligences: New horizons. New York: Basic Books.

Gardner, H. (2007). Five minds for the future. Boston: Harvard Business School Press.

Gehrke, S.J. (2008). Leadership through meaning-making: An empirical exploration of spirituality and leadership in college students. *Journal of College Student Development,* 49(4), 351-359.

Gherardi, S. (2000). Practice-based theorizing on learning and knowing in organizations. Organization, 7(2), 211-223.

Gibbard, A. (1990) Wise choices, apt feelings: A theory of normative judgment. Cambridge: Harvard University Press.

Gilovich, T. & Griffin, D. (2002). Introduction – Heuristics and biases: Then and now. In T. Gilovich, D. Griffin, & D. Kahneman (Eds.), Heuristics and biases: The psychology of intuitive judgment (pp. 1-18).Cambridge: Cambridge University Press.

Glaser, B.G. & Strauss, A.L. (1967). The discovery of grounded theory: Strategies for qualitative work. New Brunswick: Aldine Transaction.

Goffman, E. (1959). The presentation of self in everyday life. New York: Anchor Books.

Goffman, E. (1974). Frame analysis: An essay on the organization of experience. Boston: Northeastern University Press.

Goldman, A.I. (1999). Knowledge in a social world. Oxford: Oxford University Press.

Goleman, D. & Boyatzis, R. (2008, September). Social intelligence and the biology of leadership. Harvard Business Review. Retrieved November 12, 2008 from http://harvardbusinessonline.hbsp.harvard.edu/hbsp/hbr/articles/

Green, D. D. (2007). Leading a postmodern workforce. Academy of Strategic Management Journal, 6, 15. Gross, N. (2009, June). A pragmatist theory of social mechanism. *American Sociological Review*, 74(3), p. 358-379.

Grover, K.S. (2005, April). Linking leader skills, follower attitudes, and contextual variables via an integrated model of charismatic leadership. *Journal of Management*, 31 (2), 255-277.

Guzman, Patricia M. (2007) Strategic leadership: Qualitative study of contextual factors and transformational leadership behaviors of chief executive officers. D.M. dissertation, University of Phoenix, United States -- Arizona. Retrieved November 30, 2008, from Dissertations & Theses @ University of Phoenix database. (Publication No. AAT 3302617).

Habermas, Jürgen. (1987). *The Theory of Communicative Action. Volume 2. Lifeworld and System: A Critique of Functionalist Reason.* (Trans. Thomas McCarthy). Boston, MA: Beacon Press.

Hamel, G. (2009, February). Moon shots for management. [HBR at Large]. Harvard Business Review, 91-08.

Hancock, P. & Tyler, M. (2001). Work, postmodernism and organization: A critical introduction. Thousand Oaks: Sage Publications.

Handy, C. (1991). Gods of management: The changing work of organizations (3rd ed.). Oxford: Oxford University Press.

Harvey, D. (1990). The condition of postmodernity. Cambridge: Blackwell Publishers Inc.

Hautala, T. (2005, Summer). The effects of subordinates' personality on appraisals of transformational leadership. *Journal of Leadership & Organizational Studies*, 11 (4), 84 (9).

Herman, M.A. (2010). Do you see what I am? How observers' backgrounds affect their perceptions of multiracial faces. *Social Psychology Quarterly*, 73(1): 58-78.

Herold, D., Fedor, D., Caldwell, S., & Liu, Y. (2008, March). The effects of transformational and change leadership on employees' commitment to a change: A multilevel study. Journal of Applied Psychology, 93 (2), 346-357. Retrieved November 4, 2008 from doi:10.1037/0021-9010.93.2.346

Hesselbein, F. & Goldsmith, M. (2009). The organization of the future 2. San Francisco: Jossey-Bass.

Hine, C. (2000). Virtual ethnography. London: Sage Publications.

Hinkin, T. & Tracey, J.B. (1999). The relevance of charisma for transformational leadership in stable organizations. Journal of Organizational Change Management. 12 (2), 105-119. Retrieved November 4, 2008 from http://swtuopproxy.museglobal.com /MuseSessionID=9168c647d262762f69df29d74a7381/MuseHost=www.emeraldinsight.com/MusePath/Insight/ViewContentServlet?Filename=Published/EmeraldFullTextArticle/Articles/0230120203.html

Hoopes, J. (2003). False prophets: The gurus who created modern management and why their ideas are bad for business today. New York: Basic Books.

Hoyt, C. L. & Blascovich, J. (2003). Transformational and transactional leadership in virtual and physical environments. Small Group Research, 34 (6), 678-715. Retrieved November 4, 2008 from http:sgr.sagepub.com/cgi/content/abstract/34/6/678.

Huang, M., Cheng, B. & Chou, L. (2005). Fitting in organizational values: The mediating role of person-organization fit between ceo charismatic leadership and employee outcomes. International Journal of Manpower, 26 (1), 35-49. Retrieved November 4, 2008 from http://swtuopproxy.museglobal.com/MuseSessionID=20e2f470c2907d82bf13de961ea54

48/MuseHost=www.emeraldinsight.com/MusePath/Insight/viewPDF.jsp?Filename=html/
Output/Published/EmeraldFullTextArticle/Pdf/0160260103.pdf

Huber, G. (1990, January). A Theory of the effects of advanced information technologies on organizational design, intelligence, and decision making. *Academy of Management Review*, 15(1), 47-71.

Jung, D., & Sosik, J. (2006, Spring). Who are the spellbinders? Identifying personal attributes of charismatic leaders. *Journal of Leadership & Organizational Studies (Baker College), 12(4),* 12-26. Retrieved April 25, 2008, from Business Source Complete database

Kahneman, D. & Frederick, S. (2002). Representativeness revisited: Attribute substitution in intuitive judgement. In T. Gilovich, D, Griffin, & D. Kahneman (Eds.) Heuristics and biases: The psychology of intuitive judgment (pp. 49-81). Cambridge: Cambridge University Press.

Kahneman, D., Slovic, P. & Tversky, A. (Eds.). (1982). Judgment under uncertainty: Heuristics and biases. Cambridge: Cambridge University Press.

Kahneman, D., & Tversky, A. (Eds.). (2000). Choices, values, and frames. Cambridge: Cambridge University Press. Russell Sage Foundation.

Kahneman, D., & Tversky, A. (1982). Causal schemas in judgments under uncertainty. In D. Kahneman, P. Slovic, & A. Tversky (Eds.) Judgment under uncertainty: Heuristics and biases (pp. 117-128). Cambridge: Cambridge University Press.

Kallinikos, J. (2009). On the computational rendition of reality: Artifacts and human agency. *Organization*, 16(2), 183-202.

Katz, D. & Kahn, R.L. (1978). The social psychology of organizations (2nd. ed.). Hoboken: John Wiley & Sons, Inc.

Kearney, E. (2008, December). Age differences between leader and followers as a moderator of the relationship between transformational leadership and team performance. *Journal of Occupational & Organizational Psychology*, 81(4), 803-811.

Kilduff, M. & Krackhardt, D. (2008). *Interpersonal networks in organizations: Cognition, personality, dynamics, and culture.* New York: Cambridge University Press.

Konorti, E. (2008). The 3D transformational leadership model. *Journal of American Academy of Business, Cambridge*, 14(1), 10-20.

Kotlyar, I., & Karakowsky, L. (2007, August). Falling over ourselves to follow the leader: conceptualizing connections between transformational leader behaviors and dysfunctional team conflict. *Journal of Leadership & Organizational Studies, 14, 1.* p.38(12).

Kouzes, J.M., & Posner, B.Z. (2009, January). To lead, create a shared vision. [Forethought]. *Harvard Business Review*, p. 20-21.

Latour, B. (2005). Reassembling the social: An introduction to actor-network-theory. Oxford: Oxford University Press.

Law, J. (1994). Organizing modernity. Oxford: Blackwell Publishers.

Law, J. (2004). After method: Mess in social science research. Routledge: New York.

Law, J. & Mol, A. (2002). Complexities: An introduction. In J. Law & A. Mol (Eds.) Complexities: Social studies of knowledge practice (pp. 1-22). Durham: Duke University Press.

Lepelley, D.M. (2001). Exploring the adaptability of leadership styles in senior business executives: Life narratives and self discovery of factors contributing to adaptability.

(Ph.D. dissertation, Fielding Graduate Institute, United States – California). Retrieved January 28, 2009, from ABI/INFORM Global database. (Publication No. AAT 3037966).

Ling, W., Chia, R., & Fang, L. (2000, December). Chinese Implicit Leadership Theory. *Journal of Social Psychology*, 140(6), 729-739.

Lundberg, C. (1988). Working with culture. Journal of Organizational Change, 1 (2), 38-47. McShane, S. L., & Von Glinow, M. A. (2005). *Organizational Behavior* (3rd ed.). Boston: McGraw-Hill Irwin.

Manning, T.T. (2003). Leadership across cultures: Attachment style influences. *Journal of Leadership and Organizational Studies*, 9 (3), 20-30.

Marcuse, H. (1964). One-dimensional man. Boston: Beacon Press.

McLaurin, J.R., & Al Amri, M.B. (2008). Developing an understanding of charismatic and transformational leadership. Allied Academies International Conference. Academy of Organizational Culture, Communications and Conflict. *Proceedings*, 13(2), 15-19.

Mead, George Herbert. 1934. *Mind, Self, and Society. From the Standpoint of a Social Behaviorist.* Chicago, IL: The University of Chicago Press.

Merton, R.K. (1996). On social structure and science (P. Sztompka, ed.). Chicago: The University of Chicago Press.

Miller, M. (2007, July). Transformational leadership and mutuality. *Transformation (02653788), 24(3/4)*, 180-192. Retrieved April 25, 2008, from Academic Search Premier database.

Mintzberg, H., Lampel, J., Quinn, J.B., & Ghoshal, S. (2003). The strategy process: Concepts, contexts, cases (4th ed.). Edinburgh Gate: Pearson Education Limited.

Morris, L. (2006). Top-down innovation: leaders define innovation culture. Retrieved April 26, 2008 from http://www.realinnovation.com/content/c070528a.asp

Neuhauser, C. (2007). Project manager leadership behaviors and frequency of use by female project managers. Project Management Journal, 38(1), 21-31. Retrieved February 16, 2009, from ABI/INFORM Global database. (Document ID: 1258771331).

Pastor, J., Mayo, M., & Shamir, B. (2007, November). Adding fuel to fire: the impact of followers' arousal on ratings of charisma. *Journal of Applied Psychology, 92(6)*, 1584-1596. Retrieved April 25, 2008, from Business Source Complete database.

Pawar, B. (2003). Central conceptual issues in transformational leadership research. *Leadership & Organization Development Journal*, 24 (7), 397-406.

Pearce, C.L., Sims Jr., H.P., Cox, J.F., Ball, G., Schness, E., Smith, K., & Trevino, L. (2003). Transactors, transformers and beyond: A multi-method development of a theoretical typology of leadership. *Journal of Management Development*, 22 (4), 273-307.

Pillai, R., Schriesheim, C.A., & Williams, E.S. (1999). Fairness perceptions and trust as mediators for transformational and transactional leadership: A two-sample study. *Journal of Management*, 25 (6), 897-933.

Rahim, M. A. & Psenicka, C. (2002). A model of emotional intelligence and conflict management strategies: A study in seven countries. The International Journal of Organizational Analysis, 10(4), 302–326. Retrived May 1, 2009 from http://papers.ssrn.com/sol3/papers.cfm?abstract_id=429760.

Rizzolatti, G. & Sinigaglia, C. (2006). Mirrors in the brain: How our minds share actions and emotions (F. Anderson, Trans.). Oxford: Oxford University Press.

Scott, B., Colquitt, J., & Zapata-Phelan, C. (2007, November). Justice as a dependent variable: Subordinate charisma as a predictor of interpersonal and informational justice perceptions. Journal of Applied Psychology, 92(6), 1597-1609. Retrieved November 4, 2008, from http://swtuopproxy.museglobal.com/MuseSessionID=b2b3fa245bbffc63558a98d12196c/MuseHost=web.ebscohost.com/MusePath/ehost/pdf?vid=2&hid=113&sid=cb20452b-d942-433c-9ef8-3d2ea8114e8a%40sessionmgr104

Sillince, J.A. (2007). Organizational context and the discursive construction of organizing. *Management Communication Quarterly: McQ*, 20(4), 363-394.

Sloman, S.A. (2002). Two systems of reasoning. In T. Gilovich, D. Griffin, & D. Kahneman (Eds.) Heuristics and biases: The psychology of intuitive judgement (pp. 379-396). Cambridge: Cambridge University Press.

Soulsby, A., & Clark, E. (2007). Organization theory and the post-socialist transformation: Contributions to organizational knowledge. *Human Relations*, 60(10), 1419-1442.

Stone, G.A., Russell, R.F. & Patterson, K. (2004). Transformational versus servant leadership: A difference in leader focus. *The Leadership & Organization Development Journal*, 25 (4), 349-361.

Taylor, F. (1911). *The principles of scientific management.* New York: Harper & Brothers Publishers.

Taylor, V. (2007, April). Leadership for service improvement: part 3. *Nursing Management - UK, 14(1)*, 28-32.

Tekleab, A G, Sims, H P, Yun, S., Tesluk, P E, & Cox, J. (2008, Februrary). Are we on the same page? Effects of self-awareness of empowering and transformational leadership. *Journal of Leadership & Organizational Studies, 14, 3.* p.185(17). Retrieved May 01, 2008, from General OneFile via Gale

Thaler, R.H. (2000). Mental accounting matters. In D. Kahneman, & A. Tversky (Eds.), Choices, values, and frames (pp. 241-268). Cambridge: Cambridge University Press. Russell Sage Foundation.

Thompson, Craig J (1995). A contextualist proposal for the conceptualization and study of marketing ethics. *Journal of Public Policy & Marketing*, 14(2), 177.

Tichy, N.M. & Devanna, M.A. (1986). The transformational leader. New York: John Wiley & Sons, Inc.

Todorovic, W. & Schlosser, F. (2007, July). An entrepreneur and a leader!: a framework conceptualizing the influence of leadership style on a firm's entrepreneurial orientation--performance relationship. *Journal of Small Business & Entrepreneurship, 20(3)*, 289-307.

Travica, B. (1999). *New organizational designs: Information aspects.* Stamford: Ablex Publishing Corporation.

Tuomo, T. (2006). How to be an effective charismatic leader: lessons for leadership development. *Development and Learning in Organizations, 20*(4), 19-2.

Varner, I., & Beamer, L. (2005). Intercultural communications in the global workplace (3rd. ed.). New York: McGraw-Hill/Irwin.

Walumbwa, F.O., Avolio, B.J., & Zhu, W. (2008). How transformational leadership weaves its influence on individual job performance: the role of identification and efficacy beliefs. *Personnel Psychology, 61*(4), 793-825.

Wu, C., Neubert, M., & Xiang Y. (2007). Transformational leadership, cohesion perceptions, and employee cynicism about organizational change: The mediating role of justice perceptions. *Journal of Applied Behavioral Science 43* (2), 327-351.

Wren, D.A. (2005). *The history of management thought. (5th ed).* New Jersey: John Wiley & Sons.

AUTHOR BIOGRAPHIES

1. LEADERSHIP LEARNING JOURNEY

Dr. Glenys Drew works with executive staff at Senior Leadership Development Consultant at the Queensland University of Technology (QUT), Brisbane, Australia, and with senior leaders in universities, schools, colleges and 'for people' organizations in Australia, New Zealand and Hong Kong. She facilitates the renowned, valid '360 degree' feedback instrument, the Quality Leadership Profile (QLP) and its offshoot instruments, the Quality Leadership Profile for Schools and the Quality Profile for Research Leadership. The resultant feedback debrief and development conversations yield proven results for enhanced leadership insight and growth, to the credit and benefit of participating leaders and their organizations.

Dr. Drew developed and published the 'Lantern' model of leadership and organizational development which offers a guiding framework to CEOs and senior leadership teams. The model focuses on pursuing a 'well-lit' environment characterized by strategic clarity and connectedness, enhanced strategic and interpersonal communication and an ethical platform for building a positive, amenable organizational culture. She holds a PhD in executive and organizational leadership development and prior postgraduate honors in communication and literature. Further to her individual practice she undertakes research and publication and presents invited talks and workshops in the field of leadership and organizational development.

2. RECOGNIZING SKILLS FOR EFFECTIVE LEADERSHIP

Mrs. Maria M. Johnson lived in Kentucky for a number of years, where she attended Berea College for her undergraduate degree before pursuing a career in manufacturing. While working in the automotive industry, she learned a number of important lessons about effective leadership, employer-employee relationships, and the role of empathy in the workplace. After several years of service in this field, she changed directions to pursue a new challenge: teaching. She received her MA in education from the University of Kentucky and her MA in history from Eastern Kentucky University. Utilizing the methods she learned in graduate school and the leadership skills gained in manufacturing, Ms. Johnson creates a learning environment within the high school classroom that challenges and encourages students of all abilities.

3. Work Engagement in Transformational Leaders: A Multi-level, Multi-source Study

Dr. Karina Nielsen is Professor of Work and Organizational Psychology at the National Research Centre for the Working Environment, Denmark and Honorary Professor at the University of Leicester, UK. She has a PhD in Applied Psychology. She is currently on the editorial boards of *Human Relations* and *The Leadership Quarterly*, and is associate editor of *Work & Stress*. She has published her work in journals such as *Human Relations, Work & Stress, The Leadership Quarterly, Journal of Occupational Health Psychology*, and *Journal of Organizational Behavior*. Her research interests lie within the area of new ways of working and job redesign. She is particularly interested in how leaders may organize and manage work to ensure employee well-being. A particular strand of research concerns the roles of transformational leaders in improving job and individual resources in a team context to ensure employee health and well-being. She has won several awards for her research including the early career achievement award (APA-NIOSH) and a top paper award in *Work & Stress*.

4. Leadership and the Resource Dependence Theory

Dr. Tracy L. Buchman is the National Director of Healthcare Emergency Management at HSS, Inc located in Denver, CO and holds a doctorate in health administration from the University of Phoenix. Additionally, she holds several consultant and advisory positions with the Department of Homeland Security (DHS) and the Centers for Disease Control (CDC) and applies her expertise as a national level emergency preparedness site reviewer and an instructor for the FEMA Center for Domestic Preparedness course on *Hospital Emergency Response Training for Mass Casualty Incidents*.

5. Using Stress Management Training to Enhance Leader Performance and the Utilization of Intellectual Abilities during Stressful Military Training: An Application of Cognitive Resource Theory

Dr. Ronald E. Smith is Professor of Psychology and Director of Clinical Psychology Training at the University of Washington. He received his bachelor's degree from Marquette University and his Ph.D. in clinical psychology from Southern Illinois University. He completed his advanced clinical training at the Neuropsychiatric Institute and Hospital, University of California, Los Angeles and later received a Distinguished Alumnus Award from that medical center. Dr. Smith has held faculty positions at Purdue University and at Washington, as well as visiting scholar appointments at Marquette University, the University of Hawaii, the University of New Mexico, and UCLA. His major research interests are in personality, stress and coping, and in performance enhancement research and intervention. His publication record includes more than 200 scientific articles and chapters and 33 books and manuals.

6. THE INFLUENCE OF SPIRITUALITY UPON LEADERSHIP AND THE WORKPLACE

Dr. James Michael Lewis is an ordained Baptist Minister. He earned a Bachelor of Arts in Religion from Samford University, Birmingham, Alabama and later received both the Master of Divinity and Doctor of Ministry degrees from the Southern Baptist Theological Seminary in Louisville, Kentucky. He served over 28 years as a Chaplain with the US Army. For ten years he provided religious support and pastoral ministry to troops in combat units including the 82nd Airborne Division in the Persian Gulf War of 1991. Later specializing in healthcare chaplaincy, he served on staff at Womack Army Medical Center, Fort Bragg, North Carolina and Madigan Army Medical Center Tacoma Washington. He twice deployed to Iraq as supervisory Chaplain with the 30th Medical Brigade Task Force. He retired from Active Duty in 2010 at the rank of Lieutenant Colonel. He and Delores, his wife of 40 years, live near Louisville, Kentucky.

7. ETHICS: AN INGREDIENT IN EFFECTIVE LEADERSHIP

Dr. Jerry D. VanVactor, FAHRMM is a native of Hopkinsville, Kentucky and an active duty medical service corps officer in the United States Army where he is a health care logistics manager. He began his military career in 1989 as an enlisted man and later earned his commission through the U.S. Army officer candidacy program. He has been involved in a variety of leadership roles since entering the military. His education includes a Doctor of Health Administration from the University of Phoenix, Masters in Healthcare Management from Trident University, and Bachelor of Science in Health Science degrees with an undergraduate minor in Procurement and Acquisitions Management from Athens State University. He is a Certified Materials & Resource Professional and a Fellow of the Association for Healthcare Resource and Materials Management of the American Hospital Association. Dr. VanVactor is the recipient of numerous individual military awards and decorations for demonstrated professionalism and leadership excellence.

8. POLITICAL LEADERSHIP FROM A GENDER PERSPECTIVE

Dr. Chiara Rollero, psychologist, teaches Social Psychology at the Faculty of Political Sciences in Turin (Italy). She works at the Department of Psychology at the University of Turin. Her main publications concern gender differences, political participation, and Environmental Psychology. Now she is working on well-being and quality of life from a gender perspective, ambivalent sexism and objectification processes.

Dr. Norma De Piccoli is Full Professor at the University of Turin (Italy), in the Faculty of Psychology, where teaches Social Psychology and Community Psychology. She is president of the Master of Science in Clinic and Community Psychology. She directs the Laboratory of Social and Community Psychology and is responsible for several research projects commissioned by public services. Her methodological interests are related both to quantitative and qualitative approaches and field-research. Her main topics of interest are:

formal and informal aggregation in youths; social identity; social representations; language and communications; political and social participation; gender theories; health and quality of life; community intervention and health promotion.

Dr. Filippo Rutto is a Ph.D. student at the Human and Social Science Ph.D. School - University of Turin (Italy), psychologist. He has a master degree in psychology. His current studies focus on political participation from a gender perspective.

9. The Gendered Image of Power: How Male and Female Leaders Are Perceived

Dr. Chiara Rollero, psychologist, teaches Social Psychology at the Faculty of Political Sciences in Turin (Italy). She works at the Department of Psychology at the University of Turin. Her main publications concern gender differences, political participation, and Environmental Psychology. Now she is working on well-being and quality of life from a gender perspective, ambivalent sexism and objectification processes.

Dr. Norma De Piccoli is Full Professor at the University of Turin (Italy), in the Faculty of Psychology, where teaches Social Psychology and Community Psychology. She is president of the Master of Science in Clinic and Community Psychology. She directs the Laboratory of Social and Community Psychology and is responsible for several research projects commissioned by public services. Her methodological interests are related both to quantitative and qualitative approaches and field-research. Her main topics of interest are: formal and informal aggregation in youths; social identity; social representations; language and communications; political and social participation; gender theories; health and quality of life; community intervention and health promotion.

10. The Curt Flood Effect and Its Impact on Workplace Leadership

Mr. Tony Gill manages strategic projects within the corporate real estate department at Canadian Tire, one of Canada's largest retailers. In this capacity, he is in charge of implementing and managing the company's mobility program, which will transform office operations from a centralized model, to one where employees can work from a network of places. Prior to joining Canadian Tire, he managed risk and business continuity for corporate real estate at BMO Financial Group, spanning all corporate locations across Canada, the United States and globally. He is on the Editorial Board of the Journal of Business Continuity & Emergency Planning in London, and on the Advisory Board of the Telework Coalition in Washington, D.C. His work connecting risk and real estate has been published in several international journals, and he has also done public speaking engagements for several organizations across Canada and the United States. He maintains a Toronto-based consulting practice.

11. The Dark Side of Entrepreneurial Leadership and What to Do about It

Dr. William L. Tullar is professor of management in the Bryan School of Business and Economics at UNCG. He has been Research Fellow at the International Research Institute for Management Science in Moscow, Russia and visiting professor at FH Worms and FH Ludwigshafen in Germany and International Management Institute in Chisinau, Moldova. He was the recipient of the Distinguished Teaching Award for the School of Business and Economics in 2011. He has been a consultant to organizations both in the U.S. and abroad. He has published over 30 scholarly articles on a wide range of subjects in management and human resources. He is also the author of three published novels.

Dr. Dianne H.B. Welsh is the Hayes Distinguished Professor of Entrepreneurship at The University of North Carolina Greensboro, Inaugural Founder of the North Carolina Entrepreneurship Center and Founder, Director of the Entrepreneurship Cross-Disciplinary Entrepreneurship Center, and Director of the Coleman Entrepreneurship Fellows Program. She previously held endowed chairs at two universities where she started entrepreneurship centers. Dianne is a recognized scholar in entrepreneurship, family business, and franchising and has six books and over 150 publications. She is the Past President of the U.S. Association for Small Business & Entrepreneurship, and was a Presidential Appointee to the Board of Visitors for the U.S. Air Force Academy and a member of the Defense Advisory Committee for Women in the Services. She was invited by the United Nations to speak on Entrepreneurship, Commercialization, and Innovation last year and currently serves on the first NC Innovation Council. As the architect of the University of North Carolina at Greensboro's Entrepreneurship Program, she won the Best Practices Award from the Small Business Institute, the Global Consortium of Entrepreneurship Center's Excellence in Entrepreneurship across the Curriculum Award, and the U.S. Association for Small Business and Entrepreneurship's Outstanding Emerging Entrepreneurship Program Award in 2012. The Entrepreneurship Program is a recipient of the Coleman Entrepreneurship Fellows Program for the past two years.

12. Wisdom for the Common Good: Tales of Three Leaders

Dr. Shih-ying Yang is an associate professor in the Department of Educational Policy and Administration at National Chi Nan University in Taiwan. She received her ED. M from Harvard University and Ph.D. in cognitive psychology from Yale University. Her main research interests are in the areas of wisdom, leadership, lifelong learning, and Taiwanese Chinese cultural psychology.

13. Leadership Is Dead, Long Live Leadership: A Shifting Paradigm

Mr. Billy R. Brocato is Managing Editor of the Journal Rural Sociology currently at Sam Houston State University. Billy holds an M.A. in Sociology from Sam Houston State

University and has worked as an international business journalist for more than 20 years from bureaus in Tokyo, Singapore, Hong Kong, and Houston, Texas. Billy also has published professional articles on leadership, international energy commodities trading, banking, and international government relations. Billy is currently undergoing doctoral studies in sociology at Texas A&M University in College Station, Texas. Billy is a member of the Rural Sociological Society, The American Sociological Association, the Southwestern Social Science Association, the Midwest Sociological Society, and Alpha Kappa Delta-International Sociology Honor Society.

Dr. Gene Theodori is Professor and Chair of Sociology and Director of the Center for Rural Studies at Sam Houston State University. He teaches, conducts basic and applied research, and writes professional and popular articles on rural and community development issues, energy and natural resource concerns, and related topics. A central feature of his work is the development of outreach educational and technical assistance programs that address important issues relating to community and economic development. He has served as President of the Southern Rural Sociological Association and is currently co-editor of the Journal of Rural Social Sciences. Dr. Theodori received the Excellence in Extension and Public Service Award from the Southern Rural Sociological Association in 2007, the Award for Excellence in Extension and Public Outreach from the Rural Sociological Society in 2010, and the Award for Excellence in Research from the Southern Rural Sociological Association in 2011.

INDEX